George C. Lorimer

Isms Old and New

Winter Sunday Evening Sermon-Series for 1880-81 Delivered in the First Baptist

Church, Chicago

George C. Lorimer

Isms Old and New
Winter Sunday Evening Sermon-Series for 1880-81 Delivered in the First Baptist Church, Chicago

ISBN/EAN: 9783337160401

Printed in Europe, USA, Canada, Australia, Japan

Cover: Foto ©Lupo / pixelio.de

More available books at **www.hansebooks.com**

ISMS
OLD AND NEW

WINTER SUNDAY EVENING SERMON-SERIES FOR 1880-81
DELIVERED IN THE FIRST BAPTIST
CHURCH, CHICAGO

BY THE PASTOR

GEORGE C. LORIMER

MEMBER OF VICTORIA INSTITUTE, THE PHILOSOPHICAL SOCIETY OF
GREAT BRITAIN

Till at length no heavenly Ism any longer coming down upon us, Isms from the other quarter have to mount up.
Carlyle's "Past and Present"

CHICAGO
S. C. GRIGGS AND COMPANY
1881

COPYRIGHT, 1881,
BY S. C. GRIGGS & COMPANY.

TO

THE FIRST BAPTIST CHURCH, CHICAGO,

THESE DISCOURSES ARE INSCRIBED

WITH GRATEFUL MEMORIES OF

UNWAVERING AND UNCEASING KINDNESS

TO THE AUTHOR.

"My love be with you all in Christ Jesus, Amen."

WHILE it is preëminently the duty of the pulpit to expound the doctrines and precepts of Holy Writ, there are times when it should confront and challenge the insidious errors which unfit the public mind to receive attentively and believingly its expositions. Exegesis, however eloquent and elaborate, will be as powerless, morally and religiously, as the learned interpretations of dusty Egyptian hieroglyphics, if confidence is seriously impaired in the Divine origin of the Book whose teachings it seeks to unfold. The unclean spirit must be cast out, and the house be swept and garnished, before the spirit of truth will find there a welcome and a sure asylum. We invite the wayward to accept Christ and be saved, and when we chide them for not doing so, we frequently overlook the fact that they are in sympathy with forms of thought which are irreconcilable with the claims of that volume on whose authority rests the duty so earnestly enjoined. Hamilton says, "Plato in his Phædo demonstrated the immortality of the soul from its simplicity; and in the Republic demonstrated its simplicity from its immortality," a species of reasoning still in vogue, and by many highly esteemed, but which is utterly inadequate to meet the subtle and protean infidelity of our age. Never will its enthusiastic course be arrested, nor its illusions be dispelled, nor the asbestos fire it is kindling be quenched, and the Gospel achieve its triumph over both head and heart until, abandoning the *petitio principii* in our methods, we fight the enemy with its own weapons, and prove at least that it is not invulnerable.

This conviction led to the preparation of the accompanying sermons. Working for Christ in a community distinguished almost as much by its mental restlessness as by its business activity, the author became convinced if he would promote in the highest sense the religious life of the unconverted in his congregation he must diminish their confidence in certain prevailing errors, and disengage them from their fetters. His endeavors were so favorably received that he has ventured to seek for his series a wider sphere of usefulness, by giving the discourses to the press. They are not, however, printed precisely as they were delivered. They have been subject to such revision as the cares of an exacting pastorate, enhanced by the labors incident to the formation of a new church and the building of a house of worship, would permit; and they have been increased in number by the addition of several that were not included in the original course, of which the one on Buddhism is a sample, which was preached under a different title soon after the appearance of the beautiful poem which it commends and reviews.

In dealing with such themes as are presented in this volume, especially within the limits usually prescribed to sermons, an author will find himself frequently baffled by the immeasurableness of the territory he has to traverse, and by the shadowy vagueness of the land he seeks to invade. Dr. Johnson has said, "There are objections against a plenum and also against a vacuum, but one or the other must be true." Verily; but how much wearisome thinking and how much wearisome writing would be needed to answer all these objections, and how much more of both would be required to completely fathom the emptiness of unbelieving speculation, and to vindicate the fullness of Christian truth. This the author of these discourses has keenly felt; and he has done, not the best that could be done, but the best that *he* could do under the circumstances. While not attempting an exhaustive treatment of these *Isms*, he has tried to point out their startling dissonances, their thought-encircling darkness, and their comfortless, hopeless, soul-freezing tendencies; and he has tried to help his readers to grasp more deeply and feel more intensely those essential doctrines of religion that meet the necessities of our spiritual life, as the celestial poles coincide with the axis of our revolving world. As Lord Byron says in *Childe Harold*, "what is writ is writ"; and the author can only pray that it may not "die into an echo," but prove a word of hope to many a troubled heart,—a living seed, which, however lowly and insignificant, may not altogether prove either flowerless or leafless.

CONTENTS.

I.
AGNOSTICISM.
Or the Impregnability of Ignorance, - - - - 9

II.
ATHEISM.
Or the Superfluousness of Deity, - - - - - 40

III.
PANTHEISM.
Or the Deification of the Universe, - - - 62

IV.
MATERIALISM.
Or the Theory of Mindless Mechanism, - - - 82

V.
NATURALISM.
Or the World Without a Sovereign, - - - 101

VI.
PESSIMISM.
Or the Mystery of Human Suffering, - - - 127

VII.
BUDDHISM.
Or the Light of Asia and the Light of the World, - - - - - - - - - - - - - 156

VIII.
UNITARIANISM.
Or the Superhuman Manhood of Christ, - - 182

IX.
SPIRITUALISM.
Or the Modern Necromancy, - - - - - - - 205

X.
SKEPTICISM.
Or the Unreasonableness of Doubt, - - - - 229

XI.
LIBERALISM.
Or the Limits of Thought-Freedom, - - - - 250

XII.
FORMALISM.
Or the Relation of Shadow to Substance, - 267

XIII.
DENOMINATIONALISM.
Or Christian Unity in Diversity, - - - - - 284

XIV.
MAMMONISM.
Or the Savageness of Money-Greed, - - - - 303

XV.
PAUPERISM.
Or the Problem of Poverty, - - - - - - - 326

XVI.
ALTRUISM.
Or the Law of Self-Sacrifice, - - - - - - 345

ISMS OLD AND NEW.

AGNOSTICISM.

"To the Unknown God." *Acts xvii, 23.*

"And toward me now, the self-same paths I see a pilgrim steer.
Halt, wanderer! halt!—and answer me.—What, pilgrim, seek'st
    thou here?
               To the world's last shore
               I am sailing o'er,
Where life lives no longer to anchor alone,
And gaze on creation's last boundary stone.
Thou sail'st in vain.— Return! Before thy path, infinity!
And thou in vain!— Behind me spreads infinity to thee!
               Fold thy wings, drooping,
               O thought, eagle swooping!
Oh, fantasie, anchor! The voyage is o'er:
Creation, wild sailor, flows on to no shore!"
                                   Lytton's Schiller.

IN a curious book, called *The Rosicrucians*, an English peasant is represented as making an important discovery. As he was completing a trench on the close of a long day's work, his pick suddenly struck something hard, which emitted sparks. On examination it proved to be an oblong slab of granite, in the center of which was inserted an iron ring. After considerable labor he removed the stone, and found that it covered an entrance leading to subterranean chambers. Although it required no small degree of courage to do so, he determined to descend the rude and broken steps and attempt to penetrate the darkness. Down he clambered, and pressed on until the aperture above him had disappeared and the blackness of night enswathed him. He continued, however, to persevere in his perilous journey, and "at the foot of a steeper staircase of stone he saw a steady though pale light" gleaming. "This was shining as if from a star, or coming from the center of the earth." Naturally enough his alarm increased; but, resolutely hushing the voice of fear, he decided to explore the cave yet farther, and if possible solve the mystery. But as he cautiously felt his way he thought he heard noises as of horses and wagons over his head, which, combined with strange aromas that filled the cavern, heightened his bewilderment and apprehension. Awe stricken as he was, he followed the light, which grew brighter as he advanced, and gradually led him to a large, square built chamber. "Here was a flagged pavement and a somewhat lofty roof, in the groins of which was a rose, exquisitely carved in dark stone or marble." The place was solemn and gloomy, and great was the surprise of the rustic to see in the chamber the image of a man sitting in a rude chair, intently reading a huge book by the flickering radiance of an ancient lamp suspended from the ceiling. An involuntary cry of astonishment rose to his lips, and, though anxious to retreat, he actually took a step forward, and as he did so the figure started bolt upright, as if amazed at his boldness. Its hooded head was reared apparently in angry mood, and it moved as though it would address the intruder. The peasant, with that recklessness which seems to come to the human heart on the approach of danger, was not to be deterred by threatening looks, and therefore he drew nearer and yet nearer to the occupant of the stonelike throne. But as he advanced the hooded form thrust out its long arm and waved an iron baton forbiddingly;

and then, as if perceiving that the intruder would presumptuously adventure closer, it violently struck the lamp, and amid crashing detonating thunders out went the light. Enwrapped in darkness the brave peasant tremblingly stood, and realized that he had reached a boundary inviolable. He found himself in the abyss of midnight, reflecting, doubtless, on what had taken place, and slowly discerning that the effort to transcend the limits of inquiry had only resulted in distracting disorder and paralyzing portents.

Ever since man discovered the door that leads to the mysterious courts of knowledge, he has, lighted by reason, steadily pursued his way along tortuous labyrinths intent on possessing truth in its completeness, impatiently exclaiming, with the youth portrayed by Schiller, "What have I if I have not all?" Before him Nature, silent, stern, sublime, holding in its hand an inspired volume — the Bible, — has risen clearly and distinctly before his mental vision. Through the weary course of years, amid the thunderous roar of social and religious revolutions, he has drawn closer and closer to the "Giant Image," "dim gleaming through the hush of the large gloom," and has sought to penetrate its mightiest and deepest secrets. But ever has his impetuous search, "urged by the sharp fever of the wish to know," been baffled, and baffled when success seemed most assured. Triumph has quickly changed into defeat. Evermore has a mysterious hand warned back the ambitious invader of the Inscrutable, and mute lips have seemed to murmur, "Hitherto shalt thou come, but no further"; if, however, in blind intrepidity he has disdained the warning, and has continued "to rush in where angels fear to tread," darkness has settled over all his knowledge, and the harmonies of nature and of grace have grown discordant. Many a mind has been beclouded, many a soul has been saddened, "the sweet serenity of life has fled," and "deep anguish has dug an early grave," through the failure of inquiry to arrest its search at the boundary line of the impenetrable. To this boundary the Rosicrucian tradition points; and wise the man who recognizes its impassableness, and content with what of knowledge is attainable, frets not because beyond the reach of thought the pathless obscure extends.

Everywhere throughout the universe are limitations manifest. The fire-planets, that in their swift and mazy revolutions seem to sweep at pleasure through the unshored sea of space, are restrained and curbed, held to particular orbits, from which they never deviate, and beyond which they cannot circle. Oceans roll and impetuously drive their landward waves, and, dashing surgeful waters against nature's rugged barriers, threaten to submerge the earth. But all in vain their stormful rage and mad ambition. Ragged, jagged rocks intercept the lawless billows, and proudly disperse their strength in iridescent spray; and even defenseless sands check their tumultuous advance, and convert their white-capped breakers into idle, crawling, harmless foam. Plants and animals are circumscribed by zones and latitudes, or are so conditioned by some special element, that where one class or order flourishes others sicken, pine and die. Birds for the air, and fish for the water, and both for the narrower sphere within these broad domains to which they are adapted. The bald, grave eagle, around whose iron talons has been bound an iron chain, excites our pity, because he cannot rise on mighty wing to salute the burning splendor of the noon-tide sun. His ignoble fetters fatally curtail his freedom, and his straitened flight is easily surpassed by the ungainly efforts of the humblest fowl. The length of his chain determines the height of his winged ascent. But release him, set him free, and let his strong, swift pinions bear him far beyond the reach of man, and think you it will even then be possible for him to escape all trammels? No; though he soar to the gateway of the morning, he will at last reach a point impassable, and all his efforts to cleave a passage to a region higher than the sustaining air will end in sad defeat. He is, when in the enjoyment of his widest liberty, as truly caged in the circumambient atmosphere as is the silver-voiced canary that impatiently beats against the glittering wires of its little prison-house. Perhaps an ambitious fish of the intellectual order so eloquently described by Dr. Lindsay can be imagined as fretting that his existence should be bounded by the watery element. He can easily be pictured as complaining that his aspiring mind should be "cabined, cribbed and confined" within the narrow limits of sea or lake, when a vast universe stretches out immeasurable beyond. Such a member of the piscatorial family would undoubtedly contend that it is unfair to hold him captive, and prevent his mingling with happier creatures who range the earth according, as he supposes, "to their own sweet will." "Why," he might inquire, "should he be deprived of the fair fields, the fresh flowers, and sublime scenery, which yield untold delight to others?" And after much meditation on the dark problem, we can readily conceive of him as deciding to escape this thralldom, and enlarge indefinitely his sphere of action. Sapient fish! an avenue of escape undoubtedly may be found, and when least expected your hopes of emancipation be completely realized. For instance, an angler's hook promisingly flashes in the water, and if the opportunity is instantaneously improved, the reflective fish, after feeling a sharp sensation in his gill, and a rude, sudden jerk, will find himself — where? Where? — why here upon the land, gasping for breath, and hearing from irreverent lips the exclamation, "After all, I have only caught a gudgeon." The fisherman is right; only a gudgeon would fall into the error of supposing that life can be other than conditioned, or that its happiness and welfare can be promoted by ignoring the restrictions under which it has been placed.

Like the lower orders of creation, man is hedged in, walled around, and circumscribed. Law touches him on every side, and he can neither breathe nor move, feel nor act, beyond the confines of its kingdom. He can neither see nor hear if but a step too far from the object of sight and the source of sound; and constantly he discovers that his senses are only operative within a narrow and contracted circle. Indeed, man is a veritable Robinson Crusoe, "lord of all he surveys," free within certain prescribed limits, and yet a captive held within this space-girt island which we call earth. And as he is physically, so is he mentally. His mind, like his engirded body, has a well-defined capacity and sweep, but it is horizoned and rigidly environed. Fancy may roam unfettered and create a universe where it does not find one; but reason is shackled, and its strongly pulsating struggles for emancipation are ever baffled and defeated. The Scriptures insist on the comparatively narrow range of man's intellectual powers. They declare that there are questions utterly dense and impermeable to his understanding, a region of knowledge whose frontiers he may inspect, but never pass. The deeper mysteries of life and grace these Scriptures undertake to reveal, but never to explain; to make them clear to faith, not comprehensible to reason. "We now see through a glass darkly;" we "cannot find God out to perfection," and neither can we grasp the meaning of the glory that awaits us, for, as it is written, "it doth not yet appear what we shall be." When the Almighty in the book of Job is represented as answering the saintly patriarch out of the whirlwind, He affirms that His relation to the universe is unexplorable by mortal man, that the mystery of the seas is unfathomable, that the dwelling place of light is impenetrable, and the gates of the shadow of death impassable. He inquires of His suffering servant, "Knowest thou it because thou wast then born, or because the number of thy days is great?" To which the answer might have been given in David's inspired words, "Such knowledge is too great for me; it is high, I cannot attain unto it." And thus it follows that what God said to the sea, "Hitherto shalt thou come, but no further, and here shall thy proud waves be stayed," is as applicable to the mind; for thought, especially religious thought, is constantly checked by an invisible border-land which it cannot pass, and before which it must inevitably pause.

The history of theological science fully confirms this doctrine. Its honored masters have continually circled within an orbit of ideas, from whence they have never been able permanently to depart. Eccentric individuals who have desired to rank with theologians, and who have sought applause by advancing radical novelties in the realm of faith, have generally gleamed meteor-like across the ecclesiastical sky, and have gone out at last in the darkness of unbelief, or have been constrained by an uncontrollable something practically to return to the old statements of the deep questions which have perplexed man's understanding from the beginning. Neither have they, nor others, been able to do more than penetrate the surface of the doctrines concerning infinitudes, trinities, cosmogonies, redemptions, providences, eternities and immortalities on which their attention has been fixed. They have only disturbed the polish on the marble; they have never yet found a way to the real heart of the texture. Up to a certain point, adventurous inquiries have been successfully urged, but a Divine appointment, like unto that which arrests the proud waves at the sandy coast-line, has uniformly driven them back from the borders of the infinite. An impediment, somewhat like to the flaming sword that guarded the entrance to Eden's bowers, seems to protect the heavenly arcanum from too near approach. Consequently theology is fragmentary, incoherent, not exhaustive and complete; and its dogmatic statements, in comparison with the realities they symbolize, are as a spark to the sun, as an arc to a circle, and as the shrill notes of a tuneless organ to a chorus of angels. The science of Logic also witnesses to the restrictions imposed on thought. It lays down the laws of reasoning, and so clearly defined are all the processes of mental action in investigation and verification that this science has made but little, if any, advance since the days of Aristotle. What Whately, Mill or Hegel has added affects none of the fundamental principles laid down by him of Stagira; and the unprogressiveness of these principles proves that our thinking is unchangeably conditioned. And, evidently, these limitations are on our faculties, not on the truth; we, not it, are bound. We are forced to think in certain channels, and we are all conscious of meeting the same barriers, at the base of which daring speculative thought may surge a little, but which arrest with painful certitude its advance. But these barriers are within, not without; they reside in man's constitution, not in the nature of things beyond; they are due to some defect in man's understanding, not to the parsimoniousness of truth; they are determined by his character as a creature, not decreed by the jealousy of a Creator. Man is finite, and the truth he seeks is infinite; and the finite, with all its straining, can never compass the infinite. As the shell that is washed by the ocean cannot contain within itself the immensity of waters, as our little earth that is refreshed by the sun cannot hold the vast bulk of the solar world in its bosom, so neither can man's measurable capacity grasp and hold immeasurable magnitudes.

Perhaps in the whole domain of inquiry there is no truth that more fully commands the assent of reason than this, and yet there is none more liable to be perverted. Beginning with limitations which cannot be denied, it is not difficult to push the doctrine to the extreme of Nescience in matters of theology. Religious Pyrrhonism or Nihilism has more than once been the outgrowth of legitimate endeavors to measure the capabilities of thought, and in this age it is of the gravest moment that nothing should be said or done to encourage so serious a heresy.

When Paul went to Athens he found there an altar to the Unknown God. With that spiritual intuition which led so many ancient peoples to recognize above their multiplied inferior deities One Supreme Being, these philosophical Greeks perceived that the crowds of gods which filled their Pantheon could not account for this wonderful universe, and that there must be One superior to them all unto whom should be rendered homage and praise. The apostle acknowledged their scrupulous devoutness, and when he preached he revealed to them the Being whom they ignorantly worshiped. Mark this. He did not assume that they could *comprehend* the Invisible Mightiness, but he did claim that they could *know* Him. Hence the discourse which follows the text, in which the spirituality, creatorship, and sovereignty of God are affirmed.

In our times efforts are being made to rebuild this Athenian altar. A party has arisen on both sides of the Atlantic who, carrying the doctrine of thought limitations to an absurd extreme, maintain very earnestly that it is impossible to know anything of those deep and perplexing subjects which are involved in religion. They admit that there may be a Deity, a spiritual world, and a future life, but at the same time they assure us that we have no means of knowing that there are, and that, being constituted as we are, we can never expect to remedy this ignorance. Of course we can guess, wish, and dream indefinitely, but all of our speculations are only like the deceptive mirage, unverifiable and unsatisfying. Theological doctrines are but the shadows of our hopes and fears cast on the curtains of the universe, or the echoes of our own desires which we have been shouting in our folly, and which return to plague us. Man may be compared to a child wandering among the mountains, who in its fear and agony cries aloud on "Father," and hears the name repeated in the distance, and then calls "Father, seek your son," and in return catches the assuring response, "Son"; and then, with a gleam of joy in the heart, exclaims, in fond anticipation of deliverance, "Home," and backward to him comes the word, as though whispered by angel voices, "Home." But, after all, these are but echoes, and lost indeed would be the child who should heed them. Such, it is claimed, is man's position in the universe. A profound silence reigns around him, and he breaks it with the sound of his own voice, and fancies that its echo is the voice of the Invisible. Nor will he be persuaded of his error, but clings to it, imagining that he knows, when in reality he knows nothing; babbling about seeing through a glass darkly, when in fact he cannot see at all; talking of his inability to find out God unto perfection, when actually it is impossible for him to ascertain whether there is such a Being or not.

This is the creed of the Agnostic, the gospel of "know-nothingism," as it has been recently called, whose altar is reared not only to the Unknown, but to the Unknowable. Dr. Porter, of Yale College, in an article on Herbert Spencer, quotes a few verses, which give a fair idea of Agnostic belief, and which also illustrate its explanation of religion as it is found among men:

"At the end of every road there stands a wall,
Not built by hands,— impenetrable, bare.
Behind it lies an unknown land. And all
The paths men plod tend to it, and end there.
Each man, according to his humor, paints
On that bare wall strange landscapes, dark or bright,
Peopled with forms of friends or forms of saints,—
Hells of despair or Edens of delight."

Then the poet describes how the painters call upon their fellows to "tremble or rejoice," as though their pictures were realities, and how indignant they grow when some "sacrilegious hand" wipes off their landscapes and exposes the hard, cold, impenetrable wall. He portrays their anger and excitement at the desecration, and represents them as saying that it were better to have fiends and flames painted by fancy than this bare, blind, and empty obstruction.

"And straight the old work begins again
Of picture-painting And men shout and call
For response to their pleasure or pain,
Getting back echoes from that painted wall."

As a fit supplement to this poetic statement hear what Mr. Huxley has to say on man's duty and on the subjects which should engage his attention, and which should occupy his time. Whether he classes himself with avowed agnostics or not, the sentences I quote express their opinions very faithfully. In one of his Sunday evening lectures to the people he says: "If a man asks me what the politics of the inhabitants of the moon are, and I reply that I do not know, that neither I nor anyone else have any means of knowing, and that under these circumstances I decline to trouble myself about the subject at all, I do not think that he has any right to call me a skeptic. On the contrary, in replying thus I conceive that I am simply honest and truthful, and show a proper regard for the economy of time. So Hume's strong and subtle intellect takes up a great many problems about which we are naturally curious, and shows us that they are essentially questions of lunar politics, in their essence incapable of being answered, and therefore not worth the attention of men who have work to do in the world." Having quoted from Hume a passage where he recommends that volumes of divinity be given to the flames, as containing nothing but sophistry and illusion, Mr. Huxley continues: "Permit me to enforce this most wise advice. Why trouble ourselves about matters of which, however important they may be, we do know nothing and can know nothing? We live in a world which is full of misery and ignorance, and the plain duty of each and all of us is to try to make the little corner he can influence somewhat less miserable and somewhat less ignorant than it was before he entered it. To do this effectually it is necessary to be fully possessed of only two beliefs. The first, that the order of nature is ascertainable by our faculties to an extent which is practically unlimited; the second, that our volition counts for something as the condition of the order of events." (*Fortnightly Review*, February, 1869.)

This is Agnosticism, and there are reasons for believing that it is multiplying converts. There is that about it which seems so reverent, so modest, and so humble that it fascinates many minds. And then it deals so summarily with perplexities, and chimes in so harmoniously with man's devotion to the things of earth, relieving him of obligation to search for religious truth and to serve its Infinite Author, that it seems to be the real philosophy of life, and to be worthy the adoption of the wise and prudent. The temptation is, therefore, great to embrace it without due reflection, and to overlook the very grave objections which lie against its credibleness. These objections are derived from various sources, and deserve to be fairly weighed before the emptiness of Religious

Nihilism is substituted for the fullness of Christian Faith. A brief examination will abundantly establish their validity, and will conclusively show that this specious Ism is
Condemned by Science,
Refuted by Reason,
Contradicted by Experience,
Rejected by Revelation, and
Discredited by Morality.
And, surely, the strength and significance of these various protests should be candidly and conscientiously estimated by every one who desires to commit himself only to such opinions as rest on firm foundations.

The attitude of many leading scientists unquestionably is favorable to the assumptions of Agnosticism. This damaging fact I do not attempt to conceal. Already we have heard from Mr. Huxley, and in the same direction Professor Tyndall has written: "The mind of man may be compared to a musical instrument with a certain range of notes, beyond which in both directions we have an infinitude of silence. The phenomena of matter and force lie within our intellectual range, and as far as they reach we will at all hazards push our inquiries. But behind and above and around all the real mystery of this universe lies unsolved, and, as far as we are concerned, is incapable of solution." But though scientists frequently indulge in such representations, we are not, therefore, to conclude that they are warranted or approved by science itself. They are far from being scientific. Science tells a different story. It knows, and otherwise it dare not report, that as much mystery enshrouds "the phenomena of matter and force" as invests what lies behind them, and that our "intellectual range" is no more equal to the complete comprehension of the one than the other. The great preacher, P. Felix, in one of his Notre Dame *Conferences* impressively inquires, "Who has been able to penetrate the secret of the formation of a body, the generation of a single atom? What is there I will not say at the center of a sun, but at the center of an atom? Who has sounded to the bottom the abyss in a grain of sand? The grain of sand, gentlemen, has been studied four thousand years by science; she has turned and re-turned it; she divides it and subdivides it; she torments it with her experiments; she vexes it with her questions, to snatch from it the final word as to its secret constitution; she asks it, with an insatiable curiosity, Shall I divide thee infinitesimally? Then, suspended over this abyss, science hesitates, she stumbles, she feels dazzled, she becomes dizzy, and in despair says, "I do not know." And, in like manner, who has fathomed the oceanic depths of mystery in a single drop of water? This question I have often asked myself; I have sought an answer from the books of science, and having heard their dim responses, I have come to believe that there is in this familiar object, which hangs like pearls on grass and flower, which sparkles in the sun, and which sweeps in evening rains and exhales in morning dew, seas of enigmas deep enough to drown the mightiest intellects. Thought has sailed over it for thousands of years, but no coast-line has ever yet been reached, and no bottom has ever yet been found. We easily express its constituent elements, and yet we are far from realizing the terrible forces that are contained and that slumber in its bosom. Were these suddenly set free, they would devastate with the fury of a midnight tempest, and would startle us with the wild evidences of their Titanic power. As Faraday has shown, the energy of 800,000 charges of the Leyden battery is lodged in a drop of water, sufficient to produce an effect equal to a stroke of lightning. But can a Faraday explain this tremendous and overwhelming wonder? Can any mind find it out unto perfection? No; inquire as we may, we must still confess our ignorance. Oceans are necessary to engulf our ships, but a drop of water seems all-sufficient to engulf our reason.

But if an atom is as a trackless continent and a water-drop as an unnavigable sea, what shall we say to the majesty of the universe? We boastingly parade our intellectual conquests over nature, and yet, if we have not subdued an atom, how insignificant must be our knowledge of the heavens! We have above us gleaming a world — the sun — containing in its mass a volume of substance larger than that which composes the bulk of the united worlds in the center of whose mighty circle it spins and shines. Astronomers have proven that it is one million three hundred thousand times vaster than the globe; and that three hundred years would be needed to circumnavigate it, while three years would suffice, at the same rate of speed, to voyage around this petty terraqueous ball. Its heat, and the terrific energy of its heat, scientists have in vain tried to measure. They have never yet been able to convey to the mind a comprehensible idea of this tremendous force. The column of ice fifty-four miles in diameter, propelled at a rate of two hundred and ten thousand miles per minute, which Herschel figures would be needful to perceptibly diminish its intensity; or the comparison of Tyndall, that the heat of the sun every hour is equal to the combustion of nearly seven leagues thick of coal, distributed over an area as vast as its own surface, stimulates the imagination, but only astounds and prostrates the reason. Then beyond our solar system there are glowing orbs, and solitudes of unpeopled space, processions of nebulæ, unkindled suns, and embryo stars, moving at different rates of velocity and in various directions, in comparison with which the solar system is as the dew-drops pendent from the flower that lifts its tiny head on the vast ocean's verge. Sir William Herschel, in the eighteenth century, from the Cape of Good Hope, undertook with the aid of his gigantic telescope to count the stars in the Milky Way, and as the result of his investigations arrived at a totality of more than eighteen million suns. Yet even this is only an inconsiderable fraction of the unnumbered worlds which, bound by ties and sweet affinities, roll harmoniously in the ether-depths throughout the immensity of creation, whose fathomless tides seem "to flow on to no shore." Who has ever had steadiness of mind sufficient to follow their mazy courses, and who has been able to comprehend the unity which pervades the whole? Light, traveling two hundred miles a second, takes thousands of years to reach our planet from some of the cresset lamps that gleam in heaven. Venus is 27,000,000 miles from the sun; the nearest fixed star is 20,000,000,000 miles distant from the earth; and deserts of creation doubtless separate such worlds remote from the confines of yet remoter systems. But who is there that really understands what these prodigious distances and spaces signify? We represent them to the eye in figures, but no mind is capable of forming a just conception of their exhaustless meaning. They exceed the power of thought, as gravitation, about which we speak so glibly, baffles the scrutiny of the keenest intellect. An eminent French *savant* has well said on this point, "We know that bodies approach each other in the ratio of their masses, and in inverse ratio of the square of their distances; but why do they approach each other? This is what we do not know, and what we probably never shall know." . . . "As to the real cause which makes small bodies to rush toward greater ones, and the little stars to revolve around the larger, it is, we repeat, a mystery that cannot be penetrated by mortals." And thus science itself comes to a standstill at the border-land, and is incompetent to explain the wonders it proclaims; and shall we then for one moment suppose, when the subjects of inquiry are theological, that science will presume to say that the affirmation of mystery becomes the negation of knowledge? If it should do so, it would simply invalidate its own teachings; for if thought-limitations in one direction are held to prove the certitude of incertitude, logically they must do so in the other. And thus, according to such reasoning, Nescience in religion leads by a logical necessity to Pyrrhonism in science. As has been said by M. Royer-Collard, "we cannot assign a part only to skepticism; as soon as skepticism once penetrates into the understanding, it invades it throughout."

Professor Tyndall admits that the phenomena of matter and force are within our intellectual range, but denies that by them we can invade the intrenched secret of the universe that lies beyond. If he means that we cannot "find God out unto perfection" through the operations of nature, we have no controversy with him; but if he means that we cannot by such endeavors arrive at a real, though partial, knowledge of the Divine existence, we modestly but earnestly dissent from his position. Newton has said, "It no doubt belongs to natural philosophy to inquire concerning God from the observation of phenomena," and there is no good reason for doubting the soundness of his conclusion. The contrary assumption is so one-sided, so destitute of analogy, so foreign to the judgment of mankind, creating so wide and so arbitrary a distinction between the domain of matter and of mind, that it borders on the irrational. Common sense argues that, as everyone admits we can become acquainted with the laws governing physical phenomena by the study of the phenomena themselves, there is no sufficient reason to doubt that we can in the same manner arrive at certain reliable conclusions regarding the Divine existence and man's immortality. The laws that govern the various operations of nature can be known, though they are unseen; and though they may not be thoroughly understood, our information concerning them is looked upon as absolutely trustworthy. But physical phenomena lead us back to Cause as well as to law, and to a Cause adequate to accomplish what is perceived; and as in the phenomena mind is apparent, we may with the same degree of certainty believe that it is in the Cause as we believe, on precisely the same evidence, that law is, and that it answers to such or such a formula. If the reasoning in the one case is sound it is in the other, and if it is not in either, then we are incapable of verifying anything. On the one side, by the knowledge of phenomena we rise to the knowledge of law; on the other, by the same means we rise to the knowledge of Cause, and to a Cause which, comprehending in itself potentially the complex and practically measureless wonders of creation, we cannot but call God. But if it is said that such a Being cannot be clearly apprehended or distinctly defined, common sense replies that the limitations of mind account for this comparative failure, but that the inability is paralleled by the difficulty experienced in understanding fully the precise character of a law, say such as gravitation, and of formulating it intelligibly. The dew-drop that faithfully reflects the sun, gives but a meager idea of its majesty. But in addition to this, common sense protests against the exclusive attention to the physical and the disregard for the spiritual which Professors Tyndall and Huxley manifest. It insists that the phenomena of soul are as worthy of consideration as those of matter. Mind is an essential part of the universe, and no system can be sound which ignores it. If it is scrutinized and catechized, it responds in no doubtful terms to the reality of God and the immortality of man. On this internal testimony an unanswerable argument has frequently been reared. The universal consciousness is against Agnosticism, and the only question in debate is whether its testimony is reliable. Why should it be thought otherwise? If we can with safety build on the physical, why not on the psychical? They are parts of the same system of things. For all we know, the latter may even be more trustworthy than the former, and unquestionably it challenges as much attention. But if it is not to be treated as a faithful witness when it testifies to God's existence and to man's immortality, what confidence can be placed in any of its processes, without which we would be unable to ascertain anything, conceive or substantiate anything, either physical or spiritual? It is a necessity of science, as well as of religion, that the trustworthiness of mind be admitted. If it is not, then everything is uncertain; if it is, then its testimony to the supersensuous, the superhuman and divine is conclusive and unimpeachable.

We have thus shown that science, fairly interrogated, condemns the ism we are reviewing, and we are now prepared to weigh what reason has to suggest in the same direction. The Agnostic is essentially metaphysical. His stronghold is in cloudland, and his logical defenses are abstract, involved, subtle and tortuous. He speaks the language of Sir William Hamilton's *Lectures*, of Dean Mansel's *Limits of Religious Thoughts*, and of Herbert Spencer's voluminous revelations regarding the Unknowable. To him the fundamental conceptions of theology are unthinkable and self-destructive, and he triumphantly asks, "How can Infinite Power be able to do all things, and Infinite Goodness be unable to do evil? How can Infinite Justice exact the utmost penalty for every sin, and Infinite Mercy pardon the sinner? How can Infinite Wisdom know all things, and Infinite Freedom be at liberty to do or to forbear? How is the existence of evil compatible with that of an Infinitely Perfect Being? For if He wills it, He is not infinitely good; and if He wills it not, His will is thwarted and His sphere of action limited." He further insists that the Infinite or the Absolute is inconceivable: "There is contradiction in supposing such an object to exist, either alone or with others, and in supposing it not to exist; in conceiving it as one and as many, as personal and as impersonal, as active and as inactive, as the sum of all existence and as a part only of that sum," and, consequently, we find him sententiously affirming with Herbert Spencer that this is the "deepest, widest, and most certain of all facts, that the Power the universe manifests to us is utterly inscrutable."

Reason is not satisfied with these representations, and is far from consenting to the conclusion. Following in substance Mr. Mill's line of argument, it claims that while we may not have an adequate conception of the Infinite, we may be able to form a very real conception, and it illustrates this distinction by a passage from Mr. Mill's *Examination of Sir W. Hamilton's Philosophy*, in which he says, "Let us try the doctrine on a complex whole, short of infinite, such as the number 695,788. Sir W. H. would not, I suppose, maintain that this number is inconceivable. How long does he think it would take to go over every separate unit of this whole, so as to obtain a perfect knowledge of that exact sum, as different from all others, greater or less? Would he say that we can have no conception of the sum till this process is gone through? We could not, indeed, have an adequate conception. Accordingly, we never have an adequate conception of any real thing. But we have a real conception, if we can conceive it by any of its attributes which are sufficient to distinguish it from all other things. . . . If, then, we can obtain a real conception of a finite whole, without going through all its component parts, why deny us the conception of an infinite whole because to go through them all is impossible? . . . Between a conception which, though inadequate, is real as far as it goes, and the impossibility of any conception, there is a wide difference." Moreover, reason discerns in the doctrine of the Unknowable a grave inconsistency. Having expressly denied that the Infinite can be a subject of thought, it goes to work to show why it is unthinkable, and in doing so it quietly assumes certain things to be true of it which, according to its principal proposition, it has no possible means of verifying. If the Infinite is unknowable, how can the Agnostic prove that this or that idea is inharmonious with it? As it is, he proceeds on the supposition that he knows it for the purpose of obtaining the evidence that it is unknowable.

Mr. Mill has clearly brought out the fact that the Agnostic conjures up "a conception of something which possesses infinitely all conflicting attributes," and because this cannot be done without contradiction, "he would have us believe that there is contradiction in the idea of Infinite Goodness or Infinite Wisdom," on which piece of metaphysical insincerity Mr. Mill comments in these terms: "Instead of 'the Infinite' substitute an 'Infinitely Good Being,' and the argument reads thus: If there is anything which an infinitely good Being cannot become, if He cannot become bad, there is a limitation, and the goodness cannot be infinite. If there is anything which He is, namely, good, He is excluded from being any other thing, as from being wise or powerful." Having pointed out these absurdities he declares that these contradictions are not involved in the notion of the Infinite, "but lie in the definitions," definitions which have been expressly manufactured for the sole purpose of proving that nothing can be known of the Supreme Ruler of the universe. But after all that has been done in this direction success has not followed, for, as Professor Birks has exhaustively shown in his admirable treatise on *Physical Fatalism*, a work to which I gladly acknowledge my indebtedness, the very terms employed to express the unknowableness of the unknown convey an important and large amount of knowledge. Thus from the various ideas and positions of its advocates, already quoted, we learn that God is absolute not derived, infinite not finite, manifest in nature not hidden, distinct from His works not identified with them, omnipotent not impotent, and One not manifold. This is a good deal of information for a theory, which sets out to demonstrate that the Almighty is absolutely inscrutable, to afford humanity struggling to obtain light. We really are indebted. By these concessions, involved in the mazy and hazy statements of the Agnostic, reason perceives that his doctrine is untenable, and that he is confirming, though unwillingly, the positive declaration of Paul: "For the invisible things of Him from the creation of the world are clearly seen, being understood by the things that are made, even His eternal power and Godhead."

But if reason refutes, experience contradicts Agnosticism. When its supporters assert that nothing spiritual can be known, they are merely judging mankind by themselves. Because they themselves are in the gulf of night, they conclude that everybody is in the same unhappy condition. But if a few persons living inland should contend that the ocean does not exist because they have not seen it, would we be willing to allow that it is unseeable, especially when thousands testify that their eyes have rested on its grandeur? No; we would answer that the privation of some cannot be weighed against the positive observation of others. Though a hundred persons should deny that President Lincoln was assassinated because they were not present to witness the tragical event, the testimony of half a dozen who were on the spot would be sufficient to prove its occurrence. Well, all the Agnostics in the world cannot invalidate the experience of a few

Christians. All they can say is that they do not know, and that is worthless by the side of the "I do know" of Christ's disciples. His followers have communed with God, have conversed with him. They have realized the grandeur of responsibility, the awfulness of sin, and the sweetness of pardon, and they can therefore speak with authority. If it shall be said that they are self-deceived, then we are modestly asked to believe that all the world is deluded, with the exception of a few individuals who are evidently infatuated with the charms of ignorance. But is this reasonable? Why may not the few be deceived by their prejudices instead of the many be duped by their fancies? We do not deny that what we have felt may be but as the shadows described in Plato's *Republic*, which were seen by the captives in the subterranean cave when their back was turned toward the light, but shadows are ever cast by substantial objects, and proclaim reality. The reflection of the mountains in the water attests their existence and their vastness, and thus our experiences, though but as faint images of the Infinite, of eternity, of immortality, witness to sublime and imperishable correspondences. But there is another answer to this supposition. As has been elaborately stated by a New England author, religious truth is not above experiment. If you would know for yourself whether there is a God, or whether He can be communed with, and whether He can come into the soul, comply with the conditions revealed in the Bible, and you shall have the evidence in yourselves. Put away wrong doing, call upon God's name, beseech Him to verify His own being and your own immortality, sincerely desire to discover the truth, and I have no doubt but that the answer will be such that you and Agnosticism will part company forever. Dr. Walker, in the *Observer*, eloquently points out the grounds of this duty, and enforces it in a manner so masterly that I cannot refrain from quoting his words. He says:

"Man finds himself with a religious nature, the spontaneous and normal exercise of which is reverence, adoration, obedience to a Power above himself. Here are subjective conditions, which imply objective truths corresponding. As is the case with all other parts of his nature, these are not purposeless. They prompt to the investigation of that which they demand and to which they are related,—truths about God, in the universe of mind and of matter, discovered, certified, reduced to system, rendered into theology. These truths are those of the Divine personality, His character, His dealings especially with man, endowed with a nature which craves to know and honor Him. Why should man refuse to seek Him here as well as elsewhere? Is it the really scientific spirit which dictates such a course? Is it not mere caprice not only to decline investigation of these phenomena objective to the religious nature, and demanded by it, but to insist beforehand that such investigation, if made, is not and cannot be scientific? Such course, in reference to anything but religious truth, would not for an instant be tolerated. But here we are met by the objection of mystery. What is its pertinence? It is never offered in connection with other sciences. They all involve mystery, rest upon it, and are surrounded by it. What is matter? What is life? What is mind? What is spirit? '*Omnia exeunt in mysterium.*' No one, on the score of mystery, declines scientific investigation, or denies its possibility in any of these spheres of knowledge. It is only as men see or fear that they will encounter God in His claims, that such objections are offered. They do not like to retain God in their knowledge, and thus their effort is to make out that He cannot be known."

The allusion to the Bible in the foregoing paragraph

leads us naturally to our next position. Revelation rejects in toto the senseless theory of religious Nihilism. Suppose that we concede to the Agnostic that the limitations of thought are such that it is impossible for man to arrive at the knowledge of God or of his own destiny, does that preclude the possibility of its coming to him in some other way? May not that which is undiscoverable be revealed? Or, in other words, if man's capacity is as narrow and weak as Agnosticism claims, does it prove the unattainableness of religious knowledge, or does it merely indicate that an inspired Revelation is indispensable? Certainly it can never establish the former as long as the latter is possible. And that it is possible the belief of many millions that it is actual abundantly sustains. Everywhere we hear of sacred books, attributed to divine interposition, and whether only one is true, or all are alike false, they express the common conviction that the Almighty can communicate with His creatures. The ideas which fill mind and heart regarding the Supreme, the nature of obligation, and the eternity of the soul, may have been derived from this source by immediate and personal illumination, or by the inspired enlightenment of chosen men. We know, however, that the ideas are here; how they came may be open to debate, but that they have not been received from God is beyond the power of man to prove. Whether any existing revelation is in reality of Divine origin cannot be discussed here, nor is it needful, for our present aim is simply to show that, though man's resources be inadequate to meet his spiritual necessities, it cannot with reason be affirmed that religious knowledge is beyond his reach when it may be received from above. Agnosticism at the worst only establishes the necessity for a heavenly revelation, and the more fully it makes manifest our helplessness the more clearly it brings out the probability that it has been conferred. For if we are thus incapable, and if we feel so deep a yearning for light — and that we do no one can deny — that we are led to seek it by a native impulse, our highest welfare must be interwoven with it, and just in proportion as this is true must the probability be increased that the Being who has provided so liberally for all our other wants has not forgotten to bestow this last and indispensable boon.

Herbert Spencer, in his *Philosophy*, expresses the opinion " that the knowledge within our reach is the only knowledge that can be of service to us"; and it seems to me the right word to say in this connection, for in judging the claims of any sacred book we should examine whether its teachings are especially available for the moral exigencies of life, or whether they are fitted merely to gratify a prurient curiosity. The ship-master does not need accurate views regarding the origin or formation of the universe to safely navigate a vessel across stormy seas. Professional practicalities are of more importance to him. If he knows the tides, their strength and their seasons; if he is instructed in the use of the compass, its deflections and variations; if he understands taking the sun, and even how to steer without it, and if he is familiar with the capabilities of his ship, his ignorance of the true cosmogony would not disqualify him for command. The mason builds without knowing the plan of the architect, the soldier fights without inquiring into the designs of the general, the laborer in the factory pursues his task on the ninth part of a pin, and never pauses to investigate his brothers' work, or to demand from his employer a detailed account of the contracts which he is fulfilling. We all thus work on partial knowledge, and work efficiently. Thorough and exhaustive comprehension of everything connected with our daily callings none of us have, and neither is it necessary to success. It seems, then, reasonable to infer that a Revelation from God would deal more directly with the moral and spiritual practicalities than in elaborate expositions of deep truths, which, however glorious in themselves, would be comparatively of secondary value in their bearing upon life. And this is precisely the principle which determines the character of the sacred Scriptures. While they announce abysmal mysteries, they leave them mysteries; and partly, perhaps, because the intellect could not grasp their clearest elucidation now, and partly because another class of truths is of more immediate service, they devote a large portion of their contents to such matters as lead to human regeneration, elevation and salvation. Upon such points they are adequate and complete. We, therefore, have in these inspired writings all the knowledge necessary both for life and godliness. We have enough both for faith and practice, and unless we are prepared to ignore the probabilities which so strongly point to the reasonableness of a supernatural revelation, we need not inhabit tombs nor grope in darkness, and despairingly cry that we know not our duty either to God or man. Here it is made manifest, and made manifest in such a way that it is unobscured and unaffected by the unexplorable truths with which it is associated. Though clouds and darkness still enshroud God's throne, sufficient light has fallen on our path to make clear the road to heaven. There is no position we occupy, no relationship we sustain, no serious issue we have to meet, concerning which we may not, if we will, obtain the fullest information; neither is there any honest doubt, springing from a troubled conscience, that has not its antidote in the affluent provisions of Divine grace. If you would know how to approach and honor your Creator; if you would realize the claims of Christ upon your faith and love; if you would learn how to fulfill your obligations as parent, child, citizen, or friend, and if you would understand how to live and die triumphantly, you have but to consult the sacred volume, whose pages glow with simplest wisdom and with safest counsels. The Bible may be reticent where you would be pleased to have it voluble, it may be tongueless where you would have it eloquent, and obscure where you would have it clear; but though it may conceal many things from your too curious eyes, and refuse to lay bare either the secrets of a past or of a future eternity, what reason have you for complaint if it has made manifest the range and scope of present duty? This much at least it has done; and for the way in which you deal with the Heaven-given light — call it twilight if you will — which it has shed upon your path, will you have to render an account to God, not for the darkness which it has left undisturbed, and which all your intellectual power never can dispel.

Finally, morality discredits Agnosticism; for its interests are jeopardized by a doctrine that condemns mankind to total ignorance on matters of individual and social obligation, and forbids them to recognize a moral governor of the world. On this point Mr. Mill, in the work already alluded to, testifies, and certainly he is no partial witness: "My opinion of this doctrine (namely, that nothing can be known or understood of moral attributes in a Supreme Being), in whatever way presented, is that it is simply the most morally pernicious doctrine now current, and that the question it involves is, beyond all others which now engage speculative minds, the decisive one between good and evil for the Christian world." This can easily be demonstrated by the effect of this Ism on society. When it declares religious knowledge to be unattainable, it, of course, anticipates the formation of communities where it will be entirely ignored. Absolute secularism is already recommended, and the extract quoted from Mr. Huxley places him on the side of those who deem it desirable. He would have us care for our fellow-beings, would have us try to alleviate their sorrows, and diminish their ignorance. But it is legitimate to ask by what motives shall philanthropy be sustained and inspired when Agnosticism triumphs? It will then be impossible to prove that it is even a duty, and will be beyond the ability of man to show that it would not, on the whole, be better just to let the unfortunate classes perish as rapidly as possible. Carried to its logical consequences, this theory does not even offer any encouragement to education; for why, if there is no divine law imposing such obligation on us, should we trouble ourselves about others at all, and why lavish so much care on those who cannot make much progress in this life, and who can never reap any benefit from it in a life to come? Proposals to organize society on a Godless basis have always been looked on with suspicion, and indeed every effort in that direction has been fraught with evil. It has been proven, where the attempt has been made, that it is impossible to foster reverence for law, to cultivate a due sense of responsibility, to conserve safety, and property, and to promote purity and peace, apart from the recognition of the Almighty, His supremacy, and man's immortality. Many infidels have recognized this, and among them one whom we would least suspect of entertaining such sentiments. Thomas Paine has left on record his conviction that stable and wholesome government must rest on Divine truth. When, in his book entitled *Common Sense*, he is answering those who expected the speedy destruction of order in these States because monarchy was overthrown, he says: "Let a day be solemnly set apart for proclaiming the charter; let it be brought forth, placed on the Divine law, the Word of God; let a crown be placed thereon, by which the world may know that so far as we approve of monarchy, that in America the Law is king." [*P.* 47.] That is, human law must rest on the Divine for it to be clothed with authority and secure to the citizen the blessings of good government. But this foundation Agnosticism sweeps away, and we therefore feel warranted in concluding that it must be radically defective and undeserving of confidence. And here ends my argument.

Man's mind is limited, but it is not powerless; it has its zenith and its nadir, but its periphery is neither meager nor contracted; it is circumscribed in its range, but it is neither wingless nor footless. It may not be able to circumnavigate infinity, nor "gaze on creation's last boundary stone," but it can sail on its seas and know that its floods stretch limitless around. It may not be able to fathom the abyss of mystery that there is in an atom, nor lay bare the secret hidden in the humblest seed; but it can measure them both, and know in part, if not altogether. With becoming modesty may it acknowledge its inability to comprehend the Author of its being, or to find out His plans and purposes to perfection; but though it confess that it cannot do everything, it would be absurd to assume that it cannot do anything. It can know God, and learn of God, though it has no terms by which to explain Him; it can think of Him as Absolute, as Infinite, as Personal, while it may never in this life be able to fathom the full meaning of these sublime ideas. At present the mind has sufficient capacity to know the Creator, that He is, what — in part at least — He is, what He commands and what He reveals. Sufficient for present duties, present hopes, whether for time or eternity, can be acquired. And happy the man who improves the light he has. By and by, in the world to come, the veil on the mind shall be rent, the channels of thought be widened and deepened, and the soul's pinions be immeasurably strengthened, and then shall man comprehend the height,

depth and breadth of that which here and now passeth
understanding.

> "O gracious God! how well dost Thou provide
> For erring judgments an unerring guide!
> Thy throne is darkness in the abyss of night,
> A blaze of glory that forbids the sight.
> Oh, teach me to believe Thee thus concealed,
> And search no further than Thyself revealed;
> But her alone for my director take
> Whom Thou hast promised never to forsake!
> My thoughtless youth was winged with vain desires;
> My manhood, long misled by wandering fires,
> Followed false lights, and when their glimpse was gone
> My pride struck out new sparkles of her own.
> Such was I, such by nature still I am;
> Be Thine the glory and be mine the shame!
> Good life be now my task; my doubts are done."

ATHEISM.

"In the beginning God created the heaven and the earth." *Gen. i, 1.*

"Heaven's unnumbered host,
Though multiplied by myriads, and arrayed
In that glory of sublimest thought,
Is but an atom in the balance weighed
Against Thy greatness — is a cypher brought
Against infinity!
I *am*, O God, and surely Thou must be!
Thou art! — directing, guiding all, Thou art!
Direct my understanding, then, to Thee;
Control my spirit, guide my wandering heart."
Russian Ode, by Derzhaven.

THE way-worn traveler will gladly drink from the cool, clear, sparkling torrent that breaks from lofty and solitary rocky fastnesses, and rolls tumultuously over somber precipice and along jagged channel to the dusty plains, though its source may be hidden from his curious eyes, and forever remain inaccessible to his adventurous feet; and truth's mountain-stream should ever be as welcome to earth's weary thinkers, however hidden its springs may be in heights unapproachable, and in depths unfathomable.

If venerable tradition, chronicled by the Koran, repeated by Stanley, and rehearsed by Clodd, is to be credited, thus was truth,— the grandest, mightiest, and most mysterious,— welcomed by Him who is honored by Moslem, Jew and Christian as the Father of the Faithful. Born in Ur of the Chaldees, on the verge of the vast Assyrian plains, which for ages had been the seat of idolatrous sun-worship, Abraham turned from a system, custom-sanctioned and convention-hallowed, to embrace a simpler and a purer faith. The mythical story of his conversion is not without beauty and instructiveness. It represents Terah, his father, as a maker of wooden idols; and shows how the son's antagonism to the corruption of religion, which the business symbolized, developed and culminated. Being left one day in charge of the stock in trade, Abraham was profoundly impressed at the folly and superstition of a woman, who devoutly brought food to satisfy the hunger of *things* which, though they had mouths, could not eat, and which were as unable to appreciate gifts as they were to appropriate them. But his indignation grew fiercer, and his views of duty clearer, when an aged man entered his tent and desired to purchase of his wares.

"How old art thou?"

"Threescore years."

"What, threescore years!" answered Abraham, "and thou wouldst worship a thing that my father's slaves made in a few hours? Strange that a man of sixty should bow his gray head to a creature such as that."

Unable longer to restrain his scorn, and reason asserting its sovereignty over conflicting doubts, after the departure of his would-be customer he broke all the idols to pieces except one. The largest one he spared, and placed in its hands the hammer which had served him in his iconoclasm. When Terah returned he was filled with horror and consternation at the work of destruction which he beheld, and angrily demanded the name of the irreverent wretch who had dared to raise his impious arm against the gods.

"Why," quietly replied the then youthful patriarch, "during thine absence a woman brought them food, and the younger and smaller ones immediately began to eat. The older and stronger god, enraged at their unmannerly boldness, took the hammer which you see in his hands, and crushed them all before him."

"Dost thou deride thine aged father?" cried Terah. "Do I not know that they can neither move nor eat?"

"And yet thou worshipest them," exclaimed Abraham; "and thou wouldst have me worship them as well."

This rebuke was too much for the outraged parent, and consequently, according to the legend, he sent the wayward youth to the king for admonition and correction. When Nimrod heard the account of his infidelity and impiety, instead of condemning him hastily and harshly he sought to win him to some form of faith.

"If thou canst not adore the idols fashioned by thy father," said the accommodating monarch, "then pray to fire."

"Why not to water, which will quench the fire?"

"Be it so; pray to water."

"But why not to the clouds which hold the water?"

"Well, then, pray to the clouds."

"Why not to the winds, which drive the clouds before them?"

"Certainly, please yourself; pray to the winds."

"Be not angry, O king!" finally replied Abraham. "I cannot pray to the fire, or the water, or the clouds, or the winds, but to the Creator who made them: Him only will I worship." Neither would he be persuaded to adore the sun, moon and stars, for he discerned that they were not stationary, and he said, as he contemplated the heavens, "I like not things that set; these glittering orbs are not gods, as they are subject to law: I will worship Him only whose law they obey."

Science is the modern Terah. In these days it is energetically reviving idol-making, a trade which by this time ought to be hopelessly insolvent. The chief workmen who seem to be interested in this enterprise are Comte, Haeckel, Darwin, Vogt, Huxley and Spencer, and the gods they have thus far manufactured are variously called "Protoplasm," "Evolution," "Primitive Fire-Mist," "Promise and Potency Theory," and "Creation by Law Hypothesis." In these thought-idols a thriving business is being driven, and, as in the case of the foolish woman and the venerable man in the Abrahamic legend, many souls are substituting them in the place of the one ever-living and true God. They who have shaped these little mechanical deities, and who expose them to public view, do not assert that there may not be above them or behind them *Something* or *Somebody* to the mind unknown and unknowable, but they do assume that they are all-sufficient to account for the origin and order of the universe, without invoking the interposition of any hyperphysical or supernatural agencies or Agent. It is evident that the drift of such speculations is in the direction of Atheism; for when every reference to the Almighty is sneered at as unscientific, when He is practically ruled out of His own creation, and when second causes are invested with His attributes and credited with His work, the denial of His existence is logically demanded and cannot be long postponed. A superfluous Deity is the next thing to an imaginary Deity; to deprive Him of usefulness is to rob Him of being; to say that He *does not* is substantially to say that *He is not*. This is just the impression the new Terah is making on society, and the hammer of Abraham is needed to destroy the false gods that hide from the creature the reality and nearness of the Creator. Multiplied voices, like his, are demanded to denounce the fetich-worship developing from modern thought, and to point out the absurdity of scientific Nimrods reaffirming what Descartes has long since disproved, that dynamical force inheres in matter, or that law, which at the best is only a formula, can of itself enact itself, and from itself evolve a universe.

The advocates of undisguised and absolute Atheism, and the idol-makers who sympathize with them, are more or less agreed in maintaining certain propositions on the truth or falseness of which rests the decision of the grave question in debate. If the propositions referred to cannot be sustained, Atheism is without even the shadow of a foundation; if they can, then to say the least the cause of theism is seriously compromised, if not imperiled. It is assumed:

First, That the idea of God is explicable without God.

Second, That the origin of nature is comprehensible without God.

Third, That the existence of religion is possible without God.

Fourth, That the elevation of humanity is practicable without God.

These propositions, in my honest judgment, are untenable; most sincerely I condemn them, and confidently believe that their rejection can be justified.

Evolution, as taught by its greatest philosopher, Herbert Spencer, is regarded as adequate to account for intellectual and social advancement, as well as for physical development. Everything, it is claimed, that we think or feel, as well as everything we see or touch, has been evolved from lower and simpler forms or states. And thus, it is argued, the idea of God originated, and has slowly passed through many intermediate stages of growth toward grace and beauty. It is assumed that fetich-worship prevailed at the beginning; that this was subsequently refined into polytheism; and that this in its turn gradually gave way to theism; and that since the triumph of monotheism the character of the ideal, exalted to supreme sovereignty, has unceasingly improved and broadened. Primary and necessary belief in God's existence is denied, a primeval and supernatural attestation of this belief is discredited, and its beginnings are traced to human

THE EVOLUTION OF DEITY. 45

fear mingled with superstition. This notion runs through the poem of Lucretius; it is countenanced by Hume; it is expressed by Dupuis in the words "the gods are the children of men," and it is formulated and maintained by Comte.

Of course that which had so questionable an origin, in the advancing light of science cannot hope to maintain its authority. The luminous meteor, whose radiance broke through the night of ignorance, must inevitably be eclipsed by the sun of knowledge. As the idea of God, according to this theory, was first invented, or conjured up, to explain the universe, just in proportion as that can be accounted for, apart from Him, must confidence in His existence be diminished. And thus the natural bourne of Evolution is Atheism; and no God, the ultimate faith, or no-faith, of the world.

It is not to be denied that a color of truth tints this mass of assumption, but the color is exceedingly faint. We admit that the conception of Deity has grown with the elevation and enlightenment of mankind. That it has been freed from blemishes, incongruities, and contradictions, no one can doubt. The advent and ministry of Christ contributed toward this result; and the thorough comprehension of His teachings has led to the glorious views of God's fatherhood which prevail to-day. Whether they are susceptible of improvement, I know not. Probably they are. Most likely, as we know more of Christ's message, more of nature, more of self, we shall also know more of God. All this may be acknowledged gladly; all this may be true, and undoubtedly is, and yet the atheistic theory, with which it is deftly woven, be absolutely false.

The idea of God is inexplicable without God; the shadow that falls everywhere, as has frequently been pointed out, is meaningless without something to which it corresponds. Mr. Bradlaugh says, "children are born atheists"; but he overlooks what Lichtenberg declares: "when the mind rises, it throws the body upon its knees." As soon as consciousness dawns under natural conditions, an invisible being seems instinctively to be recognized. The child does not argue itself out of atheism into theism, for "it is after the heart knows Him that the reason also seeks Him." Cicero long ago deliberately declared that "there is no people so wild and savage as not to have believed in a God, even if they have been unacquainted with His nature"; Plutarch, in a passage familiar to everyone, expressed the same conviction, and it has been echoed by many authorities, both ancient and modern; and in answer to those, who claim to have found exceptions to this rule in recent times, writers such as Amberley, who is far from sympathizing with Christianity, testifies: "So slender is the evidence of the presence of a people without some theological conception, that it may be doubted whether the travelers who have reported such facts have not been misled, either by inability to comprehend the language, or unfamiliarity with the order of thought of those with whom they conversed." The universality of the idea evidently cannot be satisfactorily refuted, and if it is established it proves that it is intuitive, and its intuitiveness proves that it is the counterpart of reality; just as the reflection of a face in the water is sufficient evidence that the face itself is not an illusion. If it is interwoven with the mind, if it is part of the soul's original furniture, it is folly to talk of its having been evolved, and equal folly to doubt that it is God's own appointed witness to the truth of His existence.

It is also worthy of consideration in this connection that the alleged progress of thought from many gods to one rests on no reliable foundation. Rather are there reasons for believing that at an early period there was a widespread departure from the worship of one God to the worship of many. Theism seems to have preceded polytheism, and polytheism in its turn to have yielded to theism. From truth to error, and back again, and forever, to the truth, describes the historical stages of this mental process. As Naville, in his celebrated *Discourses*, says: "The idea of one God is primitive and fundamental; polytheism is derived. A forgotten monotheism slumbers under the multiform worship. It is the secret stock from which the latter grew; but the exuberant offspring consumed the whole strength of the parent tree."

Max Müller, in his *Essays on the Veda*, the venerable and most sacred book of India, observes "that after naming the several powers of nature, and worshiping them as gods, the ancient Hindu found that there was yet another power within him and around him for which he had no name. This he termed, in the first instance, 'Brahman,' force, will, wish. But when Brahman, too, had become a person, he called the mysterious power 'Atman,' originally meaning breath, or spirit; subsequently self." And in *The Chips from a German Workshop* he adds: "If there is one thing which a comparative study of religion places in the clearest light, it is the inevitable decay to which every religion is exposed. . . . Whenever we can trace back a religion to its first beginnings, we find it free from many blemishes that affected it in its later stages." Dr. Legge, in his valuable treatise on the *Religions of China*, fully corroborates this opinion; for he maintains against Professor Tiele's insinuation that fetichism was the earliest faith of the empire, the more tenable view that it was a theism. This he makes good, not merely by an exhaustive analysis of the primitive name, Tî, applied to the Supreme, but by quotations from the statutes of the Ming Dynasty, such as the following: "It is your office, O spirits,—inferior agencies,—to superintend the clouds and the rain, and to raise and send abroad the winds, as ministers assisting Shang Ti," who is also called "the great worker and transformer." Principal Dawson also, when describing *Fossil Men*, testifies that the creed of Stadacona, the ancient Quebec, "There is one God," was held, with various modifications, by all the American tribes. "The Great Spirit might be the Great Manitou, or Oghee-ma of the Algonquins; Okee or Omaha of the Mandans; or approaching more nearly to the familiar Aryan Theos and Deus, he might be the Teo of the Mexicans; but in every case there was a great Spirit, though there might be multitudes of inferior deities." The same thing has been observed by careful students of the Greek and Roman mythologies. Over and above their lesser and rival gods some Supreme Jove is discerned, governing and ruling, as in the hymn which the ancient stoic Cleanthes breathes to Zeus, the universal Spirit. And what is even of more weight, scholars have proven that the name of God in various ancient languages can be traced to a common root, pointing to a primitive belief in His unity. According to Dr. Fairbairn, "the Sanskrit *Dyaus*, the Greek *Zeus*, the Latin *Ju* in *Jupiter*, the Gothic *Tius*, the Anglo-Saxon *Tiu*, the Scandinavian *Tyr*, the old German *Ziu* or *Zio*," are cognates; and Max Müller writes concerning them: "We have in the Veda the invocations *Dyaus-pitar*, the Greek Ζεῦπατήρ, the Latin *Jupiter;* and that means in all the three languages what it meant before these three languages were torn asunder,—it means Heaven-father."

These facts are fatal to the theological theory of evolution. From them it seems evident that man began with the idea of one God, and gradually fell into idolatry, obscuring the original idea, but never completely effacing it. He debased the grandest and most central thought of his religion; he never quite succeeded in effecting its destruction. Were the Evolution hypothesis true this process would have been reversed; man would have started with belief in many gods, and have risen to the thought of one; but as the facts prove retrogression first and then progress, we are obliged to regard the hypothesis as unworthy of confidence. And as it fails to account for the origin of the idea of God, and as we find the idea at the very dawning of human history, and apparently native to every human soul, we are shut up to the conclusion that no explanation is possible, apart from the corresponding reality to which it points.

But if the idea of God is inexplicable without God, the origin of nature is equally incomprehensible without Him. Who is there that can form even a vague conception of how the universe came into being or was fashioned in beauty and clothed with deepest symbolism when the existence of an Infinite Intelligence is denied? Much is written about nebulæ, about plastic matter, about atoms and molecules, about ages of measureless duration, when the molten mass whence sprang all things was gradually cooling and shaping itself into suns, moons, stars and satellites; about the condensation of its particles, the radiation of its heat, and its rotary motion; about the formation of great rings, which continued to whirl and spin, like wheels, until each was broken into fragments and pursued its circumrotation around its own appropriate center. Much also has been written about the earth,—how at the beginning it was a liquid, fiery ball, with zones of vapor belting it, which turned into water and filled the cracks and chasms of the cooling crust with broad-heaving seas and deep-flowing streams; and how, after the lapse of untold ages, infusorial life appeared and the struggle for existence commenced, which in the course of time, and after throes of agony, extermination and transient conflict, culminated in the development of man from inferior species. All this is interesting enough, and it all may be true, but I defy any one to understand it apart from the creative wisdom and almightiness of God. Spontaneous motion and spontaneous generation, and the fortuitous concurrence of atoms, which have been marshaled with great pomp and royalty of language to explain this complicated marvel, but darken what they undertake to illuminate; they are but myths of science,— deep, involved, bewildering,— or gorgeous speculations, dazzling with electric brilliancy, and like the electric light creating denser and more painful shadows than they disperse. Whence came the primal force, of which so much is affirmed, and what at first disturbed the original inertia of matter? What determined the origin, the order and arrangement of the atoms or the molecules, concerning which we know so little and about which so many talk learned emptiness? We really know absolutely nothing of their essential nature, as they are invisible and intangible, and consequently are beyond the range of our analysis. How came they, then, to combine, what started them on their career, and how came it that their complicated combinations and mazy processionings produced the endless phenomena of the worlds? We wait for an intelligent reply, and we shall wait for it eternally. Holbach, in answering similar questions, was obliged to admit: "We do not know, neither do you; we never shall, you never will." But does some thinker, more intrepid than the German, reply: "Chance, necessity, is all that is logically required to account for everything"? But this accounts for nothing; it is simply a confession of ignorance, and not in any sense an elucidation of the problem. It is merely to repeat the senile and senseless affirmation that the earth rests upon "the tortoise," but to leave unanswered the more vital question, "On what does the tortoise rest?"

Claudias, in his *Chria*, represents the illuminati as saying: "Whether there be a God, and what He may be, philosophy alone can teach, and without philosophy there can be no thought of God." "Good," answers the Master; "yet, though no man can say of me with a shadow of truth that I am a philosopher, I never go through the forest without thinking who makes the flowers grow, and then a faint and distant notion comes over me of a great Unknown One, and so reverently, yet so joyfully, does my heart thrill that I could wager that I am thinking of God." He instinctively recognizes the Worker by His work, and realizes that it is too wonderful, too beautiful, too closely allied to himself and too intimately related to his happiness for it to have been the result of unpremeditating chance. And a similar impression led Lord Bacon to exclaim, "I had rather believe all the fables in the legend, and the Talmud and Al Koran, than that this universal frame is without mind; and therefore God never wrought miracles to convince Atheism, because His ordinary works convince it."

They are right; the order of nature, as well as its origin, reveals intelligent design, and design cannot be explained apart from a great Designer. I know Lucretius disputed this proposition, but Aristotle recognized its force, and since his day many a heart has been made glad by what has been discerned of Infinite wisdom in the universe. Mr. Spencer may ridicule Paley's argument, but his admirer, Mr. Darwin, has more than confirmed it in what he has written about insect agency, and of remarkable instances of contrivance and prevision. Sir Charles Bell also has done good service in the same direction. When accounting for his interest in the study of anatomy, he impressively wrote: "Everything there is so perfect, so curiously fitted, and leads you by little and little to the comprehension of a wisdom so perfect, that I am forced to believe that in the moral world things are not really left in all that disarray in which our partial view would persuade us they are."

Even Mr. Holyoake, in his *Debate* with Townley, was constrained to yield to the logic of such reasoning and "to allow that, so far as the design argument goes, it establishes a being which is distinct from nature,—of limited nature." These are his own words, found in the London edition of this celebrated controversy, published in 1852, and now somewhat rare. Hume, *Natural History of Religion*, declared "that the whole frame of nature bespeaks an intelligent Author"; and Voltaire, as is well known, fully sympathized with this conclusion, as, indeed, did Thomas Paine, and both gave it their unqualified support and testified to it repeatedly with graceful eloquence.

I shall never forget a similar testimony borne by the late Professor Peirce, of Harvard, one of the most devout scientists I ever had the pleasure to meet, who, in a lecture on the Nebular Hypothesis, delivered before a select company at the Chestnut Street Club, in Boston, dwelt on the evidences of Divine existence and wisdom which it afforded, and incidentally called attention to the fact that "the wing of the eagle is never found in the egg of a goose." Simple and commonplace as the statement was it condensed in itself an irresistible argument. One could not believe that from sources so similar pinions would unfold so differently, unless previously ordered and arranged by a thinking mind. He demonstrated that in the lowest organizations, as well as in the highest, the marks of design are too conspicuous to admit of cavil or doubt; and thus led he his hearers, eloquently and with poetic pathos, "through nature up to nature's God."

Yes, up to God, for to Him, and to Him alone, do the labyrinthine and complicated wonders of the universe point. When that awe-inspiring name is spoken, when He is looked up to and devoutly recognized as the primal, all-sufficient Cause, the problem of creation seems less involved and inscrutable. Even if His name does not altogether satisfy the head, it meets the questionings of the heart. At least every other attempted solution of the mystery is vague, irrelevant, incoherent and utterly meaningless. This alone is clear, complete and comprehensive, and is practically unanswerable. That as the sole Cause He is perfectly adequate to account for all things no one has yet had the temerity to deny. All that the Atheist claims is that nature is comprehensible without Him, not that it is incomprehensible with Him. Every one admits that He is a sufficient explanation; the atheistically inclined only try to show that He is an unnecessary one. I have aimed in these brief paragraphs to show that their position is untenable; that it does not and cannot account for things as they are; that their solutions of the problem, with His name omitted and His agency ignored, are irreconcilable with the evidences of design and with what we know of the properties of matter, and involve us in confusing contradictions and inextricable perplexities.

It may seem very singular to you that anyone should have suggested the possibility of religion with no God acknowledged in its faith or reverenced in its worship. Yet this is a favorite assumption of some quick-gaited followers of modern thought. Thus, as quoted by Mr. Mallock, "Professor Tyndall points with delighted confidence to the gospel of Buddhism as one of pure human ethics, divorced not only from Brahma and the Brahminic trinity, but even from the existence of God"; and M. Barthelemy Saint-Hilaire asserts that "there is not the slightest trace of a belief in God in all Buddhism." The Positive Philosophy advocates something akin to this. As man is the highest being which it can consistently recognize, it proposes to worship collective humanity with all the enthusiasm such a deity can inspire, and to derive from it a scheme of morals that shall put to blush the inferior ethics of Christianity. Verily the sagacious Lichtenberg was not mad when he prophesied: "This world of ours will become so refined, that it will be as ridiculous to believe in God as it now is to believe in ghosts. And then the world will become still more refined—then we shall believe only in ghosts. We shall ourselves become as God."

Now with due deference to Professor Tyndall and M. Saint-Hilaire I may be allowed to say that while Buddhism as a system says nothing about God, His existence is not denied; and most likely, by its founder, was assumed, as his doctrine was based on the Veda, in which it is fully recognized. Moreover, it should not be overlooked that the followers of Buddha did not abandon the ancient deities whom their fathers worshiped, such as Indra and Brahma, and that Buddha himself came to be regarded as the most exalted being in the universe. He who determined all the circumstances of his own incarnation, and who delivered infallible doctrine, could not fail to receive divine honors, or become as fully God to the faith of millions, as Christ is to untold numbers of His disciples. Hence such prayers as this, reproduced by Johnson from Franck's *Études Orientales*, and in use among the Mongolians: "O thou in whom all creatures trust, Buddha, perfected amidst countless revolutions of worlds, compassionate toward all, and their eternal salvation, bend down into this our sphere, with all thy society of perfected ones. Thou law of all creatures, brighter than the sun, in faith we humble ourselves before thee. Thou who completest all pilgrimage, also dwellest in the world of rest, before whom all is but transient, descend by thy almighty power, and bless us." In Thibetan Buddhism, Avalok-iteswara, its manifested deity, is said to hear and answer prayer, and that they who trust in him are secure. And in Nepaul, where Buddhism prevails, theism is not divorced from the system, but is interwoven with it, and is doubtless one cause of its vigor. As to Positivism, that is as yet an experiment; but I do not think much is hazarded in predicting that its influence will never extend beyond a limited circle of peculiar, not to say abnormal, souls. It is inconceivable that common-sense people will ever be persuaded to worship ideal humanity, or to agree in founding a church in which man shall be both priest and deity. The world is not yet a lunatic asylum, and it is not probable that it will soon so far become one as to deify the perishing and adore the impotent.

While it is not true that religions have flourished where "The fool hath said in his heart, 'there is no God,'" it is true that their worth and purity depend very largely on the conceptions formed of His attributes and character. What He is, they are. His nature as a rule decides theirs. A savage, cruel deity can hardly beget anything but a harsh faith and a cruel ritual; but a loving, merciful God will ever be the fruitful source of sympathy and tenderness in the institutions that are reared to magnify His name. He Himself will be reflected in the rites and ceremonies of formal worship as well as in the lives of His people. This principle explains the differences that separate historic faiths from each other and shows why some are gross and others refined, some animalistic and others spiritual, and indicates how important it is not merely to think of God, but to think of Him aright. It also very clearly proves that the growth of pure religion in the world can only be promoted by knowing more of Him: certainly not by denying Him altogether. And if religion is thus a necessity of our nature, which the Atheist concedes when he claims that the prevalence of his creed would not destroy it, and if, as we have argued, it is inseparable from a recognition of the Almighty, then we cannot but conclude that its character and universality demonstrate the reality of His existence.

A vigorous imagination is doubtless needed to affirm that the elevation of humanity is practicable without God; yet such is the dream of Gustave Flourens, and of a few other visionary mortals. The gentleman just named, apparently in a state of semi-frenzy, has been pleased to write. "Our enemy is God. Hatred of God is the beginning of wisdom. If mankind would make true progress it must be on the basis of Atheism;" and Mr. Bradlaugh so far approves this startling view as to say: "Atheism, properly understood, is in no sense a cold, barren negative; it is, on the contrary, a hearty, truthful affirmation of all truth. You cannot get your scheme of morality without it." Are these gentlemen drugged or mad, or has the entire race gone crazy and they alone retained their senses? Assuredly either the eleven jurymen have turned imbeciles, or the twelfth one is sadly muddled and demented. Which? It may, however, relieve our perplexities and allay our fears to learn that Mr. Holyoake has controverted these obnoxious sentiments, distinctly declaring that "Atheism, as such, gives no system of truth and no scheme of morality." These champions of a common creed may be left to reconcile their differences as best they may. It is enough for us to know, an enemy being judge, that theists are not so stupid as Flourens and his sympathizers insinuate. We doubtless have heard similar groundless tirades against the Deity nearer home. Some things in Colonel Ingersoll's brilliant invectives, and various statements in Professor Draper's uncandid criticisms, suggest that religion has really been a hindrance to human progress, and that until it is finally abolished all that is possible can never be accomplished. One would suppose that belief in God has been an unmitigated curse to the race, darkening the intellect, afflicting the heart, and burdening the life. Indeed, against it, in one form or another, these accusations have been brought repeatedly. It has been over and over again alleged that faith in God has excited fear, has paralyzed inquiry, has impeded freedom of thought and speech, has deepened bigotry, resisted science, and intensified selfishness and prejudice. If these charges are true, if theism has rendered mankind ignoble, miserable, dwarfed its growth and checked its onward march, then indeed must it be admitted that human elevation is not only practicable without God, but would really be accelerated if His name could be erased from the vocabulary of thought. But can any sane man, familiar with history and free from blinding antipathy to Christianity, admit such monstrous allegations?

That which we call morality is grounded on the being and governorship of the Almighty. In Him the source of righteousness is recognized, and from Him it derives its sanction. Right and wrong were meaningless terms were it not that they represent eternal and necessary distinctions which even the Infinite cannot abrogate, and accountability would be to all intents and purposes a fiction were it not that He lives and reigns. Obligation is only another word for theism: for it involves theism, and is inseparable from it. Doubtless it is possible for some men who have been reared in an atmosphere of Christian faith, and who have received from pious parents correct principles of conduct, to live upright lives; but it cannot be shown that a community entirely ignorant of religion and its sacred influence, and fully convinced of the certainty of Atheism, would be able to derive from it adequate motives to virtue, or would even be able to believe in virtue at all. Why should Plato have banished all Atheists from his ideal Republic, and why was Cicero so intent against them? Perhaps Voltaire may help us to a satisfactory reply. In his *Philosophical Dictionary* he says with much pungency: "I would not wish to come in the way of an atheistical prince, whose interest it should be to have me pounded in a mortar. I am quite sure that I should be so pounded. Were I a sovereign, I would not have to do with atheistical courtiers, whose interest it was to poison me; I should be under the necessity of taking an antidote every day. It is, then, absolutely necessary for princes and people that the idea of a Supreme Being, creating, governing, and rewarding and punishing, be engraven on their minds." That is, he believed, as did both Plato and Cicero, that the well-being of society depends on morality, and morality on God; and that, therefore, they who deny His existence will be far from feeling that sense of obligation which would make them honest rulers or useful and worthy citizens. This seems to have been the judgment of antiquity,—a judgment repeated by the best minds of modern times, and a judgment more than justified by those brief, disastrous periods, and by those unhappy cities, in which atheism has held temporary sway.

Morality is the source and inspiration of progress; it quickens and purifies genius and industry; it stimulates and encourages thought and endeavor. The countries where science and art have flourished are those which have adhered most firmly to its principles, and have traced them most uniformly to an Invisible Source. What discovery, what great enterprise, what beneficent revolution, what enlarged benevolence, what victory for freedom, what achievement for art, is due to the influence of atheism? Has it delivered the captive, rescued the fallen, lifted up the oppressed, strengthened the weak, defended the helpless? No; its record is unhonored with accounts of such deeds. It is a melancholy and disgraceful blank. Never has it given to the world a Plato, a Copernicus, a Galileo, a Bacon, a Milton, an Angelo, a Wilberforce, or any other great name entitled to rank with the benefactors of mankind. It has actually done nothing to advance the well-being of humanity; and yet it has in these last days the effrontery to represent itself as sufficiently beneficent to be the real and only Messiah. May we be saved from its millennium! for if it bear likeness to its past history, the wilderness and solitary place will only be more solitary, and the blossoming rose will return to desert dreariness.

Then, as to fear and wretchedness, how does it come to pass, if theism is untrue, that in proportion as it is doubted these evils grow denser in the soul? When it was rejected in Rome, suicide increased. The most distinguished men of those times felt that existence was worthless; and Schopenhauer, who in our day has elaborated Godless materialism into a poem, wailingly and sneeringly contends that "all possessions are vanity, the world a bankrupt in all quarters, and life a business that does not pay expenses." Such is the happiness that atheism offers and yields. Can there come anything but this awful and woful weariness when man is everlastingly confronted by eternal death, universal dumbness and echoing dissonances? Fear! How does atheism deliver from terror? It has banished God from thought, but has it excluded from apprehension that which these blind material forces, these overwhelming physical agencies, these subtle elements, ordered by lawless chance and frantic destiny, may do and work? In them there is no intelligence to appeal to, no mercy to call on,—only irresistible, reckless, heartless power and fate. Well may we cower before such devastating and consuming monsters, such huge, uncontrollable and soulless antagonists. In their grasp we are more helpless than infants; before their breath we are as frail as the bubble that is shattered by the gentlest breeze, or the spray-drop that glistens for a moment on the crested wave and is then beaten back into the oblivion of the deep by the triumphant wind. The recognition of Deity has inspired fear, and must; but not such terrible, hopeless fear as does ungoverned and ungovernable nature. He, at least, can be communed with; on Him, at least, the oppressed can lean; and unto Him, at least, the weary toilers can hope to go when death terminates their bitter sorrows; but nature has no heart to feel, no hand to help, and no refuge but a loathsome grave in which despair can hide its anguish.

Is it not ridiculous, then, to believe that human progress is feasible, with Godless nature, like a dead timepiece, for its guide and inspiration? If the universe is but a dial without a hand, how can we poor mortals know the time of day, or recognize the duty of the hour? Such a dumb, motionless horologe, without ever a morning chime to awaken slumbering virtue or a midnight bell to toll the doom of wakeful viciousness, would hardly promote the moral order of society or exalt the character of its members. And if my argument has been sound throughout, though proofs of the Divine existence have not been formally attempted, it must necessarily follow, as the idea of God is not explicable without Him, as the origin of nature is not comprehensible without Him, as the prevalence of religion is not possible without Him, or the elevation of humanity practicable without Him, that He must be the One everlasting reality and imperishable glory of the universe.

The reproach of the pagan world pronounced by Paul, "that when they knew God they glorified Him not as God," unhappily is not undeserved by many in our own times. Theoretical atheism generally may have been rejected, but that which is practical yet holds in bondage the large majority of souls. Inconsiderateness of Divine things, prayerlessness and godlessness, are the common evils of the age. Men and women who sincerely count themselves believers in the central truth of religion never bow the knee before God's throne; they avoid His sanctuary, and keep every thought of His presence and power as far as possible from them. They live every day as though there were no God, and act as though they stood not in the blaze of His omniscience, and were not hastening, with every fleeting breath, to His judgment seat. End, I beseech you, end this inconsistency. Learn that He who made you seeks to dwell in you; that He who rules over you would fain become your friend and guide. Though you are weak and frail, though you are poor and helpless, He does not despise you, but would glorify your being with His own, and raise you to fellowship with Himself. Think of Him, turn to Him, love and obey Him, and then will you know from blessed experience what it is to live and move and have your being in Him.

"What am I? Naught.
Nothing! yet the effluence of Thy light divine,
Pervading worlds, hath reached my bosom too;
Yes, in my spirit doth Thy spirit shine,
As shines the sunbeam in a drop of dew.
Naught! but I live, and on hope's pinions fly
Eager toward Thy presence; for in Thee
I live, and breathe, and dwell, aspiring high,
Even to the throne of Thy divinity."

PANTHEISM.

"For in Him we live, and move, and have our being." *Acts xvii, 28.*

> "Hallowed be Thy name — Hallelujah!
> Infinite Ideality!
> Immeasurable Reality!
> Infinite Personality!
> Hallowed be Thy name — Hallelujah!
> We feel we are nothing — for all is Thou and in Thee;
> We feel we are something — that also has come from Thee.
> We are nothing, O Thou — but Thou wilt help us to be!
> Hallowed be Thy name — Hallelujah!"
> *Alfred Tennyson.*

AMONG the Hindu lore collected by Viscount Amberley we have the following interesting legend: A wise father said to his son Swetaketu: "Dissolve this salt in water, and appear before me to-morrow morning." The youth obeyed, and when on the return of day he saluted his sire he was directed to find the salt that he had mingled with the water on the previous evening. He acknowledged that he could not. Then answered the parent: "Taste a little of the refreshing element, — a few drops from the top, a few from the middle and a few from the bottom. What is the flavor?" "The water is saltish," replied Swetaketu. "If so, wash your mouth and grieve not." Having done as he was bidden, he said to his father: "The salt that I put in the water exists forever; though it is not perceived by my eyes it is felt by my tongue." "Verily such is the case with truth, my child," responded the sage, who was seeking to illustrate the deep mystery of the finite-infinite: "though you perceive it not, nevertheless it pervades this body. That particle which is the soul of all, this is truth; it is the universal soul. O Swetaketu, thou art That!"

We have in this brief dialogue a hint of that strange doctrine which fills so large a place in Hindu philosophy, and which, in more logical shape, has exerted a profound influence on modern European speculations. I refer to Pantheism,—that remarkable belief of which traces are apparent in the world's most venerable religions; which renders Atheism impossible by identifying the Almighty with the universe; which substitutes all-God for no-God; which declares that God is everything, or that everything is God, and which thus makes Him the center and circumference, the essence and the substance, of every order of existence and of every species of phenomena. Glimpses of an all-embracing, all-comprehending, all-pervading Being, who is the "*anima mundi*," are afforded us in the sacred memorials of ancient faiths. *The Veda* represents Him as Essence, and thus chants His nature in its hymns of praise:

"The wise man views that mysterious Being
In whom the universe perpetually exists,
Resting upon that sole support,
In Him is the world absorbed,
From Him it issues.
In creatures is He twined and wove in various forms."

In the *Mahábhárata* Vishnu is presented as the supreme Deity, who is revealed in everything, and who in himself is everything. Thus he describes himself when holding converse with a mortal, whom he is inciting to slay his relatives by the argument that all life is illusive except the Divine, and that, therefore, he will only be destroying an appearance: "I am the soul, O Arjuna, which exists in the heart of all beings; and I am the beginning and the middle, and also the end, of existing things." Thus, also, among the Egyptians we find above their multiplied mythological gods One, and only One, to whom is given the name Ra, concerning whom George Ebers writes in *Uarda:* "Under the name Ra we understand something different than is known to the common herd; for to us the universe is God, and in each of its parts we recognize a manifestation of that highest Being, without whom nothing is in the heights above or in the depths below." . . . "Whether we view the sun, the harvest, or the Nile; whether we contemplate with admiration the unity and harmony of the visible or invisible world, still it is always with the only, the all-embracing One, we have to do, to whom we also ourselves belong as those of His manifestations, in which He places His self-consciousness." An English version of *Hermes* gives the following quotation, which throws additional light on this Egyptian conception of a diffused Divinity: "There is nothing in the whole world which God is not. He is being and non-being. He has manifested being, but He has non-being in Himself." . . . "Thou art what I am; Thou art what I do; Thou art what I say; Thou art all which is produced and which is not produced." And in the city of Alexandria the same mystical idea seems to have blended with the worship of Serapis; for when Nicocreon, King of Cyprus, consulted him he received this reply:

"A god I am, such as I show to thee,
The starry heavens my head, my trunk the sea;
Earth forms my feet, mine ears the air supplies,
The sun's far-darting, brilliant rays mine eyes."

According to this representation Serapis and nature were looked upon as one and indivisible; and similarly, in the "Boundless Time" of the Parsees, the "Bythos," or "The Depths" of the Ophites, and the "Closed Eye" of the Kabalists, we find suggestions of the

"One harmonious whole,
Whose body nature is, and God the soul."

. . . .

"To Him no high, no low, no great, no small;
He fills, He bounds, connects, and equals all."

Pantheism also, among the Greeks, had its advocates. The pre-Socratic philosophers were more or less tainted with it, though it first attained complete expression in the teachings of the Eleatics. Xenophanes, the founder of this school, says Aristotle, "casting his eyes upward at the immensity of heaven, declared that the ONE is God." Hunt, in his admirable treatise on this subject, represents Parmenides, the successor of Xenophanes, as holding to a species of Acosmism, which led him to challenge the reality of external appearances, and to assume that "thought is the same thing as being," and "that nothing, in fact, is, or will be, distinct from being." In contrast with Eleaticism, the mystical Heraclitus, a philosopher who constantly lived in a "cave of cloud," unable to discover the Absolute, taught that the universe is neither being nor non-being, but an eternal *Becoming*, and this eternal Becoming, as in the case of the Eleatics, he identified with the One. "Unite the whole and the not-whole," he argues, "the coalescing and the not-coalescing, the harmonious and the discordant, and thus we have the one BECOMING from the ALL, and the ALL from the ONE."

Not to these sources, however, but to Spinoza (1677), must Pantheism, as it influences thought in our day, be traced. This celebrated man was a Jew, dark-featured, slender, delicate, emaciated, consumptive, who was publicly excommunicated from the congregation of his ancestors on account of the belief, or unbelief, that was in him. The views, which he never took pains to conceal, not only resulted in his expulsion from the synagogue, but condemned him to a life of toil and indigence. He obtained enough for his absolute necessities by polishing lenses; and in a forlorn Dutch chamber at The Hague, forsaken by friends, and ridiculed by enemies, he worked out his philosophical system, which, while fiercely assailed and vulnerable at several points, remains a monument of its author's genius and industry. His death occurred when he was only forty-five years old, younger than Goethe and Kant were when they began to give the world the fruit of their reading and thinking. While Christians must deplore the perversion of his great talents, they should carefully avoid alluding to him as one who has no claims on their charity and respect. He was no moral monster, no hard-hearted wretch, no callous profligate. His only vice was the comparatively harmless one of smoking, his only villainy arraying spiders against each other in battle, and his principal amusement the struggle of flies caught in the web of their mortal insect-antagonists. He was reverent in spirit, devout, not to say religious, blameless in life, and uncomplaining in death. While we differ from him, then, let us not depreciate; while we combat his theories, let us not calumniate his character.

A comprehensive idea of his philosophy may be gathered, not only from his own writings, but from those of his biographers, annotators, and expositors—such as G. H. Lewes, Emile Saisset, Schelling, Hegel, Hunt, Morell, and Cousin. In his own words we have this summary: "The foundation of all that exists is the one eternal substance, which makes its actual appearance in the double world of thought, and of matter existing in space. Individual forms emerge from the womb of this substance, as of ever-fertile nature, to be again swallowed up in the stream of life. As the waves of the sea rise and sink, so does individual life arise to sink back again into that common life which is the death of all individual existence." Victor Cousin, in his *History of Philosophy*, gives the following statement of his doctrine: "With Spinoza the single substance is all, and the individuals are nothing. This substance is not the nominal unity of the assemblage of individuals, each of which exists singly, but is the single really existing substance, and in the presence of that substance the world and men are but shadows; so that from the *Ethics* may be gathered an exaggerated Theism, which leaves no individual existing as such." M. Saisset, a critic of no mean ability, describes our philosophic Jew as holding that "God sleeps in the mineral, dreams in the animal, and awakens into consciousness in the man"; and Luthardt, regarding Hegel as a disciple of Spinoza, represents him, in common with Morell (*Historical and Critical View, ii, 104, 155*), as maintaining "that the absolute is the universal reason, which, having first buried and lost itself in nature, recovers itself in man, in the shape of self-conscious mind, in which the absolute, at the close of its great process, comes again to itself, and comprises itself in unity with itself. This process of mind is God. Man's thought of God is the existence of God. God has no independent being or existence; He exists only in us. God does not know himself; it is we who know Him." That is, to sum up these various representations, consubstantiation of the finite and Infinite, of the natural and Supernatural, of the human and Divine; and transubstantiation, through which, mysteriously, one becomes the other and yet remains the same, are the two leading and all-comprehensive articles of the Pantheistic creed.

The extent to which these views prevail in our time is not generally realized. They appear with more or less distinctness in the writings of Emerson. His *Oversoul* is an eloquent, though somewhat incoherent, species of Pantheism; and in Theodore Parker's works, especially in his *Discourse on Religion*, numerous passages occur which manifest his sympathy with Schleiermacher's drift in the same direction. Cultivated people admire Spinoza, and the class of sentiments now widely current in literature, which grow out of his philosophy, are cherished on account of their poetic sweetness, little attention being bestowed on their accuracy or value. They do not pause to consider the effect morally and theologically of a system, which in many instances they are pleased with, but do not understand, and whose claims on their attention as rational beings they have never taken pains to examine. Believing, as I do, that its influence is disastrous, I desire, within the insufficient limits of a sermon, to point out its radical defects in such a way as to lay a broad foundation for a more intelligible and salutary Theism. In doing so I shall argue:

First, That Godhood without personality is Godhood without perfection;

Second, That manhood without individuality is manhood without responsibility;

Third, That morality without liberty is morality without virtue.

Fourth, That immortality without consciousness is immortality without existence.

Our notion of personality is derived from what we see of it in the world; and it must be confessed that it seems incompatible with any adequate idea of the infinite or absolute. Limitation and limitlessness cannot, with logical consistency, be predicated of the same being. To say that God is infinite, as we understand the term, is to say that He is entirely unconditioned; and for Him to be unconditioned is for Him to be impersonal; and conversely, to say that He is personal, that is, conditioned, is to say that He is not infinite; and to say that He is not infinite is to deny that He is God. This is the dilemma which has confronted everyone who has seriously considered the philosophy of Spinoza, and which has driven many into the denial of personality, that they might preserve the notion of infinitude. Nor do I see any other course open for us if we continue to employ these terms, as they are usually defined. If we regard the meaning which is assigned to them as complete and exhaustive, then we must admit that they are irreconcilable with each other. But in all candor, is it not too much to claim that human reason has fathomed the nature of the infinite, and comprehended in full all that is really involved in personality, for it to pronounce dogmatically on the possibility or impossibility of their coexistence? After all, what we really know in these directions is very vague and shadowy and much too indefinite for us to found a coherent and consistent system on. They who take the trouble to read Sir W. Hamilton, and Dean Mansel, and the replies which have been made to their metaphysical theories by Mr. Mill and Mr. Spencer, must be convinced that while we undoubtedly know that the infinite *is*, we do not know in any true sense *what* it is. As Dr. Porter says of one of the terms in debate: "Originally, and etymologically, it signifies *freed from*, or severed. This signification is purely negative, and waits to be explained by that from which it is freed." That our knowledge is not complete, accurate, scientific and sufficiently reliable to serve as a basis for an unyielding, positive theory has never been more fully demonstrated than by Spinoza himself. He writes: "I understand by God the Absolutely Infinite Being; that is to say, substance constituted by an infinity of attributes, each of which expresses an eternal and infinite essence." (*Ethics*, p. 4. Van Nostrand's edition.) But may it not be asked, in all modesty, if God is absolutely infinite, how comes it that He is "constituted"? and if "substance" is constituted by an infinity of attributes, how is it possible for it to be what Spinoza himself affirms it to be, "that which exists of itself, and is conceived by and through itself, or that of which the conception can be formed without having need of the conception of any other thing as its cause"? Now it seems evident to me, if God is substance, and if substance is that "the conception of which does not involve the conception of any other thing," then He is not "constituted by an infinity of attributes"; but if He is thus constituted, then He is not "that which is in itself, and is conceived by itself," and therefore He is not absolute, or absolutely infinite. Thus, following these contradictory statements, we arrive at the conclusion that even Spinoza could not define infinity without destroying it, and that therefore to erect a house on a foundation so unsubstantial is to provide in advance for its utter demolition.

Let the unconquerableness of our ignorance on this point be conceded, and let it also be granted that God's personality should not be likened, in every respect, to our own, but should be taken as simply denoting that He is separable from His works, and is wise, loving, merciful and free, and we shall at least feel the difficulty of reconciliation so far abated that it will cease to be insuperable. If we are not prepared to do this we shall assuredly do worse; we shall rashly sacrifice His perfection in our zeal for His infinitude; for an impersonal Deity can never be other than an imperfect one. To deny His supreme consciousness, wisdom, volition and sovereignty, as is done by Pantheism, is to rob Him of what we cannot but regard as among His chiefest glories. That devout instinct which prompts us to acknowledge Him as infinite, impels us to ascribe to Him the attributes of intelligence, and stripped of these He is destitute of what most powerfully affects the human soul for good. If He cannot be conceived as thinking, willing, decreeing, then all of His manifestations of Himself must be thought of as determined by something else,— some omnipotent necessity, some all-governing law, or some self-unfolding and self-sustaining force — so that, in reality, He ceases to be Supreme; and thus in our extreme solicitude for impersonalism we render impossible His Godhood.

But Pantheism assails His perfection at other points. If He is identified with the universe, then He is mobile, mutable and variable, and is in a state of perpetual flux and change. As there has been development in nature, so if He is one with it, there has been development in God. He is not, according to this supposition, what He has been, and is not what He will be, and therefore has not yet fully attained to what He may be, and must be. It is not correct then, if this theory is admissible, ever to say that God is, but that He is becoming; for what He is now He was not at an earlier stage in the history of the universe, and what He will be at a later period He has not been heretofore. This is not a caricature of the doctrine we are considering, for it is but another way of putting the statement already quoted, in which God is represented as arriving at self-consciousness in man. But such a conception is irreconcilable with the idea of perfection; for if, as Schelling says, "there is one force, one alternating agency, one weaving, one impulse, one tendency toward ever higher life," while it may be attained in the future it has never been reached in the past; and until it is attained, if we worship at all we are worshiping the Imperfect. It was the recognition of this outcome of Pantheistic premises that led M. Saisset indignantly to exclaim: "Away from me, vain phantoms of the imagination! God is eternally all that He is. If He is the Creator, He creates eternally. If He creates the world, it is not from chance or caprice, but for reasons worthy of Himself; and these reasons are eternal." Yes, as the

Scriptures teach, He is forever the same, and "His years have no end."

This criticism may legitimately be carried yet further; for if impersonalism is true, and God and the universe are convertible terms, then everything that exists, evil as well as good, wrong as well as right, impurity as well as purity, must be ascribed to Him,— must be traced to His nature, and be found in His essence. While we witness in the world much that is deserving admiration and homage, we cannot fail also to perceive much to fill us with pain and loathing. Deceitfulness, violence, cruelty, heartlessness, viciousness, licentiousness, lawlessness,— these rage and riot, filling the earth with bitterness and woe. From them the healthy mind shrinks with anguish and horror; it condemns the guilty, and seeks to restrain the malignant power of wickedness. But in this, if we are to credit Pantheism, it is wasting an immense amount of feeling; for that which kindles its indignation, after all, is only an expression of the Supreme whom we are bound to worship. Wrong doing, and every species of abomination, we must regard, in the light of this philosophy, as Divine effluxions, and therefore as unmeriting condemnation. But is it possible to think of such a Being as absolutely faultless? And is it possible, when we regard the necessary strife between good and evil as an actual warfare in His own members,— for such it is if both spring from His nature, and are equally its counterpart,— not to conclude that whatever else may be affirmed of Him, perfection certainly can not. Verily, when God is set forth as everything, He rapidly degenerates into nothing; when He is sought everywhere, at last He is found nowhere; and when He is refined into impersonal Infinity, He speedily becomes imperfection, unlimited and incalculable.

The sense of responsibility is inseparable from manhood, and the recognition of individuality is inseparable from responsibility. But if, as this Ism teaches, humanity is but part of the Universal Soul, and particular men but rays of the all-pervading Spirit, then individuality is practically annihilated, and with it falls everything that suggests the idea of moral freedom and obligation. Spinoza does not shrink from avowing this as his belief. He says explicitly: "Free will is a chimera, flattering to our pride and in reality founded upon our ignorance. All that I can say to those who believe that they can, by virtue of any free decision of the soul, speak or be silent,— or, to use a single word, act,— is that they dream with their eyes open." Ignorance! dreams! — Is there, then, nothing but fallacy reigning in the vast domain of right and wrong?

Let us take an appeal from such a suspicion to fact and we shall find that there is nothing more real than the consciousness of "the me" in distinction from "the thee," and of "the thine" in contradistinction to "the mine,"— terms with which the sense of moral duty is indissolubly blended. We do not and we cannot, unless it be sympathetically, identify ourselves with each other, and no effort of the imagination succeeds in making us feel that we are absolutely one with Deity. He may influence us, dwell in us even, but we never fail to distinguish between His existence and our own, and His operation is never confounded with our own volition. We discriminate instinctively and uniformly between the Temple and the Being who dwells there, and between His inspiration and our own action. No amount of philosophy or theology has ever eradicated, or even seriously diminished, this sense of individuality, and we may conclude that its vitality is due to the fact that it answers to an unimpeachable reality. In no other way can it be intelligibly explained, and any system that antagonizes with it must in the nature of things be radically erroneous. It will not be denied that obligation is a fiction, a morbid illusion, unless each man is a complete and separate existence. If he is not, then everything like moral conviction is a chimera, a deceitful hallucination. But is it not strange that such an *ignis fatuus* and fantastic mirage as this, if such it is, should have proven so incalculably advantageous to society, and should have led it forward step by step, as this has done, in the march of progress? Indeed, it is more than strange, it is unaccountable. Fancies, imaginations, are not the weapons by which the real evils of life are overcome, and illusions have never yet cleared the way for permanent advancement. Believe me, there is something more in this abiding sense of responsibility than the Pantheist will allow. It is, and endures, because man is a being, not an effluence, and is related to other beings, and is not so identified with them, or merged into them, that reciprocal rights are meaningless and reciprocal duties impossible. Obligation rests on individuality, and the realization of the one will be proportionate to the consciousness of the other; and if this is a true account of the matter the theory that strikes at either must be fatally defective. And that it is may be inferred from sentiments expressed by brilliant men who are more or less influenced by Spinoza's teachings. For instance, Goethe, in his *Hymn to Nature*, seeks to pacify his conscience in the following convenient way: "She placed me in it; she will also lead me forth. I trust myself to her. She may dispose of me. She will not hate her work. I spake not of her. No: whatever is true and whatever is false she spake it all. All is her fault and all her merit." Thus does the romantic German dispose of troublesome misgivings concerning accountability. And our American transcendentalist gives it as his opinion that "Nature as we know her is no saint." "The lights of the church, the ascetics, Gentoos and Grahamites, she does not distinguish by any favor;

she comes eating and drinking and sinning." ... "My friend suggested: 'But these impulses may be from below, not from above.' I replied, 'They do not seem to me to be such, but if I am the devil's child I will live, then, for the devil. No law can be sacred to me but that of my own nature.'" The tendency of such sentiments as these, and they are creeping into our literature more persistently and commonly than many suspect, cannot be at all doubtful. However harmless they may have been to their authors, if generally adopted and acted on by the uneducated and miseducated masses of society, they would speedily convert them into the children of Satan, and change this beautiful earth of ours into a howling Pandemonium.

In one of the propositions brought to your attention at the beginning of this discussion I ventured a statement which draws a wide distinction between morality and virtue. These terms, I know, are usually regarded as synonyms, and yet, admitting that they are, it does not follow that they are identical in meaning. They may present, as I believe they do, very different shades of the same thought. "Morality," in my opinion, suggests right conduct; but the word "virtue" expresses the real worth and merit which attaches to such conduct. A man may be moral in all of his dealings, and be influenced only by a cold, calculating spirit of policy, or he may, in all that he does, be but a fortunate creature of circumstances. There is, however, no strength of conviction in such a course of life, no firmness of principle, no resistance of evil; in a word, no "strength,"—an element which the term "virtue" always implies. If this is absent from what we call moral conduct, its chief charm is gone, and we are inclined to treat its pretensions with contempt. Probably this estimate springs from the fact that the presence of the high quality which imparts grandeur to conduct involves selfhood, the exercise of volition, the assertion of liberty. Without freedom there could be no choice of a path in life, no pursuit of the right in the face of difficulties, and no resistance of wrong even at immense personal sacrifice; and so without freedom there would in reality be no virtue; and without virtue there would hardly be anything in morality to distinguish it from mere decorum. Permit me to illustrate this distinction yet further. Let us suppose the case of one so rigidly trained in the practice of integrity, so carefully shielded from temptation, and so free, from childhood, of everything like human appetite, or passionate desire, that never a thought of wandering occurs, and never an inclination to err is felt; the life of such an one would be admirable, and would kindle our esteem, but it would never arouse in us enthusiasm and ardent praise. The morality in it would be acknowledged, and would be duly and apathetically approved, but it would not be regarded as exhibiting the grand reality of virtue. Such blamelessness must be viewed as natural, and therefore as unavoidable, and if unavoidable, as undeserving of any special commendation. But when a soul, like Plato's suffering righteous man, is surrounded with circumstances unfavorable to right-doing, when he is beset with evils of every description, when he is afflicted, crushed and wronged, and yet never deviates from the straight line of duty, we instinctively recognize something higher than mechanical morality, something exalted and noble, challenging our homage and awakening our reverence. We see that such an one might have been expected to yield to these overwhelming odds, and when he overcomes, we discern the power of volition, of freedom; we recognize a sublime " strength " asserting itself on the side of integrity, and we call that strength " virtue; " and in it we feel that our highest ideal of virtue is actualized. But suppose such choice were never possible; suppose that human beings were always creatures of necessity; that the good they performed was simply the result of forces in them, unoriginated or uncontrolled by themselves; then at the best their morality would hardly be distinguishable from immorality. If Pantheism is true, this is actually the case. There being nothing but God, and God being everything, human volition is not in any real sense free, and consequently, while there may be outwardly correct conduct, virtue in its deepest sense is unattainable. This Spinoza candidly admits. "Nothing," he says, "is bad in itself. Good and evil indicate nothing positive in things, considered in themselves, and are nothing but manners of thinking. Not only has every man the right to seek his good, his pleasure, but he cannot do otherwise." — *Works of Spinoza, vol. i, pp. 159–60.*

What shall we say, then, to a system which, in its insane endeavors to establish a metaphysical subtlety,— to uphold a conception which may be as baseless as it is perplexing,— deliberately undermines the foundations of virtue and deprives society of its mightiest incentives to noble living? We can only say that, as its speculations antagonize with what is eminently practical and vital, however sublime they may seem they are self-condemned, and are undeserving of support.

What a fiction is the immortality which Pantheism encourages its disciples to expect. To return to the universal soul, to be swallowed up in the Infinite, to be merged in the Supreme, to lose identity and consciousness, is the destiny it suavely proclaims. It is a euphonic description of annihilation, and nothing more. What discernible difference is there between this blank eternity and the coarse teachings of Materialism? According to both, the light that is in us must go out, and we return to the oblivion whence we came. The Materialist foreshadows a future for us all in the dewy grass, to be munched by the lowing herd; in the fragrant flowers, to be trampled under foot of men; in the swift sailing, evanescent cloud, or in the varied forms of animal and human life. We are to reappear in the coming generations, and our decay is to nourish their vitality. The Pantheist teaches that we shall go back, not indeed to the dull earth, but to what he is pleased to call "God." In Him we shall happily cease to think, to love, and to be. The dewdrop shall mingle with the Sea, the wandering ray shall be withdrawn into the bosom of primal Light, and the little ego be quenched in the all-absorbing and everlasting "I Am" of the universe. And, according to Emerson, all human beings, of whatever moral character, shall equally attain to this questionable felicity; for "the divine effort is never relaxed; the carrion in the sun will convert itself into grass and flowers, and man, though in brothels, in jails, or on gibbets, is on his way to all that is truly good."

But this self-oblivion and self-extinction in the Infinite One is not the intuitive hope of humanity, nor is it the promise of Revelation. The natural longing of the heart is for personal immortality,— for endless conscious existence. This is what is meant by all that poets and philosophers, untainted by Pantheism, have written on the subject, and this is what the unuttered and unutterable visions of the Beyond mean to the undying soul. To live continuously, to defy the power of death, to ascend to higher ranges of existence, to meet the great and good who have gone before, to welcome the noble and the pure who shall come after, and to enjoy eternally the fellowship of the saved,— this is the radiant hope that sustains us here and invests hereafter with its charm and glory. Why should we thrust it from us? Why should we for a moment listen to the doleful croaking of a Strauss, who, shrouded in "the blanket of the dark," mutters harshly "that the last enemy to be destroyed is not death, but the hope of immortality?" Why accept such dreary forebodings and deny the profoundest instinct of our being for the sake of a mere abstraction? Why doubt the reality of the immortality we feel for the sake of a guess about the nature of the Infinite, which we cannot verify? Too much is asked, too little is given in return; and when it is realized that eternal life must be repudiated, and virtue, individuality, and even Divine perfection, must be sacrificed if the truth of Pantheism is allowed, we do not hesitate to declare that the vastness of its demands should be sufficient proof to every candid mind of its untenableness.

In closing this study permit me to set before you two additional propositions which in my judgment express the only Theism that is rational and deserving the confidence of intelligent beings:

First, God is the source of nature, not its essence; and nature is the manifestation of God, not His fullness.

Second, God is the inspiration of humanity, not its soul; and humanity is the similitude of God, not His substance.

The first of these propositions asserts a difference between the Creator and His work. Schelling declares that "all individual finite things taken together cannot constitute God, since that which is in nature derived cannot be one with its original." This is just what I believe, and consequently I see in the great universe a revelation of its author, but not His substance nor His essence. He is above all, back of all, and through all the reality of His being and the greatness of His Godhead may be seen. Nature is His temple, and it is like that one of glass which the sun-worshipers built that their deity might stream in and be with them; it is transparent, and through its walls and through its starry roof He reveals Himself, as the light penetrates and shines through the flinty crystal. There is something that beams on you from the flower, that sparkles in the water, that gleams in the sun's radiance, and in the moon's quiet luster; something that oppresses you, and yet exalts you in the gigantic magnitudes of the heavens, and in the dense forests and overpowering solitudes of the earth, which does not answer to the names you invent to describe it. You call it "beauty," or "sublimity," or "grandeur," but you feel that these terms are inadequate, that they fall short of truth. Call it God! Yes, call it God! for God it is. It is His eyes that look down upon you from the stars, His smile that glances at you from flower and wave, His love that answers yours in every form of beauty, and His awful greatness that appeals to you in the wonders of the universe. "If," as said the Psalmist, "I ascend up into heaven, THOU art there; if I make my bed in hell, behold THOU art there. If I take the wings of the morning and dwell in the uttermost parts of the sea, even there shall THY hand lead me." Yes, there, and *there*, and *there*— EVERYWHERE. But this is not Pantheism. The Almighty is *not* heaven, but *in* heaven; *not* hades, but *in* hades; *not* the uttermost parts of the sea, but filling them with His immeasurable presence and unspeakable majesty. "Of God, and through Him and to Him are all things;" and nature that sprang from His thought, and is sustained by His power, is also "to Him,"— is His symbol, the manifold expression of His greatness. Before Him she breathes the incense of her homage, and offers to Him the tribute of her praise. She points to Him, and with her many voices cries that to Him, not to her,— not to the temple, but to the God who fashioned it and dwells in it, — should all people bring their offerings of adoring love.

Though the Almighty is not the soul of humanity He is its inspiration, for "in God we live and move and have our being." Each living thinking entity is His creation, made for Himself and related to Him. He moves upon mind and heart, begetting exalted thoughts and holiest resolves, even as it is written, "The inspiration of the Almighty giveth understanding." He is the real source of whatever has been, of whatever is great, good, noble or heroic in mind and deed. Without Him cannot anything be done that is worthy to live in the memory of earth, or worthy to receive the reward of heaven. And yet the doing is ours, not His. He inspired it, we wrought it out. He quickened, but we brought forth. His the heart-beat, but ours the hand-stroke; His the influence, ours the effluence. Here man's true dignity is made apparent. It does not consist in his being a fraction of the Godhead, but in being a distinct existence, made so truly in the Divine image that he can hold communion with his Maker, can respond to the infinite One, can receive Him, abide in Him, and live in correspondence with Him,—yea, and can grow yet more fully into His likeness, and blend so completely with His spirit, that while personality is never lost, He becomes to the soul its All and in All forever.

"Know ye not that ye are the temple of the living God; as God hath said, I will dwell in them and walk in them, and I will be their God and they shall be my people"; and know ye not "he who dwelleth in love dwelleth in God, and God in him?" When humanity shall deeply realize the truth of these declarations, conscious of its heavenly affinities, it will seek closer fellowship with the Highest, and attaining to that oneness for which our Savior prayed, it will apprehend the only Pantheism in which reason can believe or the heart rejoice,—the Pantheism which leads the devout soul to sing, with Madam Guyon:

"I am as nothing, and rejoice to be,
 Emptied and lost, and swallowed up in Thee,"

and which is alike synonymous with individual identity and immortal blessedness.

MATERIALISM.

"Let us eat and drink, for to-morrow we die." *I Cor. xv, 32.*

"For everywhere
We're too materialistic,— eating clay
(Like men of the West) instead of Adam's corn
And Noah's wine; clay by handfuls, clay by lumps,
Until we're filled up to the throat with clay,
And grow the grimy color of the ground
On which we are feeding. Ay, materialist
The age's name is. God Himself with some
Is apprehended as the bare result
Of what His hand materially has made."
Mrs. E. B. Browning.

A FABLE is current in England of a youth who picked up a piece of money lying in the highway. After this good fortune it is said he always kept his eyes fixed on the ground, hoping to find stray coins, and in the course of a long life gathered from the road and street quite an amount of gold, silver and copper. But during all this time he was depriving himself of greater treasures. As his glance never wandered from the dusty, filthy way of his feet, he never saw the starry heavens above him nor the glories of nature's scenery around him. He died poor. Though he had scraped together considerable wealth he passed into eternity without knowing that earth is something more than a dirty place where money may be found as the journey is made from the cradle to the grave.

For now some years gone Science has been disposed to walk with its eyes down-bent. Ever since it made a few important physical discoveries, such as the antiquity of the globe, the procession and progress of life, and brought to light the petrified memorials of former animal and vegetable generations, such as the siliceous fossil shells of the Galionelli, some interesting specimens of the Ichthyosaura, the Plesiosaura, Mosasaurus and the Iguanodon, its gaze has been steadfastly centered on the material. Upon that it has lavished so much attention that the universe has come in its philosophy to be the child of cosmic sparks, and reason to be the grandchild of diffused fire-mist. It is still busy looking for additional discoveries, feeling in the mire for wealth. But though it multiply its riches, it is growing poorer and poorer, for it is losing sight of God, Christ, angels, providence and immortality, and is groping its way through the world blind to the real glory and significance of creation, failing to discern that nature is the real Jacob's ladder on which celestial beings are ascending and descending, a Patmos isle in an unshored ocean, where visions of invisible realms shine through all its manifold shapes and forms.

It is not necessary to trace the rise and progress of this Ism from the time of Leucippus, Democritus and Epicurus to Feuerbach and La Mettrie, and from them to our more modern evolutionists. Whatever peculiarities or variations may have distinguished it at various points in its history, it has always been substantially the same. It has ever regarded the raw eternal matter, the elementary stuff of creation, as the only substance and as the all-sufficient cause of every variety and species of life. Its god, formerly dwarfed to the meager proportions of an atom, is now further dwindled to the insignificance of a molecule; it is, however, the same deity, only grown infinitely little. While it recognizes a scepter, which it calls "force," it acknowledges no intelligent hand to sway it; while it perceives a throne, which it honors with the name of "law," no loving, infinite Being is seen to reign there, and while in original chaos it finds a complicated laboratory it discerns no all-wise chemist regulating and determining its subtle and mysterious combinations, from which universes proceed. Materialism, old and new, when stripped of its rhetoric, simply writes "mindless" on the dateless procession of things, and teaches that these things come from nowhere, as they are eternal; are marching nowhither, as they are practically endless, and that over them is nobody, as they are self-fashioned and self-sustained. As Lucretius is reported to have expressed it, "Nature is seen to do all these things spontaneously of herself, without the meddling of the gods." And man is looked on as earth-begotten, earth-bound, and earth-destined; and his sublimer and deeper aspirations and affinities are belittled or ignored.

Unquestionably these teachings are exerting a tremendous influence on our times. Our relations with the visible are so intimate, our susceptibility to its impressions so keen, our bodily demands so imperative, and the dominion of our senses so absolute, that we are strongly drawn toward whatever promises to minister to the sway of the physical. Shakspeare wrote:

> "There's not the smallest orb that thou behold'st
> But in his motion like an angel sings,
> Still quiring to the young-eyed cherubim:
> Such harmony is in immortal souls,
> But, whilst this muddy vesture of decay
> Doth grossly close it in, we cannot hear it."

That is, we are so wrapped about with the heavy folds of dull earthiness that we cannot always detect the music of the spiritual within, nor catch its echoes in the universe without. We are, therefore, liable to be imposed on by materialistic philosophy, and to yield submission when it should be questioned and resisted. It has an ally in man himself, in the dominancy of the physical, which may account for its present prevalent potency. And very likely the character of our civilization itself has enhanced its power. Wherever we turn we find matter triumphant. Science has laid bare the vastness of its magnitudes, has subordinated its forces to human service, and has rendered possible the magnificent achievements of machinery which lighten labor and promote industry. We talk along wires, we fly along rails, we hear through our teeth, we almost see without eyes, and even the supposition of Dr. Bowen may become actual in the future,—skill may be able to construct a wooden footman whose "exact and unvarying obedience may be more than could be expected of any but a superhuman footman." If it would only give us such a Bridget, in these days of maid-servant supremacy, our joy indeed would be full. Who knows? A new aim or ambition has been developed by the successes of science, and instead of seeking primarily the culture of soul, we are concerned with the conquest and improvement of nature. Everywhere we are digging, delving, mining, projecting railroads, compassing seas, reclaiming lands, and making everything tributary to man's temporal gratification and comfort. For six days in the week we are devoted to the interests of matter, and begrudge a small portion of the seventh in which to consider the claims of spirit. Is it not, then, probable that this undue prominence given to one aspect of the universe blinds us to the reality of any other, and disposes us to give heed to a philosophy whose terms exclude everything else?

Whether I have guessed the true explanation of the present widespread influence of materialism others must judge; but there can be no doubt that its extent is such that earnest words must be spoken, and earnest efforts be made, if society is to be saved from bondage to the sensuous, and inspired anew with belief in the supersensuous and immortal. As contributing to this end, I suggest the following propositions for thoughtful consideration:

First, Materialism is too imaginative to be either scientific or reasonable.

Second, Materialism is too debasing to be either credible or attractive.

Third, Materialism is too impoverishing to be either probable or possible.

The assumptions of this Ism are numerous and bold. It asserts that matter is the only substance in the universe, or at least the only substance of which we have any definite knowledge, or about which we can argue with certainty. For its teachings, consequently, it claims implicit confidence as being necessarily beyond cavil and dispute. But surely it forgets that very wise men have questioned the reality of this visible world to which it is so attached, and of which it makes so much. The idealism of Berkeley, grounded in the non-existence and impossibility of external nature, and the belief of Faraday in the immateriality of physical objects, go far toward proving that this boasted certainty is somewhat uncertain, and that the definite, after all, is very indefinite. As Professor B. Stewart, in his *Conservation of Energy*, says: "The universe has more than one point of view, and there are possibly regions which will not yield their treasures to the most determined physicists, armed only with kilogrammes, and meters, and standard clocks;" and in another place he adds: "We know nothing, or next to nothing, of the ultimate structure and properties of matter, whether organic or inorganic." If he is warranted in this statement, how purely fanciful is the assertion that substance is one, and that it is the only, source of positive knowledge. And if this primary assumption is questionable, what shall be said of the second, that matter is capable, through its inalienable properties, of evolving inorganic forms, developing, also, organic life or growth, and even of originating thought? Here, assuredly, we have a tremendous stretch of the imagination. The ancient savage, in the dense depths of native ignorance, made to himself a mud fetich, and attributed to it divine energies. We smile at his infantile superstition, and we wonder that he could believe for a moment that a wretched heap of plastic filth could call into being the beauties and utilities of creation. But according to the Ism we are studying, this primitive superstition is the ultimate goal of science. Extremes meet. The savage and the scientist clasp hands, and the end of investigation is found at the beginning. It began with the worship of mud; it is ending with unworshiped, but deified, molecules. Wherein is the difference? Why shall we stigmatize the faith of the savage as puerile, and yet honor the theory of the scientist with encomiums, as though it were the expression of the highest wisdom? Are they not substantially the same?

While the essence of matter defies our scrutiny, for the sake of proving that it is capable of producing all that we see and feel, its simple and primary definition has been gradually enlarged. New qualities have been constantly ascribed to it, and as Dr. James Martineau quaintly says, "starting as a beggar, with scarce a rag of 'property' to cover its bones, it turns up as a prince when large undertakings are wanted, loaded with investments, and within an inch of a plenipotentiary." On which remarkable phenomenon he adds, addressing believers in its almost boundless resources: "In short, you give it precisely what you require to take from it; and when your definition has made it 'pregnant with all the future,' there is no wonder if from it all the future might be born." But the endeavors that have been put forth in this direction have never succeeded in making out that in each separate atom resides every force, every quality, every sensation known to thought, yea, and thought itself, combined with consciousness by which thought is recognized; and anything short of this is fatal to the trustworthiness of the theory in debate; for the aggregate can never be more than an expression of the unit, and the whole can never manifest what is not potentially in the parts. Locke witnesses to the validity of this position in the following words: "Whatsoever is first of all things must necessarily contain in it, and actually have, at least all the perfections that can ever after exist; nor can it ever give to another any perfection that it hath not actually in itself, or at least in a higher degree; it necessarily follows that the first eternal Being cannot be matter." The advocates of materialism, in their reasoning, constantly overlook this axiom, than which there is none more generally approved by philosophy. They are unable to show that whatever is in the effect was first in the cause, — that is, in the cause which they assign, — and, consequently, they are shut up to the illogical inference that there is something in the effect which is traceable to no cause whatever. We cannot believe that the greater springs from the less, or that something comes from nothing; and until we are convinced that our incredulity on this point is irrational, the explanation of the universe which assumes that the organic proceeded from the inorganic, order from disorder, life from death, and thought from molecular motions, we must regard as fanciful, possibly seductive, but very imaginative, and certainly immeasurably less reasonable than that which attributes all things to an infinitely intelligent and sovereign Spirit.

The assumption of Herbert Spencer that the ego, or conscious self, is merely "a group of psychical states constituting an impulse," and that of such writers as Moleschott and Büchner that thought is determined and conditioned by phosphorus, can hardly be considered other than whimsical extravagances of facetious science. Their advocates, however, at times seem to be serious enough. Mr. Huxley, for instance, appears to be very much in earnest when, in writing to *Macmillan's Magazine* in 1878, he says: "I believe that we shall arrive at a mechanical equivalent of consciousness, just as we have arrived at a mechanical equivalent of heat," and adds: "even those manifestations of intelligence and feeling which we rightly name the higher faculties are not excluded from this classification." But when the famous protoplasmist, in his *Lay Sermons*, confesses that how "anything so remarkable as a state of consciousness comes about as the result of irritating nervous tissue, is just as unaccountable as the appearance of the Djin when Aladdin rubbed his lamp," we half suspect him of indulging in a little sly humor at our expense when he penned the first of these statements, as in the second he seems to attach as much value to it as he does to one of the Arabian Nights' marvelous stories. Certainly they are not altogether consistent with each other, and on the authority of his *Lay Sermon* we may with propriety question the soundness of his doctrine in the magazine, and from the bearing of both conclude that the mechanical theory of thought is but a wild speculation, incapable of verification.

Such writers as Dr. Maudsley soberly enough maintain that "the nerve-cells, which exist in countless numbers — about six hundred millions according to Meynert's calculations — in the gray matter spread over the surface of the hemispheres, are the nervous centers of ideas;" or, according to the explanations given by others, "thought is a function of the brain, and brain secretes thought as the liver secretes bile." It is undeniable that a most intimate relation exists between mental phenomena and the brain. No one familiar with the literature on the subject would think of calling it in question. The brain seems to be in some way the organ of mind, but to identify them, or to assume that there is nothing but brain, or that it alone is the source of thought, is in my judgment to transgress the modesty of true science. This also seems to be the opinion of Professor Tyndall. In his *Fragments of Science* he expresses himself on this subject in these terms: "In affirming that the growth of the body is mechanical, and that thought, as exercised by us, has its correlative in the physics of the brain, I think the position of the Materialist is stated, as far as that position is a tenable one." . . . "I do not think that he is entitled to say that his molecular groupings and his molecular motions *explain* everything. In reality they explain nothing. The utmost he can affirm is the association of two classes of phenomena, of whose real bond of union he is in absolute ignorance. The problem of the connection of body and soul is as insoluble in its modern form as it was in the prescientific ages."—*pp. 119, 120.* And it is well known that Virchow, one of the most eminent of German scientists, when opposing the proposition of Haeckel and Nägeli that materialistic doctrines should be introduced into the system of public instruction, said very decidedly: "So long as no one can define for me the properties of carbon, hydrogen, oxygen, and nitrogen in such a way that I can conceive how, from the sum of them, a soul arises, so long am I unable to admit that we should be at all justified in importing the plastidulic soul into the course of our education."

But, assuming that various and striking considerations can be adduced in favor of what is called "Cerebral Psychology," let us note whither it tends. For instance, on this hypothesis the bulk of the head and the measure of its contents, a healthy body being granted, ought to decide the quality of a man's intellectual life. Pure blood should be more needful than what we denominate education. Physical organs should be nourished with substantial food, not with ideas. What is it that we now attempt to educate in our schools? When we set about training a boy, what portion of him is it that receives attention? Is it said that we try to cultivate the brain? But, if so, are we not employing singular methods? We are actually trying to build up, strengthen, and develop the material through the immaterial. If this hypothesis is tenable we should rather provide wholesome physical diet than innutritious knowledge; and if Moleschott is right when he says, "*Ohne Phosphor, Kein Gedanke,*" then we should feed phosphorus to our youth and cram them as full of phosphorus as possible. And yet, were their heads as full of it as the sea, it would be no guaranty of exceptional brilliancy. Men who have been deprived of nourishing food, who have toiled in poverty, have conferred on the race the most enduring triumphs of thought, and others, like Milton, Spinoza, Cervantes, Bunyan, and Burns, produced their masterpieces when in pinched want or in deep affliction; while many who were reared in affluence, who were both strong bodied and large headed,— and had all the phosphorus they desired,— have continued to the end mental drones. This ought not to be so if mechanical cerebration is true, and it cannot be explained unless it is acknowledged that the thinking subject is different from brain-tissues and nerve-centers, and at times is capable of surmounting their imperfections.

And this is a conclusion to which we are impelled by other considerations. Instinctively we discriminate between ourselves and our surroundings, and between "something" which we regard as "self" from the body in which it dwells. We are conscious of an existence which does not change with the flux and flow of the physical, and which we identify as the same in age, manhood, and youth. Moreover, this "something" is able to antagonize with the body, to resist it and overcome it; and in so doing feels a distinctness from it and a superiority over it, and finds itself haunted with ideas of the infinite, the impersonal, the absolute, the abstract, which it in vain tries to trace to "the gray matter" of the brain or to the outward forms of the universe. This "something" we call "soul," "spirit," perfectly distinguishable from the other substance by its phenomena, and which is conscious of its own existence and its own agency, and which is therefore beyond the reach of doubt. To deny its reality is to disregard the most unanswerable evidence, and prefer the region of chimera for that of fact. This is the judgment of many sober thinkers, and is expressed by "one of the most eminent physicists of England," Prof. P. G. Tait, who, as quoted by Dr. Bowen in *Literary Gleanings*, remarks: "To say that even the very lowest forms of life, not to speak of its higher forms, still less of volition and consciousness, can be fully explained on physical principles alone — that is, by the mere relative motions and interactions of portions of inanimate matter, however refined and sublimated — is simply unscientific. There is absolutely nothing known in physical science which can lend the slightest support to such an idea." Such principles certainly cannot account for the wonderful aptitudes which distinguish some children, and which under the circumstances cannot be ascribed to the influence of education, such as the mathematical ability of Pascal, which asserted itself when he was twelve years old, as the musical genius of Mozart revealing itself in an opera composed when he was only eight summers in the world, or the artistic inspiration of West, or the military instincts of Napoleon. Here we meet with a phenomenon which "nothing known in physical science" can explain, and which strengthens the conviction that this entire theory is a day-dream, phantom, fiction of fairyland, a rhapsody of visionary romancers and of scientific knights-errant, which has no foundation in the empire of facts, and should be discarded from the realm of faith unless it should be accepted on the basis of "*Credo quia absurdum.*"

Were its imaginativeness the only ground of objection we could afford, perhaps, to treat it with indifference, but unhappily it is debasing, and therefore its claims should be seriously challenged. The effort recently made by Professor Lindsay to identify the brute mind with the human is one that tends to obscure, if not to lessen, the sense of moral obligation, and to degrade the race to a lower level than it occupies at present. He relates some wonderful stories about animals, which could be matched with others equally striking, and he leaves the impression, though he does not aim to advocate any special doctrine, that man differs only in degree, not in kind, from his humbler associates. Interesting though his volumes are, they by no means succeed in bridging the chasm that separates the human from the animal. The inventive faculty, the powers of ratiocination and abstraction, the moral sense, and the gift of language, are among the chief difficulties in the way of such a result. In the *Descent of Man* we find this discriminating objection: "A moral being is one who is capable of comparing his past and future actions and motives — of approving of some and disapproving of others; and the fact that man is the one being who with certainty can be thus designated makes the greatest of all distinctions between him and the lower animals." Such testimony from such a quarter ought to counteract the effect of Dr. Lindsay's inconclusive effort to establish the opposite view. And when it is realized that no adequate explanation of either reason or speech can be given on his hypothesis, it may be dismissed as untenable. Süssmilch, in 1764, argued the impossibility of language without thought, and of thought without language; and if any such close connection exists between them as he maintained, then it is certain that, as all skill has failed to teach animals to speak, for the mere automatic imitation of sounds is not speech, what is called thought in the brute and thought in the man are incapable of being classified together. The German whom Dr. Bowen quotes as saying, "I will believe that animals have reason when one of them tells me so," in reality disposes of the whole question at issue; for when they find their tongue they will have found reason, and when that comes to pass we may, without discredit to our own intellect, acknowledge theirs.

In his anxiety to make good his position, Dr. Lindsay says: "Even as regards man himself, it must be borne in mind . . . that there are countless thousands — many whole races — that are intellectually and morally the inferior of many well-trained mammals, such as the chimpanzee, orang, dog, elephant, or horse," etc. But this is not a fair and ingenuous statement of the case; for the savage can hardly be found who entirely fails to feel the force of "ought" and "ought not;" and there is no animal in the world, however carefully trained, who knows anything about them, or is in the least degree conscious of them. But, after all, this is a question of capacity, not of training. Under the most scrupulous discipline the dog remains a dog; up to a certain point he can be taught, and beyond it he cannot go. A recent writer has represented the canine "as a candidate for humanity"; but it may be safely said that he has never yet succeeded in securing an election. On the other hand, no limit can be placed to man's development. He can advance indefinitely, and from the lowest form of intellectual life rise to the highest. The race has a capacity that is not shared by the dog; individuals may possess it in different degrees as canine aptitudes differ, but the human nature, as such, is not to be classed with the brute nature, for even in its degradation it is infinitely higher, as its possibilities are infinitely greater. These comparisons, in my opinion, are always to be deplored, not merely because they rank some men lower than beasts, but because they leave the impression on many that essentially they do not rank above them. If, however, they are to be trusted, then thought is automatic, volition is mechanical, and the ideas of responsibility and duty are illusions; our noblest and purest emotions are due to a highly sensitive sensorium and a symmetrically arranged ganglia, and all that is divine in man dies out. If, as has been maintained by an English author, "the conduct of the elephant and of the tiger depends on their structure, and so, therefore, does that of man," then we must abandon the doctrine that he has any will that can initiate action, we must abrogate the ideas of guilt and innocence, and we should seek to educate him as we train other animals, by processes suited to automata. No words can do justice to the degrading influences of such teachings. They lead men to regard themselves as creatures of necessity, whose actions are no more praiseworthy or blameworthy than those of the cat or dog, and they gradually stifle and smother the consciousness of manhood, without which no heroic sacrifices or generous deeds are possible.

As a result of this Ism we find that modern life is pretty thoroughly materialized. Of those who are striving and struggling in this and other lands, how few there are who have set before them any other object than the accumulation of wealth. For this they abandon home and friends, spend sleepless nights and toilsome days, and endure enough of pain, mortification and anguish to make them martyrs in a holier cause. True, the desire for gain is frequently subordinate to some other end; but how rarely is it anything radically better. In many cases the ambition is for means to satisfy luxurious tastes, to gratify senseless pride and vanity. Mansions, servants, carriages, horses, delicate wines, rare pictures, rich laces, and elegant appointments are valued on account of the favorable impression regarding their possessor which they are supposed to make on a world which evermore walks by sight and not by faith. It may be that love of pleasure, or of power, rank, and office, or of the windy praise of his fellows, stimulates man to strive, but even these aims are of the earth earthy. They certainly fall infinitely below what they should be. To an appalling extent the people around us live without any pronounced desire to know God, indifferent to communion with Him, and careless of their immortal destiny. They do not seem to realize that they are other than a higher sort of animal, and do not recognize any obligation to unfold the God-likeness in them, or to reveal the goodness and beauty of the Redeemer in their character and conduct. So absorbed is the ordinary mind in the terrible struggle for existence that is going on, so intently is it concentrated on sordid interests, that it is quite unfitted for spiritual concerns. Consequently attempts to read the Scriptures fail, the letters change to rows of figures, and the shortest road to affluence seems more important than finding the surest way to heaven. In prayer terrestrial riches strangely blend with the celestial, and supplications take on the tone of the market rather than the devoutness of the altar. These too common experiences, combined with the reluctance of many to go to church at all, and the anxiety of more to get out again after they have entered, show how the prevailing philosophy of our times is gradually hardening, withering, and blighting the spiritual in humanity. Can such a system be credible? Can we regard it as attractive? Credible! Can that be credible which can only be established at the cost of all that is great and good in man? Attractive! Can that be attractive which allies us with brutes, and which buries all our fair ideals in mud and slime? Attractive possibly to worms wriggling in the earth, and to swine grunting over their swill, but assuredly not to men; not at least to those who will open their eyes wide enough to recognize the quagmire into which it is perceptibly sinking them.

Already we perceive how ruthlessly this Ism plunders and impoverishes the race, and therefore only a few more words need be added on this point. Practically it robs the soul of God. Mr. Emerson, in *The Unitarian Review*, tries to estimate the extent and painfulness of this loss. He deplores "the solitude of the soul that is without God in the world," and likens it to "aimless, fatherless Cain," "who hears only the sound of his own footsteps in God's resplendent creation." To such a one "heaven and earth have been deprived of beauty, the sun of its power to cheer, and every great thought of its power to inspire." Here, indeed, is bankruptcy! Take away God, and the beggarly inventory of what is left is not worth the reading. Not satisfied with depriving us of God, Materialism also plunders life of everything that makes it tolerable. It filches from the unsuspecting soul the sense of immortality, and in return leaves some such melancholy Gospel as that which Yang Choo comforts his disciples with: "All are born and all die; the intelligent and the stupid, the honorable and the mean. At ten years old some die; at a hundred years old some die. The virtuous and the sage die; the ruffian and the fool also die. Alive, they were Yaou and Shun, the most virtuous of men; dead, they are so much rotten bone. Alive, they were Klüe and Chow, the most wicked of men; dead, they are so much rotten bone. While alive, therefore, let us hasten to make the best of life; when about to die, let us treat the thing with indifference, and seeking to accomplish our departure, so abandon ourselves to annihilation." One shudders as he reads. Yet this same death's-head philosophy, only skillfully adorned with flowers, is that which is current among high and low in Europe and America. No wonder that existence becomes insufferably wearisome, unendurable and drearisome when it is overshadowed by such a upas. The perpetual and meaningless clatter, the endless and senseless rattle of this soulless mechanism which we call life, signifying and ending in nothing, can hardly fail to evoke gloominess and despair. Hence so many are wretched who seem to have everything needful for happiness, and so many are groaning who have every earthly reason to rejoice. Prosperity, palaces, pictures, pleasures, cannot satisfy the cravings of the soul, and after the excitement is passed which was experienced in their pursuit, there is nothing to sustain and satisfy. The question is now being asked, "Is life worth living?" and it is being as frequently answered by the grave of the suicide. In the light of Materialism it is not. Why should one strive, why plod on beneath oppressive burdens, why endure the agonies and shame of time, when oblivion in the quiet grave is so easy? Apart from God, emptied of spiritual meaning and deprived of eternal hope, life is a curse, and no wonder if its unsatisfactory experiences and cruel disappointments madden the intellect, darken the heart, and drive the weary one to the repose of death. Well has Mr. Malloch summed up this intense and utter degradation when he trenchantly writes: "To bring into men's minds eternal corruption, instead of eternal life,—or, rather, not corruption, I should say, but putrefaction. For what is putrefaction but decomposition? And at the touch of science all our noblest ideas decompose and putrify till our whole souls are strewed with dead hopes and dead religions, with corpses of all the thoughts we loved

"'Quickening slowly into lower forms.'"

Can that be a true philosophy which pauperizes existence, and that converts the fair earth into a potter's field, where beggars may find a refuge with worms, and hide their tattered wretchedness in the cold, narrow bed of annihilation? True? When hell is true, when devils are not false, and when wrong and error are not deceitful, it may be true. But not till then. Not till things most certain become uncertain, the harmonies of the universe be out of tune, and the foundations of eternal verities be shaken, can such a monstrous, rapacious theory be probable to reason or possible to faith. Unhappy the soul who has been deceived by it, who has surrendered his sense of immortality to its block and ax, and who stumbles along over the ruins of once-cherished hopes and beliefs toward extinction. For him no sweet voices sing welcome in the far Beyond; for him no land of beauty unseen by mortal eye unfolds its loveliness; for him no Savior stands with extended arms inviting to the mansions blessed, and for him no endless vistas of unsurpassed and unsurpassable glory open as the scenes of time recede. No; all is dark, cold, forbidding. Every sunrise only hastens impending doom, every grave but tells of sad, irreparable decay, and every sunset is to him only the gorgeous, flaunting herald of annihilation. Annihilation is the burden of every murmuring wind; it is articulated in the rustle of autumnal leaves; it is roared in the thunder clap, and seared into his soul by the lightning's shaft that splinters to naught the giant of the woods. This is to him the one sad message of creation; and all the voices within him and without sent by the Almighty to assure him of everlasting life have turned false prophets to his heart, and mutter death, only death,—nothing but death.

While we deplore these insatiate ravages, we rejoice

that the power of Materialism is less than its malignancy. It may destroy our ideals, it may crush our hopes, it may debase our life, it may lead us to doubt the being of God and the eternity of man, but it can go no farther. It may triumph over our faith in the realities against which it strives; but it never can prevail against the realities themselves. It cannot empty the universe of God, cannot strike Him from His throne, or wrest the scepter from His hand. In this we will rejoice and be glad; yea, and we will shout for joy, because it is equally impotent in its war against humanity. It cannot dispossess the soul of immortality, cannot rob it of that endless life which is its glory, nor drown it in the seas of drear oblivion, nor doom it to the "Realm of Nothingness":

> "The stars shall fade away, the sun himself
> Grow dim with age, and nature sink in years;
> But Thou shalt flourish in immortal youth,
> Unhurt amidst the war of elements,
> The wreck of matter and the crash of worlds."

Of this we are assured, and in this confidence will we rejoice; and while we struggle with the thickening fogs of cold Materialism this hope shall sustain us, that the sun of truth, which for the moment it obscures but cannot extinguish, shall once more and forever stream through the misty veil, and with the night-scattering wings of light chase away the sorrows and the shadows which have settled on too many souls, and enshrouded them in gloom too long.

NATURALISM

"Upholding all things by the word of His power." *Hebrews i, 3.*

"There is a power
Unseen that rules the illimitable world,
That guides its motions, from the brightest star
To the least dust of this sin-tainted mold;
While man, who madly deems himself the lord
Of all, is naught but weakness and dependence."
Thomson.

ARISTOTLE thought that Anaxagoras talked like a sober man, because he rejected the transcendentalism of the Greek Pantheists, and advocated a system which recognized the reality of the visible universe, and attributed the existence and variety of material forms to the creative mind of God. Socrates, also, for the same reason, was at first disposed to admire the philosopher of Clazomenæ. "Having one day," he says, "read a book of Anaxagoras, who said the Divine mind was the cause of all things, and drew them up in their proper ranks and classes, I was ravished with joy. I perceived that there was nothing more certain than this principle." But more intimate acquaintance with his writings did not confirm this good opinion. Socrates soon discovered that Anaxagoras failed to inculcate sound views regarding a superintending and sustaining Providence, and criticised him accordingly in these terms: "He makes no further use of this mind, but assigns as the cause of the order and beauty that prevails in the world, the air, water, whirlwind, and other agencies of nature." It seems that this father of **anti-transcendental theologies**, while ascribing the origin of all things to God, did not teach that He upholds them, governs or interferes with them in any way, except, at times, to correct their derangements or to avert their destruction. His was the machine theory of the Cosmos, which represents the Almighty as imparting to the works of His hands certain forces, and subordinating them to specific laws, and then as withdrawing from them to some remote retreat in infinite solitude, from whence to contemplate with serene satisfaction, or serener indifference, their self-supporting and ceaseless operations. Such a philosophy, in which the Creator is comparable (to employ a Carlylian similitude) to a "clockmaker that once, in old immemorial ages, having *made* his Horologe of a Universe, sits ever since and sees it go," was not to the liking of Socrates. In his judgment it was radically defective, insufficient and inconclusive, stopping far short of the truth, and subversive of its fundamental postulate.

The theory of an involved, boundlessly complex, and automatic system of worlds, rejected by the Athenian sage, has been revived in our day, and has grown, and is growing, in tumultuous popularity. While Naturalism in its extreme form is atheistic, as in the remarkable treatise of Baron D'Holbach, in its more moderate, if not more consistent shape, it concedes the Divine existence. It assumes that God is, and that He is necessary to account for the beginning of things; but it discredits the belief that He is indispensable to their maintenance, takes any direct interest in the affairs of His creatures, and either can or will interfere on their behalf. Naturalism, considered as a theistic scheme, dispenses with the Almighty after He has made the universe, and assumes that, being completely made, it is abundantly able to take care of itself. Its favorite illustration, probably derived from Anaxagoras, by which it seeks to make plain to the simplest understanding the character of its teachings, is founded on the structure and action of complicated machinery. An engine, for instance, is fashioned by human intelligence and skill, arranged in harmony with particular principles, constructed to accomplish a specific end, capable of generating steam, its motive force, and supplied with adequate fuel. Then, by the same intelligence, it is started on its journey, and afterward it runs along the rails independent of its contriver, propelled by its own inherent energies and in obedience to its own fundamental laws. The engineer may be drunk, asleep, or dead; the locomotive will, all the same, pursue its journey as far as the route extends, and as long as the steam endures. This, it is claimed, is a fair description of God's relation to the universe. He called matter into being, endowed it with various properties and with all-sufficing potencies, molded, distributed and organized it according to a predetermined plan; and then, having shaped his suns and stars, and fixed the boundaries of their orbits, having rounded the earth, and furnished it with animals, plants and human puppets, and having provided for every possible contingency; that is, having finished his enormous, complicated machine, with its jagged wheels and ponderous hammers, He removed His hand, gave the word of command, and the whole began to move, and has been moving ever since. If this analogy is justifiable, then from the creative hour "not wanted" might have been written on the throne of God. For if He has from the beginning stored up in nature all the forces requisite for its operations, neither His sleep nor death would have hindered or varied them in the least, or have made any perceptible or practicable difference. And if the theory which is thus illustrated is correct, and the Creator has withdrawn from His works, having committed them to the vicegerency of all-potent second causes, then prayer, of course, is useless, providential care is a myth, and light or help from any other source than nature an absolute impossibility.

And this is just what the Ism we are examining asserts. It denounces as the fruit of ignorance and superstition the belief that God is approachable, or can in any sense be influenced by His creatures, or ever interposes in behalf of their well-being. To even entertain such thoughts is reprobated as a sign of the weakness of man's reason, and of the strength of his vanity. We are exhorted to look upon the world, to study the past and the present, that we may see how utterly groundless these conceptions are. We are told that man will be found at the period of densest mental darkness attributing every strange phenomenon of nature and every remarkable event of history to supernatural interposition; but that as he advances in knowledge he gradually discovers his mistake, and repudiates his former superstition. In our day much that was regarded as the result of superhuman agencies is easily explained by natural causes. Continually we are solving mysteries before which our ancestors trembled; and in a little while we shall be able to account for everything without falling back on God, angels, or devils. Just in proportion as the intellect expands will the domain of the semi-miraculous diminish, until it dwindles down to a point too imperceptible for faith to build on. Naturalism also asks, what more can be needed for the moral culture and religious training of the race than the wonders and glories of creation, interpreted by science and apprehended by reason? These surely must be efficacious to restrain from evil, to inspire goodness, and to kindle devotion. By their side, how mean, inadequate and powerless do cathedrals, with their tawdry decorations, and churches, with their silly preachings, appear. Why puzzle our heads and pain our hearts concerning revelations and gospels, when the true word of the Lord flames on us from the heavens and is articulated by the earth? But whether sufficient or not, this is all we have or can have; He has spoken once— in creation — He has not spoken since, and never will speak again. To expect Him to open His sacred lips for man's behoof is as ridiculous as to suppose that He is constantly interfering with the established order of the universe to answer prayer, or to bring special deliverances to individuals. Evidences of such condescension are scouted with derision. It is claimed by Naturalism that they have no existence outside of the imagination. In danger and distress men call upon God, and are not heard. The ship goes down in the night, the home is reduced to ashes in the fire, the harvest perishes in the storm, and the child dies in the parent's trembling arms, though prayers importunate and fervent ascend to the throne of Him who is believed to have power to save; yea, and minds sink beneath the burden of mystery which such a faith entails, and hearts are broken on this rock, and yet God rises not up to vindicate His name by affording help to the sufferer. How anyone, therefore, with these and similar facts before him, can cling to the doctrines of prayer and providence, Naturalistic advocates affect not to understand. Ignorance and unreason, they concede, may be deceived by them, but they cannot comprehend how men of intelligence can ever be persuaded of their truth. Judging these doctrines to be thus irrelevant, irreconcilable and irrational, they thrust them contemptuously away, and in effect write "fool" on the brow of every man who gives them entertainment.

But what shall we say of the wisdom that rejects them? Naturalism assumes an air of intellectual superiority, and looks down with patronizing pity on the unfortunate people who are unable to rise to its lofty views of God and the universe. Perhaps it may not be amiss to name some of these unfortunates, and to take the true measure of their folly. Permit me first of all to mention the venerable men who spake of old as they were moved by the Holy Spirit, and to whose influence the world undoubtedly owes much of its mental culture and moral refinement. The inspired prophets, poets and preachers acknowledge in glowing terms what is counted visionary and absurd by those who are enraptured with the idea of an impenetrable and imperturbable "Clockmaker Almighty." They delight to speak of Him as "The Great, the Mighty God, who hath His way in the whirlwind and in the storm, and the clouds are the dust of His feet; who is great in counsel and mighty in work, whose eyes are open upon all the ways of the sons of men to give everyone according to his ways and according to the fruit of his doings; and before whom all the inhabitants of the earth are reputed as nothing, and who doeth according to His will in the army of heaven, and among the inhabitants of the earth; and none can stay His hand, or say unto Him, 'What doest Thou?'" Unto Him they cry, "O Lord God of our fathers, art not Thou God in heaven? and rulest not Thou over all the kingdoms of the heathen? and in Thine hand is there not power and might, so that none is able to withstand Thee? Thine, O Lord, is the greatness and the power and the glory and the victory and the majesty; for all that is in the heaven and the earth is Thine; Thine is the kingdom, O Lord, and Thou art exalted as head above all. Both riches and honor come of Thee, and Thou reignest over all; and in Thine hand is power and might, and in Thine hand it is to make great, and to give strength unto all." "Even Thou art God alone; Thou hast made heaven, the heaven of heavens, with all their host, the earth and all things that are therein, the seas and all that is therein, and Thou preservest them all; Thy righteousness is like the great mountain; Thy judgments are a great deep; O Lord, Thou preservest man and beast; and by Thee all things consist." They confess that "the way of man is not in himself; it is not in man that walketh to direct his steps; but his goings are of the Lord; for He giveth power to the faint, and to them that have no might He increaseth strength." They rejoice to record the Savior's assuring words, "Are not two sparrows sold for a farthing? and not one of them is forgotten before God; but even the very hairs of your head are all numbered. Fear not, therefore, ye are of more value than many sparrows"; and they are always confident that Jehovah is "their refuge and strength in every time of trouble," that He will arise upon them "as light in the darkness," that "He will uphold them with His hand," that "He will make them to dwell safely," and that "in their way He will cause life, and in their pathway no death." And thus, and in a thousand other ways, they represent Him as "upholding all things by the word of His power," as being "a very present help," as sustaining, guiding, directing, and as working "all things together for good." To them He is no banished, absentee Jehovah, a rigid cast-iron Destiny, sitting listless, and watching the grinding of this acutely and wretchedly devised mill of life and death,—to them He is no dead Almighty Majesty entombed in the charnel house called the universe; no withered skeleton gleaming ghastly, like the bleached bones of the poor cardinal in Milan Cathedral, clothed with regal garments woven in the loom of eternity, and gorgeous with sun-spangles and stellar-scintillates. He is to them preëminently the Living God, the Ever Living One, the "King eternal, immortal, invisible," who is "not far from every one of us," "who is able to do exceeding abundantly above all that we ask or think," and who "worketh all things after the counsel of His own will."

That this magnificent faith of theirs is not grounded in unreason as impartial a witness as Mr. Holyoake involuntarily confesses. In his *Debate with Townly* he clearly shows the worthlessness of a Theism that excludes the Almighty from any direct interference with the affairs of His creatures. Upon this point he says, "If you tell me that God exists, that He is a power, or principle, or spirit, or light, or life, or love, or intelligence, or what you will — if He be not a father to whom His children may appeal, if He be not a providence whom we may propitiate, and from whom we can obtain special help in the hour of danger,— I say, practically, it does not matter to us whether He exists or not." That is, in the estimation of an Atheist, the Naturalist, whose Deity is, like Baal, asleep or on a journey when His creatures implore His aid, is not remarkably sagacious, as he is holding to a creed from which he has eliminated everything that renders it important, advantageous, and profitable. Thomas Jefferson is another such impartial witness, who, though skeptically inclined, had not discernment enough to perceive the senselessness and childishness of the supernatural. In his *Notes on Virginia*, when writing of the helpless condition of those who suffered from human cruelty and tyranny, he exclaims: "Doubtless a God of justice will awaken to a sense of their wrongs, and either by disseminating a sense of humanity in the bosoms of their oppressors, or by His exterminating thunders, show that this world is not governed by a blind fatality." Is it not singular, if such expectations are as illusory and extravagant as Naturalism claims, that so keen-sighted and long-headed a man as Mr. Jefferson should have been deceived by them? But if it is said that this is accounted for by his lack of scientific knowledge, how shall we dispose of the views announced by Newton, who cannot justly be charged with such ignorance? Upon this subject he pens these immortal words: "This most beautiful system of the Sun, Planets and Comets could only proceed from the counsel and dominion of an intelligent and powerful Being. . . . This Being governs all things, not as the soul of the world, but as Lord over all. The Supreme God is a being eternal, infinite, absolutely perfect. We know Him only by his most wise and excellent contrivance of things and final causes, we adore Him for his perfection; but we reverence and adore Him on account of his dominion. For we adore Him as his servants; and a god without dominion, providence and final causes is nothing else but Fate and Nature." Evidently he did not regard faith in the personal oversight and rulership of the Almighty as subversive either of common sense or of scientific accuracy. Leibnitz, also, expresses the conviction that "God is a good governor as well as a great architect;" and Niebuhr, in his *Lectures*, writes: "As the consideration of nature shows an inherent intelligence, which may also be conceived as coherent with nature, so does history, on a hundred occasions, show an intelligence which is distinct from nature, which conducts and determines those things which may seem to be accidental, and it is not true that the study of history weakens the belief in a Divine providence. History is, of all kinds of knowledge, the one which tends most decidedly to that belief." (*Vol. i, p. 146.*) And Morell confirms this testimony when he says: "To the man who looks unbelievingly upon Divine providence the world's history is a problem that can never be solved." (*Hist. of Phil., vol. ii, p. 571.*) These, then, are some of the names in the great army of simpletons, numskulls, and fanatics who, misled by their own shallowness and obtuseness, indulge in unphilosophical, irrational and nonsensical dreams of an ever-present Infinite Spirit, who "upholds all things by the word of His power," and who works in and through all things to the honor and glory of His name. But is it suggested that these are among the brightest names in the world of thought? Is it so? What then?

What is the real significance of this fact? Does it not indicate that, measured by the capacity of the men, there must be less of absurdity and fatuity in the doctrines they avow than their critics are willing to acknowledge? And may it not, also, indicate that the much-talked-of unreason, after all, is to be found entirely on the other side?

Let us see.

The argument for God's existence is equally an argument for His governance. If intuition discerns His being, it also perceives His activity. The primitive faiths of mankind rather identified the Infinite Spirit with the universe than separated Him from its operations. They saw Him in the phenomena of nature as well as in the movements of history. He was over everything and in everything. Pantheism far more than Naturalism expresses the idea which filled the mind of the earliest races, and which imparted to the most ancient religious systems their distinctive character. Doubtless among ignorant tribes the intuitive recognition of Providence was crude, and led to many superstitious and foolish thoughts and observances. And not a few people of narrow and limited culture err in the same direction still. As Shakspeare expresses it:

> "No natural exhalation in the sky,
> No scope of nature, no distemper'd day,
> No common wind, no customed event,
> But they will pluck away his natural cause
> And call them meteors, prodigies, and signs,
> Abortives, presages, and tongues of heaven."

But the strength of these superstitious feelings only goes to show how vigorous and clear the intuition is. We ourselves must be conscious of the fact that just in proportion as we realize distinctly the existence of the Almighty, we seek to draw nearer to Him, to commune with Him, and to commit to Him our ways. Has not this been your experience? If you have ever taken pains to analyze your idea of God, as the reality has emerged from the mists of vagueness you have instinctively bowed the knee before Him, and lifted up your heart in homage. It would seem, then, that the recognition of His sovereignty and supervision springs from something interwoven in the soul's texture, native to it and originating with it, and that, therefore, it is as worthy of confidence as is the testimony of that untaught voice within us which proclaims the certainty of His being.

But if we shift the ground of belief from what we feel within to what we behold without the result is the same. Discerning thought in the constitution of nature, we are led by a mental necessity to impute it to a Cause, and so to reach the conclusion that Infinite Intelligence is the only adequate explanation of creation. But is not thought as manifest in the operations of nature as in its construction? We cannot have failed to observe their regularity, their order, and their apparent submission to the supremacy of law. Not perhaps the unvarying action of a steam engine, or the undiversified movement of a watch; for nature is not without deviation from the strict line of its march, and its regularity is not precisely an endless, monotonous repetition. While all organizations correspond to certain types, no two of them are exactly alike; while each succeeding day and season resemble the preceding, they are not in every respect the same; and though the earth from the beginning must have been subject to the physical laws which reign at present throughout the realm of matter, yet under them what transformations have taken place in the past, and probably what equally radical changes will take place in the future. We have in the administration of the universe diversity in unity, sameness and variation, retrogression and progress; in a word, everything to assure us that, while it is governed by law, it is law in the hands of a free intelligent Being, who knows how to bring about modifications of old processes and even new effects without transgressing its limits or disregarding its authority.

The Christian poet asks

> "How should matter execute a law,
> Dull as it is, and satisfy a charge
> So vast in its demands, unless impelled
> To ceaseless action by some ceaseless Power,
> And under pressure of some conscious cause?"

And Reid has well answered: "The laws of nature are the rules according to which the effects are produced, but there must be a cause which operates according to these rules. The rules of navigation never navigated a ship; the rules of architecture never built a house." (*Essays, iii, 44.*) Sir John Herschel, in his address to the British association (1845), drew a similar distinction. He reminded his hearers that "a law may be a rule of action, but it is not an action;" . . . and that "we can never substitute the rule for the act." And Mr. Wallace, regarded as a Darwinist before Darwin, from the consideration of many peculiar phenomena arrives at the same view: "Natural selection is only a means by which the Creator worked." . . . "A superior intelligence has guided the development of man in a definite direction, and for a special purpose, just as man guides the development of many animal and vegetable forms;" . . . and "it, therefore, implies that the great laws which govern the material universe were insufficient for his production." (*Wallace, p. 360.*) I have no doubt if common sense would have sanctioned a different conclusion our scientist would not have been slow to embrace it; and the fact that he and others have been obliged to admit the impotence of mere law, strengthens my position that its reign, especially when taken in connection with the variety of operations that occur under it, of which man's development is a fair illustration, makes unanswerably for belief in God's imperial executive functions; or, in other words, for the reality and completeness of His all-wise providence.

Another line of thought, suggested by a remark of Mr. Wallace, can hardly fail to carry conviction to the mind of the most dubious. He alludes to the fact that man has guided the development of many animal and vegetable forms. This is indeed true, but probably very few pause to consider its significance. Horace Bushnel has said: "Not all the winds, and storms, and earthquakes, and seas, and seasons of the world have done so much as man to revolutionize the earth." He discriminates between humanity and nature. The latter he looks upon as having no power of improvement within itself, but as subject to the action of soul, "thoughtful soul," and as receiving from its touch new aspects and new features. This is the idea of the Psalmist: "Thou hast made him (man) to have dominion over the works of Thy hands. Thou hast put all things under his feet." That is, the creature is the viceroy of the Creator in the terrestrial world, and in miniature, and in some small degree figures to the understanding how it is possible for his Sovereign to interfere in the course of things for special ends, such as the answer to prayer, without disregarding their constitution or disarranging their laws. We know that man has improved vegetation, has added freshness and beauty to the grass on the lawn, has enriched the fruits on the boughs of the orchard, and multiplied the colors and increased the fragrance of plants. He has bettered soils, moderated the severity of the seasons, turned rivers, joined seas, and rendered tributary to his service those strange forces seen only when in operation, and only in useful and available operation through the influence of intelligence. But in all of these manifold endeavors and conquests has any law been trifled with? Has the uniformity of nature been imperiled, or its integrity been jeopardized? When man has flashed the electric spark, charged with his thought, through the heart of mountains like St. Gothard, and under the surging billows of oceans like the Atlantic; when he has drawn the lightning's shaft from out the stormy cloud, and dispersed its anger through the air, or buried its fury in the earth; when he has confronted the devastating lava flowing down the fissured sides of ancient volcanoes wreathed in sulphurous smoke, diverting its fiery tide into channels which his skill has dug, as was done by the Viceroy in 1794 to save Portici from Vesuvius; when he has grappled with the might of the pestilence, wrung from the bowels of the earth her hoarded treasures, or extracted from the plant the soothing anodyne, has he outraged nature, has he disregarded her mandates or deranged her courses? No; she is just as fair, as orderly, as regular as ever. Effects have been produced which, left to herself, never would have been produced, and which are to be traced to the influence of intelligence, which is able to subject nature, without subverting her, to its ends and aims.

And can man do so much and God do nothing? Is the mind of Deity less potent than the mind of humanity? If the creature can find a way to communicate with his fellows across wastes of water and deserts of sand; if he by some simple anæsthetic can alleviate pain; if he by a thousand ways can avert calamities, or bring deliverance to those who are in danger, cannot the Creator, by means undiscoverable to us, by agencies and instrumentalities which lie beyond the range of our vision and the tests of our chemistry, hear the helpless when he cries, and open up unexpected avenues of escape? If, in a word, man is himself providence to the lower world, what is to hinder God from being providence to the higher? Surely nature must be as pliable to His touch and as plastic to His thought as it is to the being made in His image! Is He Himself never to exercise that power which He has intrusted to His child? And if that child, in its folly, can sway it without occasioning anarchy in the universe, cannot the Father, in His wisdom, do the same, and even more wonderfully and abundantly, without incurring the suspicion of inconsistency, fickleness, or lawlessless? This we infer from man's relation to nature, and it is as though God had introduced it before our eyes, that we might thereby be assured that He Himself is thus allied to us, and that, in as real a sense, though perhaps more mysteriously, He guides and controls all things according to the counsel of His own will. And as long as the similitude is perpetuated we shall believe that the Invisible One can hear our prayer, can come near to us in trial, can succor us in temptation, can comfort us in sorrow,—can and will; yea, will and does.

The reasonableness and value of the system we are considering may also be tested in another manner. It claims that nature is all-sufficient for moral, reformatory, and religious inspiration and guidance, and that God will in no case interpose to supplement this first volume with a second. But is the first really sufficient? When it has been relied on exclusively has it brought forth the fruits of righteousness? Has it promoted human brotherhood, renovated society, and multiplied altars of devotion? If it has not,—if in these particulars it has failed,—then the assumption of moral potency put forth in its behalf is baseless, and the inference that God will not shed additional light on the path of His creatures is purely gratuitous. We have not to seek far or long to discover that on these points Naturalism romances, and that this spiritual power is more imaginary than real. Undoubtedly the works of the Almighty influence wonderfully the human mind. They exalt, overawe, delight and expand the soul; they sometimes hush to silence, or awaken praise, create ennobling images or kindle poetic fires; but it is exceedingly questionable whether they ever do more than render active what is already latent in the man. But be that as it may, though nature may quicken the muse of the poet and the genius of the artist, and although it may at times stimulate devotion, it is practically powerless to reclaim the wanderer from right, to purify the heart of the vicious, or to restore hope to the despairing. The sun that rolls resplendently in space, whose brightness is the shadow of its Creator's glory, subtle and penetrating though its light may be, invading chambers of densest ignorance and inundating dens of vice, never yet has flooded the benighted intellect with healing radiance or quickened into moral fruitfulness the barren conscience. The humblest roadside preacher in his poverty has made more converts to virtue's cause than has the king of day in all the affluence of his insufferable splendor. Ocean in its vastness,—a world of water rising in mists and ascending in waves to salute a world of fire,—awakens not with the thunder of its rolling billows the penitence of the prodigal; and neither does its majestic and appalling power rescue the dissolute and depraved. The sweet, saintly life of a Christian mother has done more to save the sea-boy from eternal ruin than all the mighty, headstrong waters that swirl in tempests or sleep in calms. They who dwell among the mountains, who inhabit solemn solitudes, who gaze on the untrodden snows of altitudes beyond their reach, and who are familiar with the antheming winds as they traverse the pine forests whose roots cling to inhospitable rocks, are no better, no purer, than they who tread the muddy streets and gaze continually on the blank, monotonous houses of great cities. The poorest mission in the most squalid quarter of a dense metropolis will do more real work in a year for virtue and piety than the beauty of Chamounix or the savage grandeur of the Engadine will accomplish in an age. Morally, the Sunday-school children of a country are worth more than all the stars that shine in heaven or all the flowers that gleam on earth, and in things pertaining to spiritual regeneration the Judsons and Cloughs are of more value than the Himalayas; and every Christian laborer consecrating the meagerest talents to the Master's cause is of more importance than wooded dell, savage glen, majestic cataracts and cloud-crowned mountains.

It will not be denied that men of genius, who have been most susceptible to nature's influences, have been among the most godless. Who is there among the poets that has surpassed Goethe in depth of sensibility, or who could more vividly portray every phase of beauty and sublimity, and yet his life was far from saintly? He trifled with female affections through many foul and filthy years; and philosopher as well as poet though he was, he restrained not the hot winds of passion from ravaging his soul like a Sirocco's blast. Your heroic Byron, whose majestic verse reveals a heart as impressionable to the loveliness of stream and bird and flower as Geneva's placid lake, which he describes so tenderly, is to the luster of the stars, was a wayward spirit, and continually gravitated downward toward the frail and sin-stained. Robert Burns, too, who could discern the grace and purity of the mountain daisy, and who in his poems could enshrine the stern grandeur of his Scotia's scenery, failed not to put in practice one part at least of his ribald song, "to riot all the night." Painters, who are supposed to drink in inspiration from the Creator's works, and musicians, who feel their tender harmonies, have afforded in their dissolute conduct sad proof that there is an infinite gulf between æsthetical sentiments and ethical principles. And even where nature has been idealized into a deity, or transformed into an altar, and where piety has sought to do it honor, as in the case of the Chaldeans and the Greeks, the worship has not been free from sensuality, or the worshipers from licentiousness. A fatality seems to attend every naturalistic system of religion. Whatever may be the explanation, whether it is to be accounted for by its utter inability to reach the conscience, or by some other and here nameless impotency, the fact still remains that it ever tends toward looseness in morals and weakness in virtue. Witness the truth of this statement in the lives of those who, in Europe and America, have fallen under the influence of such writers as D'Holbach, and who, thrusting from them the teachings of Christianity, have come to regard man as the universal priest, and the world as a veil hiding from mortal eyes an Infinite Unknown. While some among them are undoubtedly men of purity and rectitude, the rank and file have little share in these high qualities. They are too frequently careless of moral obligation, and too indifferent to right for them to be classed with the pure and noble. While they talk much of nature, they are rarely found in communion with her; while they extol her, they do not desire her company. Not in cathedral forests will you find them, nor treading the solitudes of the temple-hills, pouring out their souls in the presence of the Unseen, and seeking with trembling faith the Infinite One. No; their thoughts are not concerned with such sublime pursuits and such exalted themes. Generally they are found with agitators who would overthrow society, who would trample law and order under foot, and who would welcome bloody revolution in the interest of crazy schemes of progress. Not from the pure air or from the sublimities of creation do they expect to derive strength for manly duty and comfort for weary hearts, but rather from the wine-glass and the beer-barrel. They lounge in saloons, guzzle in concert-gardens, and beclouding their mental and moral faculties with the fumes of untold quantities of liquor, go forth to drunken slumber, or to moody discontent, and are ready for the heroic task, which they not infrequently perform, of shooting into crowds of helpless, unarmed people, or of brutally murdering defenseless women.

It is a significant fact, not unworthy of note in this connection, that the wrathful and stormful aspects of nature, which sometimes overwhelm the human heart with terror, rarely, if ever, produce permanent spiritual results. Occasionally thay may impel toward a better and more religious life, but they invariably stop short of the sacred goal. They need to be supplemented by something else, something that will deepen the impression received, and carry it forward to an abiding moral transformation. Thus it was the gospel of Christ, not the tempest that alarmed Martin Luther in the forest, that effected the conversion of the monk, and prepared him to be a reformer. The earthquakes in New England, which startled so many people into a desire for union with the church, as was abundantly proven, failed to implant in the soul the principles of godliness and righteousness. An intelligent Scotchman related to me on one occasion what he had experienced when alone near the summit of the Rocky Mountains. He said that he was so oppressed with the grandeur of the scene that he wept, and found himself doing what for years before he had neglected — praying. Here was a hopeful case surely. After all, then, we have an instance of conversion through the ministry of nature. Not so fast. This man when narrating the circumstance to me treated it as a pleasantry, as an incident to be merry over, and interblended coarse expressions and oaths in his speech. Evidently the transient emotion had produced no lasting improvement. I remember once the crew and passengers of a ship, during an Atlantic hurricane which threatened destruction, becoming violently penitent and devout, and when the danger abated rapidly returning to their folly and their irreligion. I have seen a city stricken with Asiatic cholera draped in sadness, mourning over its wickedness, supplicating God with self-reproaches and with vows of self-amendment, and when the frost announced the return of a healthier season I have seen the people of that city as proud, oppressive and corrupt as they were before. A company of sailors related to my church the dealings of God with them which led them to desire baptism. Their ship had been caught in the whirl and might of a typhoon in the China Sea. They gave themselves up for lost. Grim darkness covered them, the wind howled round them, the seas swept over them, and prospect of deliverance there was none. "They were at their wits' end," and then called they upon God, and as they lifted their despairing eyes they saw through a sudden rent in the pall of death above them a bright star shining. They hailed it as a happy omen. It comforted them in their distress, inspired them with courage, and helped them by its soothing influence to weather the terrific storm. If any set of men could have been made better by nature, surely these sailors ought to have been transformed into saints. But they were not; and never did they rise to the higher life until some young Christians boarded their vessel at the wharf and guided them to Jesus. In their case, as in many others, the humblest colporteur proved a mightier and more effective moral force than the sublimest typhoon. As I have reflected on such instances, the conviction has grown that the extirpation of sin and the renewal of the heart in goodness require something more than glare of lightning, stroke of thunder, or fury of devastating tempest.

Nay more, if we estimate this Ism by the ethical and religious principles which it necessitates, and which in its name are presented as the theological doctrines of the material universe, we shall be persuaded that morally it is worthless. The first article of its creed declares that there is no supreme God, at best only a supreme unknowable Unknown, with whom it is impossible for us to hold communion, and who of course can take no possible interest in His creatures. Its second resolves the doctrine of providence into fate, and attributes the mysterious influences that dispose us toward the right, or incline us toward the wrong, to physical sources. They are identified with atmospheric changes, the moon's phases, the stars' motions, the earth's perihelion, the sun's periodic convulsions, with variations of the temperature, the scenery that surrounds us, the food we eat, and the fluids we drink. These teachings are suggested as worthy substitutes for the doctrines of God and His government — how elevating! As a third kind of article, we are assured that the Bible idea of moral liberty is a myth, and that we should believe in its stead that of mechanical or chemical necessity, and regard thought, opinion, emotion, desire, volition, as the result of changes in the tissues of the brain, or as determined solely by the weight and size of that remarkable organ. How reasonable! Very! On these exalted notions, however, Shakspeare, in his *King Lear*, has ventured to express the opinion — an opinion so dark and depreciatory that it must be attributed to the benighted condition of the unhappy age in which he lived: "This is the excellent foppery of the world, that when we are sick in fortune (often the surfeit of our own behaviour) we make guilty of our disasters the sun, moon, and stars: as if we were villains on necessity; fools by heavenly compulsion; knaves, thieves, and treacherous by spherical predominance; drunkards, liars, and adulterers, by inforced obedience of planetary influence; and all that we are evil, by a divine thrusting on." Of course if the poet had only lived in these enlightened days he would have seen differently, and would have extolled what he has ridiculed. Unhappy poet! blind to the most luminous of doctrines!! Alas for dim-sighted genius!!! Then, we are informed, fourthly, that man sprang from one-celled amœbæ ancestors of the Laurentian period; that after developing into skullless vertebrates, such as the amphioxus, and proceeding upward through amphibian forms, he appeared among the mammals, and having for a season borne the simian image, emerged into the shape which now he wears. How ennobling! Fifthly, it is affirmed that sin is only disease, or better, a circuitous route to perfection; that moral qualities do not inhere in human conduct; and that it is wrong to suppose that there is anything sacred in marriage, or anything heinous in infanticide. How liberal! Then, by way of climax to this singular Confession of Faith, we are encouraged to believe that the universe is infinitely miserable, but that man inevitably shall attain to happiness in the rottenness and oblivion of the grave. How cheerful! Yea, how delightful, charming, and edifying! Perfectly splendid! These are the principal dogmas and precepts of the New Theology. What an advance on the antiquated doctrines of Paul, and the narrow statutes of Moses. How exalted! Immeasurably beyond the Tridentine Decrees, or those other wretched decrees of Dort, or the melancholy articles of the Westminster divines! Certainly, if they are not transcendently above every other confession, descendently they surpass them all.

But let us see whitherward these remarkable teachings tend. I must confess, if the only Almighty is blind force, if man is a creature of circumstances, if the only law to be obeyed is the irresistible, if the rule of marriage is affinity, and if the end of life is personal gratification, that I cannot see from whence we are to derive our inspiration to virtue and piety. Piety, purity — they wither under the blighting influence of such ideas. They crucify lofty feelings and noble aspirations, and can hardly fail to promote the growth of vice and crime. If man is but an advance on the brute he will probably be inclined to rend and tear as the brute; and if marriage is destitute of the sacred element it will gradually pass into what Herbert Spencer calls "Promiscuity," and Sir John Lubbock defines as "communal" wedlock; and if maternity is a curse which no divine law imposes, infanticide will inevitably become as common in America as in Tasmania; and if wrong-doing is but an unavoidable accident, idlers, drunkards, and the whole *canaille* of devildom will feel that no other course is open to them but to follow their disordered appetites and turbulent passions. Surely this frightful and alarming tendency of principles professedly derived from nature by philosophical Naturalism proves conclusively that as a theology it is utterly inadequate to conserve the moral and religious welfare of society.

And in view of this utter break-down of its most pretentious and serious claims, are we not warranted in rejecting the entire system? We feel assured that we are. How much more rational the belief that, beholding our helplessness, the loving Father should confer on us an adequate Revelation, that the Unseen should refuse to remain the Unknown, and the Inconceivable continue the Inaudible. "He who made the eye, shall He not see? He who made the ear, shall He not hear?" And He who made the tongue, shall He not speak? If he has found lips in the mute rocky ranges, breath in the whispering breezes, and a vocabulary in suns, stars, seas, solitary deserts, and crowded cities wherewith to proclaim His eternal power and Godhead, seeing our dire spiritual necessities, it is reasonable to conclude that to meet them He will not despise our poor, stammering language, nor disdain to use it as the vehicle of His mighty thought. It is incredible that the speech-maker should be Himself the Speechless, or that the author of multiplied vocables should be unable to articulate His holy will. Wise men of all ages, such as Socrates, have expressed the conviction that a direct Revelation is among the most probable and possible, as it is among the most indispensable, of heaven's gifts. If it is said that this reasoning will carry us to the unorthodox conclusion that His communications cannot be restricted to the contents of one volume, I can only answer, so be it. I shall even then be only repeating the sentiment ascribed to Zuinglius by the author of *Heathen Religions*, that "the Holy Ghost was not entirely excluded from the more worthy portion of the heathen world." But while I am prepared to accept the consequences of my argument, and to reverence the signs of God in any sacred book, there are adequate reasons for maintaining that the volume known among us as the Bible contains the completest, the most fully inspired, and the best authenticated revelation ever given to the race. All others are as stars in comparison with the sun, as the cold luster of the pole in comparison with the brilliancy of the tropics, as the opaque whiteness of the pearl in comparison with the transparent beauty of the diamond. Rousseau acknowledges its moral power; Goethe confesses its unparalleled spiritual excellence; Theodore Parker magnifies it as the purest fertilizing stream that ever flowed through our desert world; Huxley esteems it indispensable to sound ethical education, and Amberley extols it beyond any other work existing among men. From these considerations it is reasonable to conclude not only that Naturalism is untenable, but that He who "upholds all things by the word of His power," also has conferred on us a revelation to lighten our darkness, and that in its supreme and perfected form it is contained in the Holy Scriptures.

Their light is needed in navigating the vague uncertainty called life; apart from their luster the universe is a dubious phantasmagoria, and aside from their spiritual vivifying warmth the world is as those hyperborean regions where winter is added to winter, where ice is piled on ice, where the sea is imprisoned in eternal repose, and where the congealed mass is swept by shivering winds. Without the Bible the soul remains doubt-riven, and "at best but a troubled guest upon an earth of gloom." The study of nature imparts not moral strength, and the conquest of nature brings neither peace nor joy. Could we penetrate the innermost laboratory, hidden in the abysmal depths of the unseen, and witness chemical combinations resulting in suns, stars and constellations, and could we disengage ourselves from old ideas and satisfy ourselves that toiling time, laborious law and moiling matter are sufficient to account for the origin and order of all things that make up this marvelous universe, we would turn from the great discovery saddened and dispirited, like children who, seeking a father, have stumbled on his grave, and like children conscious of their orphan state we would cry out in sharp agony of despair, God! God! God! So unsubmergeable are our religious instincts, and so unquenchable our religious aspirations, that could we prove the unprovable assumptions of Naturalism we would revolt from the unwelcome demonstration, and in our wretchedness bewail the loss of confidence in that Book whose sublime revelations have filled our thoughts with Divine images and our lives with the consciousness of saintly fellowships.

It is related of the great Plotinus that he sought in many directions for truth; that he communed with sciences and philosophies, climbed the heights of speculation and fathomed the depths of reflection, but received from all no satisfactory reply. He approached the verge of skepticism, and was on the point of embracing the cheerless creed that there is nothing certain but uncertainty when he heard of a strange teacher in the city of Alexandria. A man had appeared among the cultured people of that city who, though of humble rank and a porter by trade, had undertaken to lecture on philosophy, and to him Plontinus came. The young skeptic, to whom nature had been tongueless, sat at the feet of the earnest thinker, Ammonius the carrier, and from his lips received the message that opened to his mind the realities of truth. Plotinus represents many young men to whom these words will come. They have read themselves into a chaos of doubt; and they are half persuaded that they have been abandoned by their Creator to the mocking Titans of error. Why seek further? Hear this, ye young: a greater teacher than Ammonius is here. He once lived among men in lowly form, and He yet lives in the immortal revelations of this Sacred Book. Like the inquiring Alexandrian, humble your intellect and learn of Jesus, who spake as never man spake; sit at His feet; permit the supernatural to supplement and complete the natural, and then you shall go forth enriched with truth,—knowing God, knowing self, knowing, also, how God and self touch each other and come into sacred commerce,—and then shall you be able to brighten the pathway of others with the reflection of that light which fills your soul with peace and joy.

> "God's voice, not Nature's,—night and noon
> He sits upon the great white throne
> And listens for the creatures' praise.
> What babble we of days and days?
> The Dayspring He, whose days go on."

PESSIMISM.

"Now no chastening for the present seemeth to be joyous, but grievous; nevertheless, afterward it yieldeth the peaceable fruit of righteousness unto them which are exercised thereby."
Hebrews xii, 11.

"Because the few with signal virtue crowned,
　　The heights and pinnacles of human mind,
Sadder and wearier than the rest are found,—
　　Wish not thy soul less wise or less refined.
True, that the clear delights that every day
　　Cheer and distract the pilgrim are not theirs;
True, that though free from Passion's lawless sway,
　　A loftier being brings severer cares;
Yet have they special pleasures,— even mirth,—
By those undreamed of who have only trod
Life's valley smooth; and if the rolling earth
To their nice ear have many a painful tone,
They know man does not live by joy alone,
But by the presence of the power of God."
Lord Houghton.

PAIN and anguish fill a large place in human life. Their harsh voices cannot be silenced, neither can the rattle of elegant carriages, nor rush and din of commerce, nor the clamor of ambitious, eloquent tongues, drown the solemn pathos of their discourse. Their baleful presence stealthily glides everywhere, and everywhere their shadow falls. They walk unopposed through the ranks of watchful guards, and deliver to kings their sad messages, and they pass unhindered into humble, peaceful homes, and speak the awful word that withers their beauty and blights their peace. No life can build them out, no foot can speed fast enough to elude them, no hand can strike vigorously enough to repel them, and no subtle skill can evade them, nor any bribe of affluence corrupt them. They are everywhere, they have all times; yea, they have all means at their disposal, for they can impart a scorpion's sting to our delights and poison-venom to our hopes. The house we build to shield us from the storm may but furnish fuel for the fire that shall consume our prosperity and rob us of our dear ones; the adornments which afford us harmless pleasure may but serve to supply a motive to the assassin's knife; the children we have reared with so much fondness, and on whose multiplying years we have looked with fond anticipation, may only prove a perennial affliction to our sanguine souls, and the high emprise, rich in promises, may be but the herald of death and desolation. So closely interwoven is suffering with all our movements, so strangely interblended with our felicity, so inseparable, apparently, from our gladdest and serenest hours, that every earnest soul has felt the truth of what Shelley wrote:

> "We look before and after,
> And pine for what is not,
> E'en our sincerest laughter
> With some pain is fraught,
> Our sweetest songs are those which tell of saddest thought."

It ought not, therefore, to occasion us much surprise if many minds take on a despairing mood, and if many tongues adopt the language of despondency. So difficult is it for humanity at times to discern the silver lining in the cloud that overshadows, so hard is it to realize, under certain conditions, that the thick pillar which precedes us, as it did the Jews, is guiding to Canaan's promised land, that nothing is seen but the somber shadows of the savage wilderness through which our pathway lies. And when the shekinah hides the Christ of comfort from our longing eyes, it is hard, if not impossible, for us to recognize its brightness, or to perceive in it the symbol of Jehovah's presence.

Sometimes an hour's grief makes us quite forget a life of gladness. We take our happiness unconcernedly, but we rage and storm against our miseries. The shortest night eclipses the radiance of the longest day, and one hour of storm is all-sufficient to drown the recollections of long, sweet years of calm. Ah me! that it should be so; that we should so chafe and fret, droop and sink when adversities sweep over us as to unhinge our reason and evoke our bitterest ingratitude. That they work in many souls such dire results witness the exaggerative views concerning earthly miseries which prevail in various quarters, leading to dreary pessimisms and snarling cynicisms, and which would crown man's life with the morose and sullen cypress.

Pascal has said, with pathetic eloquence: "Man is so great that his grandeur appears from the knowledge of his own misery. A tree knows not that it is wretched. True, it is sad to know that we are miserable, but it is also a mark of greatness to be aware of this misery. Thus all the wretchedness of man proves his nobleness. It is the unhappiness of a great lord, the misery of a dethroned king." And yet, unless he understands the cause and the end of his dethronement, it were better for him to be unconscious of his loss. That it is given him to realize the fact and the depth of his afflictions surely indicates that he is capable of ascertaining their meaning and of falling in with their design. If he is great enough to perceive their reality, it is only reasonable to believe that he is also great enough to so far comprehend their significance as to deal with them intelligently. Of this he has himself been profoundly persuaded; and hence, during all the centuries man has been looking through his tears on the problem of suffering, and with aching heart and weary brain he has been painfully seeking its solution. And in this attitude his moral grandeur comes into a clearer light than it does when he is simply presented as gazing in mute, unquestioning melancholy on that which he shrinks from and of which he cannot possibly be oblivious.

The theory of Pessimism, snarled, croaked and moaned by a few elegiac, querimonious philosophers in response to the saddened "Wherefore?" of humanity, that misery is the natural, unavoidable and irremediable condition of the race, has never succeeded in satisfying the intellect or in pacifying the heart. It has failed to reconcile men to their trials as it has to qualify them to endure their severity. As a system it is a slander on the goodness of Deity, accusing Him of malignancy or charging Him with impotency, and as an explanation it is simply an exaggeration of the mystery which it undertakes to unfold. To say, as it does, that the universe is "a gigantic blunder," "an escapade of the Absolute," or "immeasurable *lusus naturæ*," and that happiness is only a fitful gleam of light to render the prevailing gloom more intense and unendurable, or to intimate that the end of life is to go down into nothingness, is to asperse the character of God and to leave the question that perplexes untouched and unanswered. The theory is irrational in its terms and paralyzing in its influence. It implies a Headless universe or a heartless Ruler; a reign of cruelty without motive and without advantage, and a creature helpless to resist and powerless to overcome the fiendish tyranny beneath which a merciless fate has placed him.

Pessimism begins with the repudiation of the optimistic system advocated by Leibnitz in his *Essai de Théodicée*. It denies that the Creator had from a variety of possible worlds chosen to make this one as the best, but that He had made the worst, and that actually it is worse than none at all. Nevertheless, according to Von

Hartmann, though the existing world is worse than none at all, still Leibnitz was correct in asserting that it is the best possible, for every possible world is necessarily a bad one. Yea, he argues that it would have been better if the world could have been worse than it is, for if it had been only slightly more wretched humanity before this would have taken its fate in its own hands, and by a supreme act of annihilation would have put an end to the tragedy. It is assumed that all existence is an evil, and that pleasure is negative while pain is absolutely positive. Schopenhauer looks on what he calls "will" as the cause of all things and the source of universal misery. "Will" in his doctrine stands both for creation and Creatorship, only it is not to be identified with personal volition, but with an abstract, mysterious Infinity composed of numberless and limitless wills. He further declares that it is the nature of "will" to be restless, dissatisfied and corroding, that its greed is insatiable, and that, as a consequence, suffering is unavoidable and inextinguishable. As long as will continues to will, the weary round of disappointments must follow, for no conceivable object can yield more than momentary enjoyment, and therefore, until the will is made to cease willing, black-browed misery must reign. But the cessation of will means the cessation of existence, and only in such an amiable climax can Schopenhauer discern the true solution of the problem of evil. Von Hartmann substitutes for Schopenhauer's metaphysical fiction what he calls "The Unconscious," which is made up of infinite will and omniscience, and which was harmless until it began to create; but from the unfortunate hour when it first called matter into being the deplorable history of pain began. The fearful blunder of creation originated with an unexplainable schism in the Unconscious; Will broke away from its primitive harmony with unconscious Reason, and this wretched universe was the result. The Unconscious attained to the Conscious in man, and is now busy seeking by every means to return to its primal unconscious blessedness. This desired end, it is believed, will be consummated through the discovery of the utter emptiness and hollow illusiveness of life, which will decide men to cease caring for themselves and determine them no more to propagate their species, and which very likely will be carried into effect by a unanimous and simultaneous act of self-destruction. Thus the mischievous misadventure of the Creative Power will be effaced and canceled in the nothingness of annihilation. But even this poor hope is questioned by Herr Bahnsen, a Pessimist more radical and thorough-going than Von Hartmann, who insists that as the human race by annihilating itself could hardly annihilate the power which originated all things, the world and existence must continue irrational and miserable throughout eternity. Delightful logic!

If, as is implied throughout these speculations, the universe is one vast tragic theater, the object of which is no-happiness to any one, conducted by a Superhuman Energy resembling a designing mind in everything but consciousness, it follows that life is an unqualified curse. And this inference is elaborated with a dreary enthusiasm, and a pertinacious devotion to details, which is edifying if not convincing. "Human life," says Schopenhauer, "oscillates between pain and ennui"; and having expressed the thought that these states are its ultimate elements, he adds, "driven by the fear of ennui, men and women rush into society, thinking to gain a fleeting pleasure by escaping from themselves. But in vain; their inseparable foe renews his torments only too surely." In the same direction he also writes: "The history of every life is a history of suffering, for the course of life is generally but a series of greater or less misfortunes."—"The real matter of the world-famed monologue in Hamlet may be thus summed up: Our condition is so wretched that utter annihilation would be decidedly preferable." "If, finally, all the terrible pains and sorrows to which his life is ever exposed could be brought before the eyes of each, he would be seized with horror; and if the most obstinate of optimists were led through the hospitals, lazarettos, and surgical operation rooms; through the prisons, torture-chambers, and slaveholds; over the fields of battle and places of execution; if then, those dark abodes of misery, where it creeps out of the view of cold curiosity, were opened to him; and finally, a sight were afforded him of the starvation of some Ugolino — he would surely at last perceive what kind of *meilleur des mondes possible* this is." And to these gloomy outlines he adds a few dark shadows, which impart a lurid completeness to the picture: "The present is forever becoming the past; the future is quite uncertain, and ever short. Thus is man's life a constant lapse of the present into the dead past, a constant death." —"Further, it is plain that our bodily life is but a continually checked process of dying, an ever postponed death." "At length death must conquer; for by the very fact of birth we are made over to him, and he is only playing awhile with his prey before swallowing it." It is in vain that we suggest to Schopenhauer and Von Hartmann that possibly when the ignorance and impiety of the present are overcome, the future may be prolific in happiness; for they meet all such encouraging hopes with the forlorn assertion "that misery grows with consciousness." Hence they remind us that "the more intelligent the man is the more completely does he attain the full quantum of misery; he in whom genius lives suffers most of all"; and more than this, adds Hartmann, "with all our boasted progress the evils of existence are just as great and just as hopeless as they were centuries ago." Thus all expectation of improvement in the condition of humanity is utterly baseless; and we are shut up either to asceticism for the extinction of the will, which is the root of all our trouble, as commended by Schopenhauer in theory, though unapplied by him in practice; or to utter worldliness, that the illusions of life may be speedily demonstrated, a course seriously advocated by Von Hartmann, and by him consistently pursued.

While this morbid creed is remarkable, the favor with which it is being received is even more so. Dühring claims that it is "the most sober philosophy of the century"; and Dr. McCosh, in the *Princeton Review*, calls attention to the fact that "Of late years German students have been wandering after Schopenhauer and Hartmann; and American and British youths, seeing the crowd, have joined them, and been gazing with them." But beyond the student classes the popularity of Pessimism in some of its forms is startling. Many persons in every community who do not subscribe to all of its positions unreservedly, yet sympathize with its estimate of life and its views of death. Thousands who have never heard the name of the system, and to whom it is meaningless, have already accepted its dreariest expectations and its darkest consolations. Grief, trial, disappointment, raises the question in minds inaccessible to Von Hartmann's speculations as to whether, after all, life can be called a blessing. The ambiguity of the term "happiness," as it is commonly used, and the inadequacy of multiplied pleasures, however pure and refined the pleasures may be, to answer to any definition, have prepared the way for the blank denial which Pessimists pronounce. It is welcomed as on the whole more rational than any other answer, if not as gratifying. Moreover, the dissolute orders of society hail it with delight. In Paris it is currently reported that books upon this subject are being widely read by the demireps and scoundrels, who find in them some solacement for the virtue and integrity they have bartered for fleshly joys. Such works, therefore, have a large audience, and I am inclined to the opinion that it will increase before it diminishes. Not improbably literary men will be tempted by the avidity with which the more sentimental aspects of this Ism are received by the people, to multiply literature on the subject, and thus to disseminate even more widely than at present these doleful, lugubrious, sunless, and tenebrious views. Most likely the night will thicken before the daybreak comes, and society return to a kind of philosophic chaos before God shall once more say, "Let there be light." Such being the melancholy outlook, it is surely the duty of earnest inquirers to do all in their power to mitigate, if they cannot arrest, the impending gloom; and this can only be done by challenging the Pessimistic theory, and suggesting in its stead a more rational and satisfactory explanation of human suffering.

That the doctrine of the Unconscious is a metaphysical figment, which hardly deserves the attention of serious criticism, no one who is seeking clear views and not mere entertainment from dialectical gymnastics will for a moment question. It is difficult to believe that any person in sober earnestness can expect such a tissue of absurd speculations as Von Hartmann has put forth in the name of philosophy to commend themselves to common sense. When that Infinite Indefiniteness which is substituted for the Almighty is represented as divided, the Will breaking away from the unconscious Reason, and the unconscious Reason then seeking to overtake and annihilate the pernicious Will, into what incoherencies and contradictions of thought are we thrown! How can the Will, apart from conscious intelligence, create, and how can intelligence, deprived of will, determine? To will anything implies a conscious conception of the thing to be willed, and will can no more will without intelligence than intelligence can will without will. But according to Von Hartmann we are to credit that the universe sprang from the independent activity of a will without plan and without knowledge, and that now an intelligence, which was once unconscious, is seeking to counteract the maleficent blundering of this will, although by the terms of the preceding proposition not a vestige of volitional energy is left to it wherewith to execute its benevolent intentions. Such an astounding cosmogony destroys itself. Its terms are irreconcilable with each other, and contrary to the fundamental principles of thought. Assuredly neither this involved hypothesis nor that of Schopenhauer possesses any advantages over the Theism of Scripture; neither is as intelligible nor as rational, and neither is as satisfactory to the heart nor as useful to the life. We may, therefore, dismiss the cloudy metaphysics of Pessimism as fanciful and profitless, and direct our attention to its more obvious teachings and tendencies. That these are equally unworthy of confidence may be inferred from the peculiar circumstances which have always attended the origin and progress of the theory. Never, as far as I can ascertain from its history, has it appeared among a people in the more youthful and natural stages of national development. It has only risen, like a grim shadow or unearthly monster, in after years, when civilization has introduced artificial methods of estimating things, or general corruption has seriously impaired the tone of buoyancy and hope. When religion has been asphyxied by impurities, when manliness has been atrophied by defective intellectual nourishment, and tenderest affections have been gangrened by lascivious·indulgence and moral filthiness, then has this hideous Philosophical Nightmare disturbed the repose of much afflicted peoples. Among the Hindus it followed on the decline of the healthier Vedic-Faith, and was simply the expression of the wretched degradation into which entire tribes were falling. Brahmanism was not the first religion of the East. The first, if we may judge from the remnants of its literature which have descended to us, was jocund, elastic, taking bright views of life and destiny, and wholly free from Pessimistic taints. But wars, ambitions, the growth of caste, and the multiplication of other evils, undermined its strength, and in its place arose the gigantic and gloomy worship which for centuries oppressed India. Even this system was not without some advantages, but they quickly disappeared, and in a time of densest darkness the reformation known as Buddhism was inaugurated. This took its color from the age in which it originated, and while it corrected some abuses and protested against more, it taught that evil is the very essence of existence, that even in the lives of the greatest gods misery is feared, and that all worlds have been made in vain and are doomed to wretchedness. Among the Greeks and Romans this wormwood-faith never prevailed; and even Diogenes went not as far in cynicism as Gautama. These nations were not sufficiently morbid for it to take root in their intellectual soil. Too cheerful, too active, too discerning for such an insalubrious creed to suggest itself to them, it was reserved for the grave-minded, grim-brooding and tobacco-beclouded Germans to revive and naturalize it among Europeans. And this was not effected in recent prosperous, united times; but when disastrous wars, social depressions and commercial stagnations had prostrated the nation, had darkened its mind, and crushed its heart, Schopenhauer wrote of the great earth-sorrow. If it shall be thought singular that it should retain its vitality in these days of "unexampled prosperity," let it not be forgotten that we have drifted into materialism and secularism, and that in a different way, but just as truly, our century is as diseased as the last, and that to the unwholesome condition of both must we ascribe the beginning and the advancement of Pessimistic philosophy. Now, from these facts its seems legitimate to conclude that there must be something abnormal in a theory which is thus identified with abnormal conditions of society. As we have seen, it flourishes only in a sickly, pestilential social atmosphere, and it is no more than reasonable to suspect that it simply exhales the poison of its surroundings, and is, therefore, a death-bearing tree, under whose shadow no mind should be tempted to seek repose.

It should also be remembered that it is natural for man, whatever he may profess, to act on the belief that life is not only desirable, but is really worth taking no small degree of trouble to enjoy. This was evidently the rule of Schopenhauer's conduct, however it may have run contrary to his creed. He was no ascetic, and some of his most ardent admirers approximate more closely to his appreciation of the good things to be found in this world than to his intellectual ability. Further, it should not be overlooked that many who charge themselves with the task of exposing the hollowness of existing institutions, and who point out most distinctly the unutterable woes of the race, are not Pessimists, and have no sympathy with their lugubrious estimates, but, like Rousseau and Byron, believe in the attainability of happiness, and, like Carlyle and Heine, acknowledge a supreme, satisfying Something somewhere. They who are most extreme in their denunciation of shams are most fully persuaded of an ultimate outcome in goodness and blessedness. Why, then, accept the ungladdening theory of life, painfully elaborated by a few moaning philosophers as an impartial statement, and why should we attach so much importance to their tearful array of horrors, when, on the whole, human consciousness testifies to a clear excess of enjoyment over suffering?

An apostle speaks of our afflictions as "light" in comparison with the "exceeding weight of glory" that awaits us. But, though the sufferings of the present are not worthy to be compared with the blessedness in reserve for us, we are not to conclude that here and now the contrast is not as marked. Inspiration assures us that "God's mercies are new every morning and fresh every evening," and David reminds his soul, in language we may all adopt, that He redeems its life from destruction, crowns it with loving-kindness, and satisfies it with good things, so that its youth is renewed like the eagle's. According to the entire tenor of Holy Writ, the pleasures of existence far outweigh its miseries. The consciousness of being, the sense of personal freedom, and the realization of individual power over nature, all yield the most enduring satisfaction. Placed in a world where we have dominion over the works of God's hands, we find them serving us and constantly ministering to our enjoyment. The sun not only lights our way by day, but suffuses our thoughts with images of splendor. The stars not only shed their radiance on our darkness, but penetrate our minds with subduing and sacred influences.

Every beautiful object in the universe, be it above, around or within us, has "a perpetual joy-producing power." The unobtrusive majesty of the heavens, the stern grandeur of the hills, the mobile loveliness, culminating at times into sublimity, of the ocean, the modest gorgeousness of the flowers, whose varied hues remind us of the words of Ruskin: "Of all God's gifts to the sight of man, color is the holiest, the most divine, the most solemn;" the somber trees, glittering rainbows, golden sunsets, and the endless forms that diversify and glorify the world, appeal to our deepest emotions, and create the impression that Spirit is manifested in all, and is seeking to charm us from our griefs, and exalt us above our sorrows;

"There is a pleasure in the pathless woods,
There is a rapture on the lonely shore,
There is society where none intrudes
By the deep sea, and music in its roar."

Compared with these sources of enjoyment, how meager, trivial and contemptible our crosses, burdens and disappointments appear. These we have always and ever accessible, the others occasionally and temporarily. But am I reminded that a speck in the eye will obliterate the beauty of a universe, and a defect in the ear will drown its harmony, and a grief-drop in the heart submerge the ocean of consolation that gleams around it calmly? True; but we should not overlook the fact that the misery is incomparably less in magnitude than these measureless and fathomless springs of delight, and that the latter offers more than a compensation for the former.

But in addition to the blessedness which God has committed to nature for the comfort of His creatures, we should realize that He has enriched our life by the gift of His Son our Lord. Christ is called the "Consolation of Israel," and consolation He is to all mankind. I fear we do not consider the magnitude of this gift as we should, and I am very sure that no language can do it justice. There is not only that which is amazing in this descent of God from Himself, but there is in it something assuring and comforting as well. The Incarnation attests the interest of the Almighty in the race, indicates that its loathsomeness cannot repel His love, or its waywardness alienate His heart. It was the apprehension of this fact that produced so mighty an impression on the ancient world. As Macaulay says, "It was before the Deity embodied in a human form, walking among men, partaking of their infirmities, leaning on their bosoms, weeping over their graves, slumbering in the manger, bleeding on the cross, that the prejudices of the synagogue, and the doubts of the academy, and the pride of the portico, and the fasces of the lictor, and the swords of thirty legions, were humbled in the dust." The people of all classes and conditions realized that however fallen and degraded they were, God had not abandoned them, was not ashamed to wear their likeness, or unwilling to stoop to their level, that they might be lifted up nearer to His. This conviction brought with it a sense of personal elevation, and a desire, more or less pronounced, to do something worthy this compassionate condescension. Thus ought it always to affect us. But whether it does or not, it yet remains true that the Incarnation articulates many precious assurances. It removes all suspicion of a malignant purpose in creation, or of an evil will potent to create, and of an unconscious reason impotent to restrain. When feeling friendless and forsaken, it assures us that God is mindful. When sadly oppressed with a sense of personal unworthiness, it reminds us of the value the Almighty attaches to humanity; when disheartened by the repeated losses of fortune and friends, it reveals inexhaustible affluence in the Supreme; and when death invades, and things of earth are fading from the sight, and its charms have perished from desire, the Incarnation proclaims anew the amazing union of God with man, pledging alike his immortality and felicity.

These sources of pleasure would hardly be available were it not for another,—one that lies within the reach of all and which imparts to everything a charm, even glorifying the storm-cloud with the rainbow's brilliant hues. You have frequently heard the preacher in rugged phrase urge the people listening to his words to "repent and be converted." Possibly you have been disposed to sneer at his earnest exhortation, and to hold in derision the duty he enjoined. And yet the change expressed by the now familiar term "conversion" is of all others the most precious for this life, whatever may be its relation to the life hereafter. When the Scriptures describe it they employ the most radical figures of speech to convey an adequate idea of its grandeur. They call it a "new birth," a "resurrection from the dead," and they liken it to the opening of blind eyes, and to freedom from a prison-house. These words imply a total transformation of the man. His restored sight enables him to see evil in its true light, and he shrinks from it and saves himself from many sorrows; his soul, emancipated from the grave of dull materialism, rises to the consciousness of a spiritual universe and clearly discerns that "life is more than meat and the body than raiment," and being freed from bondage to tyrant passion, he gladly accepts the yoke of Christ and rests securely in His grace. It is this change that enables us to appreciate and appropriate the beauties and joys that nature, and religion, too, lavish so abundantly upon us. Thomas Carlyle, albeit not a Christian after the straitest sort, and somewhat unorthodox in his speech and thought, yet in his *Reminiscences* can recall a day, forever notable in his calendar, when he was transformed from his old self into something higher. In referring to this period, he writes: "This year I found that I had conquered all my skepticisms, agonizing doubtings, fearful wrestling with the foul and vile and soul-murdering mud-gods of my epoch; had escaped as from a worse than Tartarus, with all its Phlegethons and Stygian quagmires, and was emerging free in spirit into the eternal blue of ether, where, blessed be heaven, I have for the spiritual part ever since lived. . . . What my pious joy and gratitude then was let the pious soul figure. In a fine and veritable sense, I, poor, obscure, without outlook, almost without worldly hope, had become independent of the world. What was death itself, from the world, to what I had come through? I understood well what the old Christian people meant by 'conversion,' by God's infinite mercy to them." He adds: "For a number of years I had ... a constant inward happiness that was quite royal and supreme, in which all temporal aid was transient and insignificant, and which essentially remains with me still, though far oftener eclipsed and lying deeper down than then." In almost identical terms have all the saints,— the Pauls, the Augustines, the Bunyans, the Newtons,— recorded the marvelous dealings of God with them; and similar the experience of every man who yearns for knowledge of a higher world than this poor, noisy, muddy one of sight and sense. Think not, then, lightly of this gracious change, but, inspired by the words of the gruff-grim cynic, seek that spirit which will make God's beneficence clear and dear to you forever. Not alone, however, should the Divine provisions for our happiness by their magnitude be measured; they should as well be estimated by their multiplicity. They are manifold, reaching in particular to every relation and condition of life; so numerous are they that they cannot be counted up in order or followed in their bearings. As the universe in vastness, they are also like the universe in endless variety and completeness. Not a sorrow, not a burden, not a temptation, not a bereavement, not a disappointment, not a care, not a groan or tear, but has its antidote in God's rich and inexhaustible resources, which are available for human comfort. You cannot imagine a state of evil, of grief however deep, of wretchedness however profound, but the Almighty has anticipated. He has given us exceeding great and precious promises, and with the promises the more precious realities, and by these we may judge how completely he has provided against the ills from which we suffer, though we never may be able to explore their deep and loving wealth of meaning.

But while these manifold sources of happiness may be

admitted, there yet confronts us the huge problem, not without difficulties, perhaps not wholly without inexplicalities, of human suffering. What can be said about it? What can be offered by way of solution? Evidently nothing on the part of Pessimism, for the repeated picturings of its intensity, in which it indulges, do not possess the first element of elucidation. The Bible may not be able to remove all mystery, but its account of the matter is certainly less demonstrably false and less palpably fabulous.

According to its teachings God is love; and all the processes of severity in His government are in harmony with this spirit. He is seeking the well-being of his creatures, and as they are moral agents, and as they are in sin, suffering becomes an essential condition of their progress. Unquestionably it is represented by the Sacred Book as retributive, but it is also described as being disciplinary and corrective. While it is in some sense the result of transgression, and while in some cases it simply serves to mark the heinousness of iniquity, and to brand it with its true character in this world and in the world to come, it is broadly designed, in this life at least, to restrain, to rebuke, to rectify, and to reclaim. It is a measure of reform, a means of development, a refining and elevating force in the education of man. This is especially the view of Paul in the chapter from which the text has been chosen. He compares the dealings of God with us to those of an earthly father with his children. Chastening he alludes to as a sign of sonship; and argues that it is inflicted not for the pleasure of the parent but for the profit of the child. He declares that it is a proof of love in Him who orders it, should be recognized as such by him who receives it, and should be endured and valued on account of "the peaceable fruit of righteousness" which it is fitted to produce.

This explanation is, in my opinion, worthy the most

serious consideration of every tried and tired searcher for truth, bringing to the mind content and to the soul comfort.

It is deserving of note that this view does not seek to lessen or to hide the grievousness of affliction. Truly is it said by the apostle in the text, that "no chastening for the present seemeth to be joyous." He does not misrepresent its real character. It is in itself an evil, whatever good may flow from it; it is a curse, although it may yield a blessing. Man cannot bring himself to desire it, and can hardly refrain from shrinking at its approach. It were unnatural for him to covet adversity, disease, and disaster; or to welcome among his household treasures the destroyer death. Who is there that does not instinctively try to avert calamity and to evade correction? The child does not anxiously seek the rod, though healing may result from its stripes; and neither do we pine for chastisement, though assured that it is administered for our profit. Poets, philosophers, painters have rightly interpreted this feeling when in their works they have sought to express the human fear of suffering. The dread of it, the aversion to it which is common to us all, they reproduce in their representations of its character. We see in their conceptions, whether wrought out by pen or chisel, that which gives pain, not pleasure, or at the most only painful pleasure, which repels while it fascinates. The lamentations of antiquity over the misery of life do not enliven our spirits or gladden our heart. When Homer plaintively declares that no creatures are more miserable than men; when Pindar represents them as a shadowy dream, or Sophocles compares them to a vapor's shade; or when Pliny says that many have thought it the best lot never to have been born, we are not thrilled with delight at our condition, nor find ourselves inclined to rejoice. Rather, if we are endowed with a contemplative mind, we are filled with melancholy and overcome by sadness. However heroic Prometheus may awaken in us a sense of awe and admiration, we have no yearnings for his rock and vulture; and however the Laocoon may impress us with its sublimity, we would not willingly take the place of the tall, massive, central figure, around which is twined the serpent's slimy folds, and whose face reveals the agony of despair. Niobe in tears awakens no desire for partnership in her grief; and whatever other forms ancient or modern art has given to suffering, they elicit from us no longing to realize them in our own experience. Upon them all we read the verification of the apostolic statement: "Now no chastening for the present seemeth to be joyous, but grievous."

That this is so should not occasion us anxiety or distress. I suppose that there are those among my readers who regard their lack of avidity to receive afflictions as a sign of unpardonable weakness, or of absolute degeneracy. Because Paul once said that he gloried in tribulations, they may have formed the impression that they, too, should contemplate them with delight. But if they will only recall the entire passage where this expression occurs, they will perceive that it was uttered in view of the patience and the hope which sufferings are calculated to produce, and not because of anything pleasurable in the sufferings themselves. He gloried in the one for the sake of the other; but he was far from contradicting in his letter to the Romans the sentiment of our text, which he addressed to the Hebrews. That we feel the sharpness of God's rod, and cry out under the weight of His hand, are not evidences of inbred corruption, but of our human sensibility, without which the design of chastisement would fail. God means us to be pained when He sends painful afflictions; He means us to weep when He touches the springs of sorrow, and he means us to moan when the plowshare goes through our heart. If we did not feel the miseries we experience, if we would just as soon be freighted with them as with joys, if our natures were indifferent to either; that is, if we were impervious to impressions, then the possibility of their influencing us for good would cease. This sensitiveness, which morbid souls interpret as something inconsistent with piety, is the condition on which the beneficent action of chastisement depends, just as ductability and pliability are required in the material on which the plastic hand would exercise its skill. We do not plow adamant. "The hard rock that breaks the share will not nourish the seed, but the soft earth that yields to the sharp iron will bear the harvest;" and the brittle stone that shivers beneath the sculptor's chisel grows never into form of beauty, while the white marble, which resists and yet succumbs, gracefully receives the fairest ideal that ever haunted poet's soul.

Let us not, then, mourn because we shrink from evil; for that shrinking proves that the evil will not be in vain when it comes. Neither let us despond if, while the storms rage and beat upon us, we fail to discern their justice and beneficence. When driven by their fury it is natural that we should be blinded, confused, and startled; and it is equally natural that we should be incapable of candid thought and reasonable judgment. Yet I have known persons, when the whirlwind had smitten a fellow-being to the ground and left him mourning in dire distress, wonder why he was not comforted by their pious platitudes and sustained by their wearisome conventionalisms. Yea, they have even affected solicitude for the spiritual condition of him who, when crushed, maddened, and lacerated, could not reply in set phrases to their jargon about resignation and submission. Believe me, it is no time for words when the wounds are fresh and bleeding; no time for homilies when the lightning's shaft has smitten and the man lies stunned and stricken. Then let the comforter be silent; let him sustain by his presence, not by his preaching; by his sympathetic silence, not by his speech. "Afterward," when the storm is spent, he may venture to open his mouth; "afterward," when the morn has dawned, he may seek "to justify the ways of God to man;" for "afterward" the sufferer will be prepared to hear, and "afterward" the sufferer himself may be able to extract sweetness from bitterness, music from mourning, songs from sorrow, and "the peaceable fruit of righteousness" from the root of wretchedness and woe.

The ultimate profitableness of chastisement is the next aspect of the subject suggested by the text. Paul assures us that it is not necessarily barren of results, but that it "yieldeth";—"tribulation worketh patience; and patience, experience; and experience, hope;" and "these light afflictions which endure but for a moment shall work in us a far more exceeding and eternal weight of glory." Not in vain need our sufferings be; not in vain need our tears be shed; but from them we may reap immortal blessedness and imperishable fruit.

It is a fact that strikingly points in the direction of this conclusion, that the most powerful and progressive nations are those which have been called to pass through the severest trials and the most painful convulsions. The life of Greece grew and became strong by these means; the Romans advanced to their commanding position along the highway of war and revolution, while England has secured and preserved her greatness at the cost of ease and quiet. She has lived in a hurricane for a thousand years; she has been devastated by civil wars; she has been prostrated by commercial panics, and has rarely enjoyed a season of absolute repose. The same is true of America, only in a less degree. The miseries incidental to the revolution seemed to develop sterling virtues; the war for the Union elevated the tone of our national character; and the recent prostration of our business interests, that entailed untold sufferings on the people, failed not to yield us enduring profit. And what is thus manifest in the history of nations is equally apparent in that of individuals. The men whom we count great were not unacquainted with privation, grief, and agony. They grew in volcanic soil; they were fostered by the fœhn, and were nourished by the desert. Genius has ever had to be crucified that it might rise from the dead on the third day; virtue has ever had to wear the crown of thorns for it to inherit the diadem of praise. The mystery of grace has been constantly reëxhibited in the lives of poets, artists, and reformers. Rich in ideas, they have had to become poor in fortune that we, through their poverty, might be made rich. I do not now recall any great production or any sublime endeavor that was not preceded by suffering of some kind. Pascal sorrowed deeply before he thought sweetly; and he thought painfully before he wrote sympathetically. Milton had tasted of misfortune's cup and had braved the storms of four and fifty years before he could sing of Paradise and of man's woeful fall. Poor Jean Paul but expresses his own experience when he says that the bird sings sweeter whose cage has been darkened, for his song broke not on human ear until he had struggled long with the thick, chill shadows of poverty. Carlyle was a dreary dyspeptic before he accomplished anything great in literature; and but for Robert Hall's spinal malady the world might never have been thrilled by his matchless eloquence. A gentle, humble poet once declared that his soul was in his poems; but it is only after familiarity with anguish that the soul seems capable of conceiving ideals above mediocrity and worthy of being actualized either in stately verse or in gleaming marble. Perhaps this accounts for the fact, to which Stolberg calls attention, that the faces of the immortal antique statues of gods and men wear an expression of severe and serious melancholy. This also may explain the pensive sadness that marks the loftier and deeper poetry. The anguish that disciplines mind and heart, and of which is born their most magnificent creations, necessarily leaves trace of its sighs and tears on page and canvas and on sculptured stone. And perhaps it is owing to the unendurableness of this inward agony that so many of earth's gifted ones speedily succumb to death after they have charmed the world with the plaintive melody of their sweetness. The fires that quicken their powers consume their life; the conflicts that develop their strength undermine their vigor, and the sorrowful strife that violently rouses slumbering greatness, and that achieves at a stroke undying fame, shortens the number of their days.

> "The mightiest tone that music knows
> But breaks the harp-string with the sound;
> And genius still, the more it glows,
> But wastes the lamp whose life bestows
> The light it sheds around."

If chastisement is thus efficacious in awakening genius, it is natural to conclude that it is potent in perfecting character. According to the testimony of Paul in this chapter, it is sent upon us that we may be made partakers of God's holiness. As common opaque substances crystallize through the action of fire into sapphires, emeralds, and other precious stones, so the carnal man, through the power of suffering, may be transformed into the spiritual. As I have seen the dull, leaden clouds and the chilly rains at evening time transmuted by the setting sun into golden mountains and into mists of fire, and seen every water-line of the shower changed into an effulgent thread connecting earth with heaven, so have I known the declining orb of prosperity to surcharge the gloomy thoughts and driving passions that darkened the firmament of the soul with a strange light,—a light that converted night into day and scowling deformities into shapes of beauty. Of Christ it is written that He was "made perfect through suffering;" and, while the declaration may specifically refer to His official qualification as mediator, it can hardly be supposed to include nothing else. Remember it is also said: "For in that He Himself hath suffered, being tempted, He is able to succor them that are tempted;" "For we have not an high priest which cannot be touched with the feeling of our infirmities, but was in all points tempted like as we are, yet without sin." Here His ability to rescue us from our trials is attributed to His own experience in trial, which is but another way of saying that He attained this height gradually and through the instrumentality of painful vicissitudes. We are told that "He grew in wisdom and in knowledge," and the school wherein much of it was acquired was evidently the school of suffering. And there also must the disciple learn; and many who have returned from its solemn courts have given abundant proofs that they have not submitted to its discipline in vain.

Among the personal advantages which they seem to derive from its severe regime may be mentioned increased self-reliance, patience, sympathy, charity, and devoutness. These precious graces have frequently glorified and crowned the characters of those who have been "tempest-tossed and afflicted." Their dreary failures and disasters, which leave them friendless in the hour of need, which alienate from them human support, and which convince them of the selfishness of their fellows, throw them back on their own energies and the helpfulness of God. Whatever reserve force slumbers in them is quickened, stimulated, and brought into action by their trial, and they become conscious of a new manhood born of the tempest. In their solitude they look to the Invisible, and their spiritual sight, clarified by their tears, discerns in Him unchanging Fatherhood. By the hands of faith, made sensitive through pain, they feel for Him in the darkness, and discover that "He is not far from every one of us." Losing man, they find God; ceasing to lean on their fellow-beings, they come to realize how to rest in self, sustained by that arm whose strength is measureless. The disappointments experienced, and the evanescence of earthly possessions and of earthly joys rudely forced upon them by consuming blows, refine their natures of worldly ambitions and desires, and gradually enable them to bear without murmuring the misfortunes of their lot. They are brought to value time less, and eternity more; to give place to more of heaven in their hearts, and to less of earth. And as their sorrows multiply their patience grows, until, with sweet, unruffled quiet, they can confront the ills of life, and, though inwardly wincing, can calmly pursue their way to the restful grave, while their old, harsh voices are softly cadenced into sweetest melody like the faint notes of an angel's whispered song. As patience deepens, charity and sympathy increase. They draw near to others, pitying their woes and forgetting their sad follies. Their own weaknesses make them considerate of their fellow-beings, and their own loneliness makes them kind and thoughtful. Griefs melt their stubborn hearts to tenderness, failures humble their pride to lowliness, afflictions and bereavements subdue their bitter discontents, and fill them with sweet harmonies of love and peace. Schiller sublimely sings:

> "If, in the woes of actual human life,—
> If thou could'st see the serpent strife
>   Which the Greek art has made divine in stone,
> Could'st see the writhing limbs, the livid cheek,

> Note every pang, and hearken every shriek,
>   Of some despairing, lost Laocoön,
> The human nature would thyself subdue,
>   To share the human woe before thine eye; —
> Thy cheek would pale, and all thy soul be true
>   To man's great sympathy."

And they who have learned in the school of anguish, and of whose graces I have spoken, have attained to the poet's ideal, and measurably to the image of Him who "was made perfect through suffering."

But not all who pass its portals are thus enriched. That they are I have not presumed to intimate; such a thing I dare not here affirm. The text does not teach it, the Bible does not warrant it. Chastisement does not necessarily "yield the peaceable fruit of righteousness." It is conditioned; it is promised only to those who are "exercised" by their trials and calamities. Many a time have men and women been made harder, colder, unkinder, and more irreligious by the bitterness of their lot. They have been taught, but they would not learn; they have been bereaved, but they grew no better; they have been deprived of their health, friends and fortune, but they were drawn no nearer heaven. Ah me! it is a sad sight to see one who has lost this world and is careless of the other, who has no hope here and none in the hereafter; who after all the scourgings he has endured has gained no wisdom and no profit. Sad indeed to think that he may so have perverted the meaning of God's discipline as to see in it only unjust harshness and cruelty, and hence to have grown under it cynical, morose, discontented and defiant. Such people I have met with. Complaining, murmuring, fretful; their hearts clothed with blackness and their faces with anger, they would not believe anything good of God, but, rushing into Pessimistic folly, have cherished their maddening thoughts of injury to the last. They have preferred to think of Him as a tyrant, and themselves as outraged victims, whose only recourse is moody melancholy. But how vain and foolish in this manner to rebel against suffering. Every creature has to meet it, has to bear it, and all our defiant talk is of no avail. If we will, we can pluck a fragrant flower from the thorn-bush; if we so determine, we can obtain the fairest colors from the mire; but if we are lacerated to death by the sharp spines of the one, or are buried in the ooze of the other, we have only ourselves to blame. Whosoever is rightly "exercised" by his afflictions will find them working together for good; whosoever is not, will find them working together for evil. What I suppose the apostle means by this expression is simply that the wise man will lay his trials soberly and seriously to heart, will seek to trace their origin and discover their design. He will meditate upon them, not in the proud spirit of him who disdains correction and feels that he is above chastisement. He will ponder them, not in the mood of one whose vanity has received a shock, and whose self-esteem has been mortified. No, not like these; for these are they who stumble on in arrogant folly to the end.

He who is "exercised" aright will realize that he has much to learn, and that God alone can teach. Conscious of his sonship, he will feel that he has a right to enjoy his Father's discipline and care, and that God would be dealing with him as an alien were He to forego its rigid administration. He desires the interest of Divinity in his welfare, though it may lead to bitter experiences, and he calls upon Him to deal with him as a child lest he should prove an outcast. Believing in the Father's love and wisdom, he is assured that no unnecessary stroke will fall, and no useless or unendurable loss be inflicted. When the darkness thickens, when misery increases, when sun, moon and stars fail from his little heaven of earthly joy, he will meekly bow beneath the rod, or draw closer to the hand that wields it, and will look up into his Father's face to discern the meaning of the scourge. And when by faith he sees that the Father's face is sadder than his own poor human heart, he will cease from all repinings, and will put away everything that grieves a love so tender and severe.

It is this spirit that converts afflictions into blessings, and it is this spirit that perceives the reason why our life is beset by ills, and is burdened with unnumbered cares. When it is fostered ghastly Pessimism will cease to haunt, and a healthier philosophy of the evil in the earth prevail. Cultivate it, one and all; cultivate it as you would taste some drops of happiness in this weary world, and cultivate it as you would carry with you a nature refined from sin to that world where the ministry of chastisement is unknown. And when the gates of this school of suffering forever close in death, may the portals of heaven open to your rejoicing souls, and there the peaceable fruit of righteousness eternally be yours.

BUDDHISM.

"He was not that light, but was sent to bear witness of that light." *John i. 8.*

> "The Scripture of the Saviour of the World,
> Lord Buddha,— Prince Siddârtha styled on earth,—
> In earth and heavens and hells incomparable,
> All-honored, Wisest, Best, most Pitiful;
> The Teacher of Nirvâna and the law."
> *Edwin Arnold.*

JOHN was not the only herald of the light. Others before him were as the gray of morning to the rising of the king of day. In other lands, and in times remote, prophets and reformers, some of whom were even looked upon as saviors, had appeared, preparing the thought of the world, both by their doctrines and their lives, for the approach of Him who should be alike its Teacher and its Redeemer. Such were Confucius, Lao-tse, Zarathustra, and, perhaps beyond all others, that personage now becoming widely known through the poem of Edwin Arnold, entitled *The Light of Asia,*— Gautama Buddha.

During the past few years western nations have become profoundly interested in the religions of ancient India. There is in them so much that is giantesque, mystical and majestic that they fascinate as well as inform the European and American mind. Especially are Christian scholars drawn to them, because of the parallelism they furnish to some of the great truths taught in the Bible, and which seem to indicate a common Aryan origin, and to point to a primeval unity of faith. An additional value is also being attached to them, as they afford a scale of measurement by which the character of Jesus Christ and the dignity of His mission can be graduated. You are doubtless aware of the fact that modern infidel writers and speakers are accustomed to group in one class the founders of all religions. They represent them as putting forth the same claims, as doing substantially the same work, as pursuing practically the same career, and as being entitled to about the same respect. In their artificial category they include our Savior. Their avowed design is to create the impression that, ranking with a definite order of men, He is worthy of no higher homage than they. Taking, for instance, the life of Buddha, they paint in vivid colors his self-abnegation, his temptations, his exalted ethics, the sufferings he endured, the confidence he inspired, the worship he received, and the superstitious myths to which he gave rise, and they argue from analogy that if such a life is explicable without recourse to the supernatural, that of Jesus Christ can be accounted for without its aid. To not a few this reasoning is conclusive; and if the followers of Christ were not as familiar with the literature of the subject as their adversaries, not to say more so, they themselves might begin to question the soundness of their faith. But possessing this literature, and indeed having themselves done much toward its formation; having such commentaries, translations and expositions as are presented in the works of Burnouf, Koeppen, Weber, Bigandet, St. Hilaire, Spence Hardy, Dr. Field, Tiele, Max Müller and S. Johnson, not overlooking the smaller and more modest contributions of Rhys Davids and Edward Clodd, they perceive that the claims of Jesus cannot be disposed of in this summary manner. "Than Buddha," writes St. Hilaire, "there is, with the sole exception of the Christ, no purer nor more touching figure among the founders of religions. His life is without blemish; he is the finished model of the heroism, the self-renunciation, the love, the sweetness he com-

'mands." The justice of this high tribute Christians are not inclined to question; but having before them the books that are authoritative on the subject, they insist upon the magnitude of the "exception," and point out, what their antagonists fail to recognize, that the contrasts between the purest and noblest religious reformer of antiquity and Jesus Christ are more numerous and radical than the comparisons. Any conclusion, therefore, that does not take into consideration this fact they hold to be entirely unreliable and unsatisfactory.

The poem of Arnold has suggested to me a special study in this direction. While he draws no inferences unfavorable to orthodox conceptions of Christ, nor indeed alludes to Him at all, but writes from the standpoint of a Buddhist who had never heard that name, his very reticence, combined with the spirit of the poem as a whole, is liable to be misconstrued by the reader, and to leave the impression that its author regards his hero as hardly inferior to any other spiritual leader known to history. I do not say that this thought was in his mind when he wrote, but it certainly comes to us as we read. But whether the thought ever occurred to Mr. Arnold or not, it may tend to counteract whatever subtle influence his book may exert in the direction of infidelity, to place Him who is called "The Light of the World" by the side of him who is termed "The Light of Asia;" and unless I widely err, such apposition will assure the most wavering faith that "a greater than Buddha is here."

The Veda, a name signifying " knowing," or "wisdom," the sacred song of the Aryas who were scattered along the banks of the Indus, is a collection of about a thousand hymns ("*Mantras*," or "mind-born"), composed by various Rishis, and dating back to a venerable antiquity. Johnson, in his work on *Oriental Religions* (Trübner's edition), to which I am indebted for various facts and for several quotations which appear in this discourse, regards this sacred book, in some of its parts at least, as three thousand years old, and as expressing the Hindu faith of "still earlier times." Max Müller, whose *Sanskrit Literature* and *Chips* have been of the highest value to me and have been freely used in this study, claims that its earlier portions cannot be assigned "a date more recent than 1300 to 1500 before our era." The Veda has been called "the oldest of the Bibles," and it has been termed "historical" on account of the realism of the picture it gives of the Aryas after their descent into India. From it, therefore, may be gained a very clear idea of the earliest manifestation of the religious sentiment. These primitive worshipers seem to have recognized life as a desirable possession, to have been continually influenced by implicit trust in the Unseen, and by childlike awe of its inscrutable power; to have regarded men as equal, and between whom the discrimination of caste should not be tolerated; to have never countenanced the horrid practice of burning wives with their dead husbands, and never to have built temples, venerated idols, honored priesthoods, or to have admitted human sacrifices in their religious rites, no explicit mention being made of such bloody offerings in the Rig-Veda. They adored the Light, beholding in its manifold manifestations, from the spark that expires on the hearth to the sun that flashes in the heavens, "an all-productive cosmic energy." According to Muir's translation, the worshiper sang: "Arise, the breath of our life has come! The darkness has fled. Light advances, pathway of the sun! It is Dawn that brings consciousness to men; she arouses the living, each to his own work; she quickens the dead. Bright leader of pure voices, she opens all doors; makes manifest the treasures; receives the praises of men. Night and day follow each other and efface each other as they traverse the heavens, kindred to one another forever. The path of the sisters is unending, commanded by the gods. Of one purpose, they strive not, they rest not; of one will, though unlike. They who first beheld the Dawn have passed away. Now it is we who behold her; and they who shall behold her in after-times are coming also. Mother of the gods, Eye of the earth, Light of the sacrificed, for us also shine!" These are beautiful lines, and equally beautiful and radiant are the deities who are interwoven with the mystic conception which underlies them,—Ushas, the morning; Saramâ, the dawn; Savitri, the sun; and Agni, the fire, who is spoken of as the child of the two pieces of wood rubbed together, and as the herdsman's friend and protector. And yet Müller finds in the Veda a Monotheism which precedes its Polytheism, " a remembrance of One God, breaking through the mists of idolatrous phraseology." In the tenth book we have the declaration: " Wise poets make the Beautiful-winged, though He is one, manifold by words;" and the desire to express this intuitive sense of unity is brought out in such passages as these: "Among you, O gods, there is none that is small, none that is young; you are all great indeed;" "Thou, Agni, art Indra, art Vishnu, art Brahmanaspati;" "That which is One the wise call many ways. They call it Indra, Mitra, Varuna, Agni, the winged heavenly Garutmat." And Johnson, who regards the Rig-Veda as "the potentiality of all religions," as "the prophetic star-dust of historic systems," says that in it "there are hints of a Father of all the gods, Dyaushpitar; of a Lord of Creation, Prajâpati; of a generator and lord of all Prayer, Brahmanaspati." " Indra contains all the gods, as the felloe of a wheel surrounds the spokes." The Pantheistic idea reveals itself evidently in these ever-changing forms of Deity, though it is modified by the personality implied in the hymns and prayers, and by the views which are incidentally expressed regarding man's immortality. For, as Johnson writes, quoting from the Veda: "Death was Yama's kindly messenger, 'to bring them (men) to the homes he had gone before to prepare for them, and which could not be taken from them.' It was far in Varuna's world of perfect and undying light, in the 'third heaven,' in the very 'sanctuary of the sky, and of the great waters,' and in the bosom of the Highest Gods. That which men desire is the attainment of good in the world, where they may behold their parents and abide free from infirmities, 'where the One Being dwells beyond the stars.'" And hence the impressive Vedic hymn still in use at Hindu funerals, given by Clodd:

> "Forth from about thee thus I build away the ground;
> As I lay down this clod may I receive no harm;
> This pillar may the Fathers here maintain for thee;
> May Yama there provide for thee a dwelling."

The Rig-Veda was followed by three other books, known as the Sâma-Veda, the Yajur-Veda and the Atharva-Veda, and they make up the four parts of the Hindu Scriptures. These additional books show considerable, though gradual, departure from the primitive and simple beliefs of the first, and around all grew up a body of literature devoted to exposition, ritual and theology, which pretty thoroughly obscured them. This period of development may very properly be designated the era of corruption, and it is identical with the rise and progress of Brahmanism. It is impossible to fix with any degree of accuracy the date of this movement, but for our purposes we may accept the opinion of various scholars that it could not have begun much later than the eighth century B.C. Originally the title "Brahman" simply meant a singer of songs, but in the course of time it came to denote a religious officer, a member of the sacerdotal caste. I suppose the transition occurred something in this way: Memorizing the Vedic hymns, and chanting them in public worship, they doubtless acquired influence, and gradually came to be invested with a distinctively religious character. Finding themselves honored on account of their service, a little ambition mixed with cunning would easily accomplish the rest. Flattering by turns the ruler and the ruled, slowly and covertly pushing their claims to consideration, they could hardly fail to capture the dignity which assumption and arrogance aspired to possess. With their establishment in power, strange doctrines, degrading distinctions, and novel rites made their appearance. The caste system was inaugurated. No longer were men equal, but divided by sharp, impassable barriers. They were distinguished into Brahmans, or the learned; Rajanyas, or the princes and warriors; Vaisyas, or the commonalty, and the Sûdras, or slaves, this latter class being doomed to a life of the deepest misery. Then came fully developed Pantheism and clearly defined transmigration. The doctrine entirely unknown to the oldest Vedic books, that the soul of the imperfect must be born again, in the form of a plant, animal, or man, until the highest stages of self-renunciation and freedom from everything material have been reached, and then sink and disappear in the soul of the universe, was openly advocated and implicitly believed. The Brahmans also taught that the complete extinction of the several appetites, and the abstraction of the mind from external objects, were necessary to prepare the mind for this hoped-for absorption in the Universal One. Moreover, they introduced childish mysticism, narrow formalism, debasing superstitions, unnatural and arbitrary requirements and cruel and bloody rites and sacrifices, and to complete their malignant work they elaborated a metaphysical theology, and founded a hierarchy whose very shadow was an unmitigated curse to untold millions. Thus they corrupted the primitive religion of India; influenced it for evil just as Romanism in a subsequent age degraded Christianity, misinterpreting the Scriptures, perverting its doctrines, and ingrafting on its simple worship the most abominable observances. (*Vide* Tiele's *Ancient Religions*, Trübner's edition.)

It was when this apostasy had attained its greatest power, when the old childlike gladness of the people had been turned into sorrow, when existence itself had come to be regarded as a curse, that Siddartha, of the family of Gautama, appeared on earth.

> "All honored, wisest, best, most pitiful,
> The teacher of Nirvâna and the law."

Various opinions prevail in the East and among Western scholars regarding the date of his birth, many favoring 623 B.C., while Koeppen, and with him others, place his death from 480 B.C. to 460, and his birth some sixty or eighty years previous. The Thibetans differ among themselves very widely, referring his death to various periods, ranging from 2422 B.C. to 546. The Chinese and Japanese are agreed on the tenth century, while the Singhalese are confident that he appeared in the sixth. Mr. Arnold adopts 620 B.C. as the time of his nativity, which event he localizes on the borders of Nepaul. His father was King Suddhôdana, and his mother Queen Maya, and they reigned in Kapilavastu. Their son, Siddartha, while distinguished preëminently as Buddha, was not the only being to whom that sacred name was applied. The title itself, derived from "budh," to know, a term in Hindu philosophy synonymous with "mind," signifies "the enlightened one," and if tradition may be believed was borne by others before him and will be borne by others in the future. Among the peoples of the Himalayas the theory prevailed that for millions of years each age had received a Buddha to dissipate its darkness. Thus Kasyapa preceded Gautama, and Maitreya is to follow him.

"Fahian reports three" of a date earlier than that assigned to Mr. Arnold's hero, and "describes a tower in Oude where the relics of one of them were preserved," and consequently the exalted personage whose life is recorded in the poem was but one of a distinguished line of sacred men who have appeared to reveal the way of salvation to the race.

The legends represent Gautama, after thousands of preparatory births, deciding to leave the deities with whom he was associating, and to be born once more into the world.

> "Yea!" spake He; "now I go to help the World
> This last of many times; for birth and death
> End hence for me and those who learn my law.
> I will go down among the Sâkyas."

He chooses his parents, a certain king and queen of great dignity and piety. When the natal hour arrived strange signs announce the advent of a Buddha.

> "The queen shall bear a boy, a holy child,
> Of wondrous wisdom, profiting all flesh,
> Who shall deliver men from ignorance,
> Or rule the world, if he will deign to rule."

"A gray-haired saint, Asita," hears the Devas singing songs, and, Simeon-like, speaks of the infant in the following mystic and prophetic terms:

> "O babe! I worship! Thou art He!
> I see the rosy light, the foot-sole marks,
> The soft, curled tendril of the Swastika,
> The sacred primal signs thirty and two,
> The eighty lesser tokens. Thou art Buddh,
> And thou wilt preach the law and save all flesh
> Who learn the law, though I shall never hear,
> Dying too soon, who lately longed to die;
> Howbeit I have seen thee."

He addresses the queen, and having told her that "she

has grown too sacred for more woe," after seven days he promises she shall "painless attain the close of pain."

> "Which fell; for on the seventh evening
> Queen Maya smiling slept and waked no more,
> Passing content to Trâyastrinshas-Heaven,
> Where countless Devas worship her and wait
> Attendant on that radiant motherhead."

The childhood and youth of Siddartha were distinguished by unusual precociousness. He excels his teachers in learning, perplexes them by his wisdom, and yet preserves his modesty of manner. His chief instructor was overwhelmed at his miraculous knowledge.

> "But Viswamitra heard it on his face,
> Prostrate before the boy; 'For thou,' he cried,
> 'Art teacher of thy teachers,—thou, not I,
> Art Gûrû. Oh, I worship thee, sweet prince!
> That comest to my school only to show
> Thou knowest all without the books, and know'st
> Fair reverence besides.'"

He likewise excels in feats of noble horsemanship, and in other manly arts, and, indeed, proves himself to be as gallant a knight as he was a consummate scholar. But his heart, though strong, was not insensible to compassion, and he begins his works of mercy by rescuing a wounded swan from the arrow of his cousin that had "killed the god-like speed which throbbed in this white wing." Up to this time the poor bird's grief was the only grief that he had seen; but visiting with his father many of the fairest spots in the country, his keen eye detected the conflict and the sorrow that was half concealed beneath the attractive show.

> "The Prince Siddârtha sighed. 'Is this,' he said,
> 'That happy earth they brought me forth to see?
> How salt with sweat the peasant's bread! how hard
> The oxen's service! in the brake how fierce
> The war of weak and strong! i' th' air what plots!

> No refuge e'en in water. Go aside
> A space and let me muse on what ye show.'
> So saying, the good Lord Buddha seated him
> Under a jambu tree, with ankles crossed,—
> As holy statues sit,— and first began
> To meditate this deep disease of life,
> What its far source and whence its remedy."

But the King was not pleased with these musings, and was not at all satisfied at the prospect of his son treading the lowly path of self-denying pains; and, therefore, having advised with his ministers, he determined to marry him to some worthy maiden as speedily as possible. His plans in this particular were successful. Siddartha at first sight falls in love with the beautiful Yasôdhara, and afterward he confesses that during a previous life on the earth he had met with and loved her, and that this affection would be eternal:

> "Lo! as hid seed shoots after rainless years,
> So good and evil, pains and pleasures, hates
> And loves, and all dead deeds, come forth again
> Bearing bright leaves or dark, sweet fruit or sour
> Thus I was he and she Yasôdhara;
> And while the wheel of birth and death turns round,
> That which hath been must be between us two."

After the wedding the king settles his son in a magnificent palace, in the description of which the poetic genius of Mr. Arnold asserts itself, and seeks to absorb his mind in pleasure. But after awhile he grows weary of dancing girls, and marbles, and pearls, and desires to see the world. His father gives his permission, but directs that the city and country be radiantly adorned, and that the blind and maimed, the sick and feeble, be kept indoors. But his precautions were all in vain, for while his son was rejoicing over the artificial signs of the world's happiness,

"Slow tottering from the hovel where he hid,
Crept forth a wretch in rags, haggard and foul,
An old, old man, whose shrivelled skin, sun-tanned
Clung like a beast's hide to his fleshless bones.
Bent was his back with load of many days,
His eyepits red with rust of ancient tears,
His dim orbs blear with rheum, his toothless jaws
Wagging with palsy and the fright to see
So many and such joy. One skinny hand
Clutched a worn staff to prop his quavering limbs,
And one was pressed upon the ridge of ribs
Whence came in gasps the heavy, painful breath.
'Alms!' moaned he, 'give, good people! for I die
To-morrow or the next day.'"

This miserable creature excited Siddartha's pity, and led him to make inquiries, the results of which were not conducive to his peace of mind. He returns to his palace, but he is restless. Dreams haunt him, and the impression deepens that he is destined to aid the suffering race. He thinks continually "how love might save its sweetness from the slayer, Time." He goes forth again and beholds the terrible evils of society, the sufferings of the world, "the vastness of the agony of earth and the vainness of its joys." He is appalled, affrighted. To him the gods seem weak, as they do not save when sad lips cry:

"Oh! suffering world,
Oh! known and unknown of my common flesh,
Caught in this common net of death and woe,
And life which binds to both! I see, I feel
The vastness of the agony of earth,
The vainness of its joys, the mockery
Of all its best, the anguish of its worst;
Since pleasures end in pain, and youth in age,
And love in loss, and life in hateful death,
And death in unknown lives, which will but yoke
Men to their wheel again to whirl the round
Of false delights and woes that are not false.
      *   *   *   The veil is rent

> Which blinded me! I am as all these men
> Who cry upon their gods and are not heard
> Or are not heeded — yet there must be aid!
> For them and me and all there must be help!
> *   *   *   I would not let one cry
> When I could save! How can it be that Brahm
> Would make a world and keep it miserable,
> Since, if all powerful, he leaves it so,
> He is not good, and if not powerful,
> He is not God?"

Henceforward his palace is a prison to him, its pleasures weary him, and at last he determines to abandon all and seek the way by which he can save mankind.

> "Oh, summoning stars, I come! Oh, mournful earth!
> For thee and thine I lay aside my youth,
> My throne, my joys, my golden days, my nights,
> My happy palace — and thine arms, sweet Queen!
> Harder to put aside than all the rest!
> Yet thee, too, I shall save, saving this earth;
> And that which stirs within thy tender womb,
> My child, the hidden blossom of our loves,
> Whom if I wait to bless my mind will fail.
> Wife! child! father! and people! ye must share
> A little while the anguish of this hour
> That light may break and all flesh learn the Law."

An affecting description is given of his parting from his beloved Yasôdhara, of the disgust which he experiences at the sight of the sleeping dancing girls, and of his ride into the night. The poet represents him as saying to his horse:

> "Be still,
> White Kantaka! be still, and bear me now
> The farthest journey ever rider rode;
> For this night take I horse to find the truth,
> And where my quest will end yet know I not,
> Save that it shall not end until I find."

The yellow robe and the mendicant's lot are chosen, and "couched on the grass, homeless, alone," "subduing that fair body born for bliss," he meditated long and watched. He became an itinerant, lived on charity, and mortified his flesh "until sin's dross was purged away," and "he was winged for glorious spheres and splendor past all thought." In the course of his wanderings he teaches a poor woman, who mourns for her child, to accept death as the inevitable.

> "'My sister! thou hast found,' the master said,
> 'Searching for what none finds,— that bitter balm
> I had to give thee. He thou lovedst slept
> Dead on thy bosom yesterday; to-day
> Thou know'st the whole wide world weeps with thy woe:
> The grief which all hearts share grows less for one.
> Lo! I would pour my blood if it could stay
> Thy tears and win the secret of that curse
> Which makes sweet love our anguish, and which drives
> O'er flowers and pastures to the sacrifice,—
> As these dumb beasts are driven,— men their lords.
> I seek that secret: bury thou thy child!'"

He teaches a king the sin and folly of animal sacrifices, and impressively affirms that all life is sacred; and to a poor Sudra lad, the victim of caste, he says:

> "'There is no caste in blood,
> Which runneth of one hue, nor caste in tears,
> Which trickle salt with all; neither comes man
> To birth with tilka-mark stamped on the brow,
> Nor sacred thread on neck. Who doth right deeds
> Is twice-born, and who doeth ill deeds vile.'"

But the hour comes when, under the Bôdh tree, Siddartha is assailed by manifold temptations. He struggles there with the varying forms of evil until, through the thick air of the conflict, he at last discerns the dawning light. The mystery of life is explained, the means of deliverance are revealed, and the perfect knowledge by which he hopes to save others as well as himself is finally and fully gained. The poem picturesquely traces his subsequent career, his visit to his childhood's home, the veneration he inspired in his father, the doctrines he taught, the countries he subdued, the peaceful death he died, passing

"Unto Nirvâna, where the Silence lives."

The account thus given by Mr. Arnold is, in all of its essential features, verified by recognized authorities, and may be accepted as substantially correct. From it, as well as from other sources of information, we gather that Siddartha, after a youth spent in luxury, became a self-denying, holy man,— one of the few historic characters whose purity was transcendent. He evidently struggled hard to subdue sin in his members, and gloriously triumphed. Let us not detract from this ancient Indian sage in the least, but gratefully acknowledge his resplendent moral beauty. He was also a reformer,— the Luther of his times,— the stern enemy of caste and of animal sacrifice. Around all life he shed a hallowed influence, the priestly orders he subverted, and magnified the importance of the individual. He gave a system of ethics to his country that has only been surpassed by the sublimer code of the Nazarene. Burnouf reproduces ten commandments of which Siddartha is reputed the author, which forbid killing, stealing, unchastity, falsehood, intemperance, irregularity in eating, attendance on exhibitions of dancing and dramatic representations, perfumes, sleeping in a large or high bed, and the acceptance of gold or silver. While some of these precepts are exceedingly curious, most of them are wholesome and of universal application. They reveal deep spiritual insight into the necessities of the race, and justify us in assigning to their author a very high rank among the moral teachers of mankind.

The doctrines of Buddha cannot as easily be determined as his ethics. Mr. Arnold, in various places in his poem, brings to view his own conceptions of what the illustrious reformer taught. According to his interpretation the misery of existence was the starting point of Siddartha's teachings. Doomed to *be* until sin should be quite purged away, and passing from one form of life to another, and through various worlds, the people for ages had thirsted to be delivered from this bondage, and to attain the blessedness of extinction. The doctrine of transmigration Buddha advocated, though, according to Arnold, it is very questionable whether he proclaimed "nothingness as the issue and crown of being." The word "Nirvâna" represents this final state, whatever it may be, and the passages in the poem which refer to it breathe a Pantheistic spirit and leave the impression on the reader that absorption in the Universal Soul was the hope set by Buddha before his followers. The poet puts on the lips of his hero the words:

"The aching craze to live ends, and life glides —
   Lifeless — to nameless quiet, nameless joy;
Blessed Nirvâna, — sinless, stirless rest, —
   That change which never changes."

In another place he adds:

"Seeking nothing, he gains all;
   Foregoing self, the universe grows 'I':
If any teach Nirvâna is to cease,
   Say unto such they lie."

Here we have a refined Pantheism, and the closing lines of the poem confirm this view:

"The dew is on the lotus! — Rise, great sun!
And lift my leaf and mix me with the wave.
Om, mani padme, om, the sunrise comes!
The dewdrop slips into the shining sea!"

Mr. T. W. Rhys Davids does not believe that the hope preached by Buddha was peacefulness in the eternal deeps of annihilation. He says: "Nirvâna is the extinction of that sinful, grasping condition of mind and heart which would otherwise be the cause of renewed individual existence. That extinction is to be brought about by, and runs parallel with, the growth of the opposite condition of mind and heart, and is complete when that opposite condition is reached. Nirvâna is therefore the same thing as a sinless, calm state of mind, and if translated at all, may best perhaps be rendered as 'holiness,'—holiness, that is, in the Buddhist sense, perfect peace, goodness and wisdom." Bunsen advocates a similar explanation, and Johnson says: "Etymology at least fails to bear out the confident assurances of Burnouf, Koeppen, Weber and others, that 'its extinction of the lamp of existence' means absolute annihilation. Nirvâna is from *nir*, separation from, and *vâ*, wind. The simplest and most natural meaning seems to be, not 'blown out,' but 'no more waving,' as from the presence of wind, no more restlessness and change. It is familiar to Brahmanical literature as synonymous with words signifying release, emancipation, the highest good." Colebrook defines it as "profound calm." And this rendering seems to be sustained by *The Dhammapada*, or "Path of Virtue," which is supposed to contain exact accounts of what Buddha really taught. According to this record Nirvâna is "the uncreated, the ineffable, the immortal"; "the place of repose and bliss, where embodiments cease"; "the other shore, beyond the power of death, where one is thoughtful, guileless, free from doubt and from all desires, and content." "The true sage is he who knows his former abodes, who sees heaven and hell, who has reached the end of births, and is perfect in wisdom." "Tear away attachments (self-love) from thy being, as an autumn lotus with thy hand, and make thy way open to Nirvâna, to rest." (*Vide* Johnson.) In view of these interpretations, we may credit the Reformer who is called by Arnold "The Light of Asia" with teaching his disciples to look for something more than nonentity as the end of all their strivings, though it may not be transparently clear whether he grasped the sublime conception of personal immortality, or discerned merely its vague, shadowy semblance. Probably his doctrine was but little different from that of the Bhagavadgitâ, and there we find unmistakable traces of Pantheism, as in the following passage from Thomson's translation: "As the all-penetrating ether, from the minuteness of its parts, passeth everywhere unaffected, so this spirit in the body. As one sun illumines the whole world, so does the one spirit illumine the whole of matter. O Bhârata! They who thus perceive the body and the soul as distinct, and that there is release, go to the Supreme." Most likely Gautama's sentiments were similar to these, and, as Arnold represents him, he may have taught concerning the self-conquering man:

"Never shall yearnings torture him, nor sins
 Stain him, nor ache of earthly joys and woes
Invade his safe eternal peace; nor deaths
 And lives recur. He goes

"Unto NIRVANA. He is one with Life,
 Yet lives not. He is blest, ceasing to be.
OM, MANI PADME, OM! the Dewdrop slips
 Into the shining sea!"

The reader of the "Light of Asia" will be struck by the almost total absence of reference to a Supreme Being. This is one of the distinguishing features of Buddhism. Its author added nothing to the world's knowledge of God. On the supposition that this is explained by the adoption of the Vedas by Siddartha, and that he believed in the Deity and divinities they praise, he is relieved from the charge of Atheism, but it still remains strange that he did not supplement their revelations with some additional light. Professor Tyndall is positive that he "divorced ethics not only from Brahma and the Brahminic trinity, but even from the existence of God." I have also seen it stated that Dr. Judson declared that "there was nothing in his system to redeem it from the charge of absolute Atheism." But to these representations Dr. Johnson answers: "It is certain, whatever may be true of metaphysical statements, that neither Nihilism nor Atheism characterizes the mass of Buddhist literature, the rites of the Buddhist church, or, as a whole, the sects into which it has become divided. It would, indeed, be fatal to our hopes for human nature if we could be forced to believe that four hundred millions of at least partially civilized people have made a religion out of the love of nonentity, or, indeed, out of mere negation in any form. The apparent Atheism of the Buddhist is, in substance, opposition to the idea of an external God, limited and individual, acting in imperfect human ways." And in support of this view he informs the reader that "The temples of Nepâl afford proof that the belief in a supreme, all-seeing Buddha, represented by two Eyes as symbols of intelligence, was current in these regions at least as early as the beginning of the Christian era. The Nepâlese say that 'Swayambhu, the self-existent, called Âdibuddha, was when nothing else was. He wished to become many, and produced the Buddhas through union with his desire. Âdibuddha was never seen. He is pure light.'" From these statements I think we may with safety conclude that at least Siddartha recognized a Supreme Impersonal existence, into whom all purified souls should at last be absorbed, and that the great object of earthly life should be such an abnegation of self as to prepare the soul for its return to its everlasting home in God.

The path to be pursued by which this end is to be attained is in essentiality one of works. Hence our poet sings:

> "Evil swells the debts to pay,
> Good delivers and acquits;

> Shun evil, follow good; hold sway
> Over thyself. This is the Way."

But Siddartha is no Redeemer, no sacrificial priest, no Savior in the highest sense, doing for humanity what it never could accomplish for itself. He is only a great teacher, a wonderful seer who discerns the origin of evil and who points out how the race may effect its own deliverance. In reality he does nothing to help the individual. He makes more vivid the mighty barriers between man and unbroken peace, and then leaves to him the inexecutable task of removing them:

> "Nought from the helpless gods by gift and hymn,
>   Nor bribe with blood, nor feed with fruits and cakes;
> Within yourselves deliverance must be sought·
>   Each man his prison makes."

Such is the Gospel that he teaches. He tells the world that there are paths, steps, commandments, all of which are beautiful in theory and in practice, and he commends them to the race. But he might as well urge an individual to lift himself from the ground in his own arms, or to walk while he stands still, or to sleep while he wakes, for not more impossible are these physical performances than are the various duties he enjoins. Who among the living can ever hope to effect escape from the evils of his lot by the method set forth in this exquisite recipe for their extinction?

> "The third is *Sorrow's Ceasing.* This is peace
>   To conquer love of self and lust of life,
>   To tear deep-rooted passion from the breast,
>   To still the inward strife;
>
>   For love to clasp Eternal Beauty close;
>   For glory to be Lord of self, for pleasure
>   To live beyond the gods; for countless wealth
>   To lay up lasting treasure

Of perfect service rendered, duties done
    In charity, soft speech, and stainless days:
These riches shall not fade away in life
    Nor any death dispraise.

Then Sorrow ends, for Life and Death have ceased;
    How should lamps flicker when their oil is spent?
The old sad count is clear, the new is clean;
    Thus hath a man content."

We can have no possible objection to these recommendations; but if eternal felicity rests on their being met and fulfilled in our own strength, unhappy are we! What humanity needs is positive Divine help to right doing, not a mere eloquent elaboration of what it is to do right. This is the special weakness of the whole system, and explains why with a magnificent code of ethics the millions of its adherents are cursed with ignorance, superstition, and moral defilement. They have fallen back from the herculean and hopeless endeavor to perfect their own righteousness; and in sullen despondency they sink deeper and deeper into the mire. No help for them in Buddha, only pitiable revelation of their bottomless misery. Assistance must come to them from some other quarter, if at all; for as to their Siddartha he is only a great talker, and not a great doer, and what they need preëminently is work done for them, not words spoken to them. Nevertheless, while his system is fairly open to this criticism, and short as it comes of the truth, yet, considering the age in which the prophet lived, it reflects high honor on his name; and if we will but realize how exalted were the ethics that he taught, how singularly unselfish was his spirit, and how fully he kept before the people their need of a savior,— although the conception he formed of a savior's mission was meager and erroneous in the extreme — we may with confidence ascribe to him the additional honor of being an adumbration of

Him who, in the fullness of time, "was born of a woman, born under the law that he might redeem them which were under the law, that they might receive the adoption of sons."

Behold! a greater than Buddha is here! If we compare Jesus or rather contrast Him with the founder of Buddhism, His infinite superiority will still appear — a superiority as marked as that of solar light over the soft-shining stars, the phosphorescence of the sea, and the flame-fires that blaze from earth's vestal altars — a superiority that reaches up to Divinity, and requires Divinity to explain. Unlike Siddartha, Jesus was born in poverty, enjoyed few, if any, advantages of education, and was from the first an outcast in the world. His youth tasted not the pleasures that affluence and rank procure, nor His manhood the sweet flavor of adulation lavished so freely on aged Siddartha. Like the Hindu, He engaged in the sublimest of endeavors — to save mankind — but how unlike his method. The sage retires to the wilderness to gather moral strength for his enterprise; to save himself before he tries to save others. Jesus from the first is perfect, sinless, and pursues His mission among crowds of men, mingling with them freely, and too pure to fear taint from any. Buddha wears a peculiar garb, ostentatiously is indigent, and cruelly ascetic. Jesus distinguishes Himself by no professional badge; does not court poverty, but endures it; and is genial, social and companionable. They are both sympathetic, self-sacrificing; but the one is appreciated in his lifetime, revered by princes, respected even by the priests against whose ritual he preached, and dies at an advanced age, venerated by Asia; while the other is misjudged, misunderstood by His contemporaries, is rejected by the sacerdotal orders, betrayed by His disciples, and at last is crucified as a malefactor. What an infinite difference! What a chasm to be bridged! Surely no highly-painted theory of naturalism is equal to such a task! This Jesus, this peasant's child, this untaught, untutored man, this mechanic, who mingled freely with the humblest and the vilest, this citizen of a despised nation, born in an obscure town and reared in a wretched village, insulted, rejected, murdered, has become, in fact, what was foreseen and predicted He would be — the "Light of the World." The light not of one country, but of all; not of one race, but of every race. Even in that India where Buddha taught, converts throng to hear His word; and, speaking for the Brahmo Somaj, its leader, Chunder Sen, declares that the Star of Bethlehem is rising on the night of Asia; that Christ it is who holds India loyal to the British throne; that Christ, not bayonets, reconciles the people to English rule, and that Christ, not earthly kings, shall dominate the thought and life of all the millions who have for ages listened spellbound to Gautama's wisdom. How shall we explain this mystery? If it is even difficult to account for Buddha's triumph by Buddha's life, though its circumstances were not unfavorable to success, what shall we say of Christ? He, against whom surroundings, condition, rank, yea, everything of an external nature, militated, achieves a world-wide victory, and the mystery thickens as the issue becomes more assured. What shall we say? How reach the truth? Outward circumstances of His life fail to supply the answer, and we are shut up to the inevitable, that in Jesus we meet an element higher than the human — the divine; and that, if the career of Buddha is a wonder, that of Jesus is a miracle; yea, the unapproachable and stupendous miracle of the universe.

This conclusion increases in force when we contrast the teachings of these spiritual heroes. The puerilities that mingle with the sublime ethics of Siddartha find no place in the code of Jesus. He wastes no breath on the height or length of one's bed, and decries neither innocent amusements, nor the art of music. He seeks not to rob life of its joys, its simple pleasures, or its sunny gladsomeness. Unlike Siddartha, He represents existence as a blessing, a heavenly boon, to be prized and cherished, and to be returned unstained to the keeping of its Author. Unlike Siddartha, He lives with God, communes with Him, walks with Him, and ever seems to be looking beyond the infinite azure into the smiling of His face. Of this Almighty Being He freely talks to His disciples; calls Him father, His father, theirs. The sage of India brings with him no word from the eternities concerning Him "in whom we live, move, and have our being." Jesus reveals His very nature, reveals His innermost heart, and shows that He who is Spirit incomprehensible is comprehensible love. He announces as the most glorious heritage of humanity the privilege of access to His presence, the possibility of commerce with His spirit, and of rest in His favor. The world was no longer lonely after Christ had spoken. God became a living presence everywhere. His smile rested on all His works, and even the shadow of the valley of death became transformed into radiance through the sunshine of His countenance. Blessed forever be His name who lifted the veil of mystery from the universe, and enabled saddened eyes to see a face beyond — the Father's face — beaming with tenderness on His creatures!

Not as Siddartha did Jesus speak of the soul's eternal destiny. No Pantheistic subtlety, no consciousless immortality, no "dewdrop slipping into the shining sea," was the burden of His high discourse. "He spake as never man spake." To all the teeming millions of this earth, to every human unit — however insignificant and debased — he proclaimed an existence endless. The flight of untold ages, all the vast cycles of a future, with which the unmeasured and immeasurable past is but as a watch in the fleeting night, and all the convulsions, upheavals, destructions, and re-creations of this complicated universe shall set no limit, find no grave, and shall bring neither decrepitude nor death to any human soul. Immortality, personal immortality, the reality of being, not its dream, is the glad message that fell from His sacred lips on the ear of a breathless world. But sad would have been His words, though radiant with the hope of life, had they been unaccompanied by that grace which "opens the kingdom of heaven to all believers." How should the sin-stained and polluted hope to enter into the invisible, on whose portals, thrones, and crowns is written one appalling word, whiter than light and fiercer than flame — Purity; "Without holiness no man shall see the Lord." Drown, drown, in a wail of lamentation the voice of immortality; let not its whisper excite our fears, let not its breath smite the little joy we have on earth. What has a sinner to do with immortality? Who craves to live eternally, carrying with him the plague of guilt to torment him evermore? Better Nirvâna, better Nihilism, better anything than such an immortality as this. Cruel would it have been in the Master to promise this, more fitting to be spoken by a devil than a Christ, and deserving more the anathema of a world than its benediction. But His gracious lips were not closed forever when He pronounced the word "immortal." They parted once more, and proclaimed "salvation." Salvation! Not the salvation Siddartha taught — salvation painfully wrought out through many births, in many worlds, by each sin-afflicted soul. No! the salvation Jesus preached, Jesus won, and freely gives to all who will accept the gift. This was the gospel that He spoke; this was the gospel that thrilled the world with joy; and this is still the gospel that conquers human hearts, and sweeps onward to crown the race with glory.

What think you of such a gospel? Do you say that

its magnificence explains the mystery of Jesus? Granted; but what explains the magnificence of the gospel? Here is sublimity your Siddarthas never dreamed of, here are moral magnitudes your Buddhas never measured. Yet are these Hindu teachers so great that under their names we write "inspired," and exalt them far above all others of their race? What then shall we, what must we, write under the name of Him "who brought life and immortality to light," and how much higher than the highest shall we exalt Him? Faith answers, and reverent Reason says "Amen,"—"GOD OVER ALL, BLESSED FOREVERMORE."

To test the soundness of this stupendous inference, let us carry the grave inquiry into the following discourse; and it may come to pass that even captious and self-sufficient Doubt will recognize DIVINITY veiled and hooded in the humanity of Christ.

UNITARIANISM.

"And Pilate saith unto them: Behold the man!" *John xix, 5.*

" Like us a man, He trod on earthly soil,
He bore each pang, and strove in weary toil;
He spake with human words, with pity sighed;
Like us He mourned, and feared, and wept, and died."

" Yet all thy fullness, Father, dwelt in Him,
In whom no shadow made the glory dim;
Such strength, O God! from Him to us derive,
And make, by life from Him, our death alive."
John Sterling.

SOMETIMES words express more than their author intends, or are susceptible of a deeper meaning than he imagined when they fell from his lips. Thus when Caiaphas said that "it was expedient that one man should die for the people, and that the whole nation perish not," he had not the remotest idea that his language was prophetical, and that he was not only predicting the death of Jesus, but was actually shadowing forth its great design. Yet, if the apostle is to be credited, such was the case. And when Pontius Pilate, the sixth Roman procurator of Judea, a cold, cruel, calculating ruler, morally enervated and incapable of vigorous rectitude, after the scourging of the obscure Nazarene in the Prætorium, had brought Him once again into the presence of His furious accusers, hoping, by the pitiable spectacle of His sufferings, to excite compassion and obtain His liberation without compromising himself, he could not have anticipated that his exclamation, "Behold the man!" would form the text of many a sermon, and would be regarded as an unconscious tribute to an exclusive and exceptional personal grandeur in the prisoner worthy of attentive thought throughout successive generations. Yet this is exactly the impression made on many minds. The words of the governor are so concise and direct that, if the emphasis is laid on the definite article, his speech sounds like the voice of inspiration testifying to the unique, unprecedented, and unapproachable manhood of Jesus. It is as though he said: "Behold the flower of humanity, the bright consummation and circled completeness of the race, the one being who cannot be compared with any other, who is as high above all others as the heavens are higher than the earth, and who gathers in Himself and expresses in Himself the diverse excellences of all the generations past and of those yet to come. Behold Him, who should be called preëminently *the Man*, as in Him the ideal perfection, toward which countless weary souls have been struggling, is actualized; and the impossible dreams of spiritual beauty, which have haunted the minds of the noblest and the purest, are fulfilled." The proud Roman, of course, had no such thought as this when he presented the outraged Jesus to His enemies; but it occurs to us as we ponder his language, and it has come to be the faith of reflecting and reverent millions.

To the Unitarians the world is largely indebted for the elevated and now widely prevalent conception of Christ's manhood. There was a time when His character was painted in somber, threatening colors, that displayed the awfulness of majesty more than the sweetness of mercy. He was to the middle ages a harsh, implacable judge, a far-off, isolated king, whose reluctant benediction was only obtainable through the interposition of hearts more tender than His own. A few gifted souls discovered the injustice of such delineations, but the majority of Christian people adhered to them even after the Reformation. Protestant theology in its earlier stages reproduced them, modifying them slightly in some particulars, while it amplified them in others. The human figure it presented was morally sublime, but it was too mechanical in its splendid righteousness, too automatic in its wonderful beneficence, and too frigid, stiff, and angular in its saving sympathy for it to be a faithful portrait of the Redeemer. But with the growth of Unitarian sentiments the rigid lines of this likeness have been softened, its stateliness has been relaxed, and into the whole composition has been thrown a tender light, like that which gleams from the eyes of the infant Jesus and irradiates the faces of the cherubim in Raphael's Madonna di San Sisto. Herder and Channing, and possibly Theodore Parker, are entitled to much credit for this transformation; though in my opinion the more orthodox school, represented by such writers as Horace Bushnell and Frederick Robertson, is to be commended for recent endeavors in the same direction; and even the rationalists Strauss and Renan, have not failed to furnish some valuable material toward the completion of this work. But, while the labors of all are to be acknowledged, to Unitarians must be assigned the high honor of leadership in the movement to restore the true manhood of Jesus to the thought of the world. Whatever the shortcomings of their theology may be in other respects, at least in this it harmonizes very fully with the teachings of the New Testament; and however it may fail to generate a deep spirit of piety, it admirably succeeds in presenting to society the most exalted model of human duty. So impressed am I with what I recognize as their influence on literature, art, and philanthropy, that it is to me the most ungrateful of tasks to question the wholesome effect of their views on devotion and spirituality. Yet it will hardly be claimed by their most ardent admirers — and among them I venture to class myself — that in these latter respects their churches approach the standard supplied by the authors of the Gospels and Epistles. And if they do not, the failure must be largely due to some defect in their doctrine, and particularly to some radical inconsistency in their treatment of Christ's essential nature. This, I am persuaded, is more than a mere suspicion. There are reasons for believing that the most exalted conception of manhood does not exhaust the apparently infinite meaning there is in Christ; that it is at best but a fragment, a Torso requiring another and a sublimer conception for its completion, and which, like the Torso at Rome, while delighting and refining, must always fail to produce in mind and heart the same great effect that the unbroken figure would. It is just at this point where Unitarianism, especially of the advanced type, is seriously at fault. It takes for granted that the humanity of Jesus is the all of Jesus; that He is man and only man, and that when this is said everything is said.

But how can such a question as this be decided? How can it be shown that He who is the subject of these doubts is anything more than the crown and glory of the race — its supreme development, and its grandest representative? He appears in history as a man. He exhibits in His life all the essential attributes of a man, and at the last He suffers and dies as a man. Why, then, should it be imagined that He is anything higher? As it was said during his ministry, "Is not this the carpenter, the son of Mary, and brother of James, and Joses, and Judas, and Simon? and are not his sisters here with us?" Yes; and yet they who asked these questions were astounded by His wisdom and perplexed by His mighty works. They were not sure of their ground; neither are we. Permit then an additional inquiry. Why did the astronomer Leverrier affirm the existence of an unseen orb, and predict its appearance in the heavens at a certain time? And why was Christopher

Columbus so fully convinced that beyond the waste and darkness of unknown seas another continent would be found? The answer is not difficult. The student of the skies inferred from the irregular movements of the planet Uranus the existence of a disturbing body; and the brave navigator was led by what he knew of one hemisphere to infer the indispensableness of another. They reasoned from the known to the unknown, from the seen to the unseen, from the part to the whole, and the result in both cases justified the soundness of the process. And in a similar way evangelical thinkers, having fathomed the depths and scaled the heights of humanity, and having measured by sixty centuries of history what it is capable of producing, have been forced to conclude that such a manhood as friend and foe attribute to Christ is deeper than its depths, higher than its heights, and entirely beyond its power to generate; and consequently, that it calls for another and a more heavenly orb to explain its eccentric movements, for another and grander continent to balance the lowly one of earth, for another nature than the human to account for it rationally, even such a nature as that toward which the testimony of Scriptures manifestly points.

In pursuing this line of argument it is important to recall some special features of a character which favor so startling and astounding a doctrine. And among them there is perhaps none more impressive than its blamelessness. Jesus challenged his enemies to convict him of sin, and with the exception of a few querulous critics, like Schenkel and Strauss, the impossibility of doing so has been acknowledged. This at once differentiates Him from the race; for iniquity is a universal malady, from which not even the noblest philosophers, such as Plato and Socrates, and the purest of religious reformers, such as Buddha and Mahomet, have dared to claim exemption.

How comes it, then, that Jesus is the only being saved from this contamination? He appears in the world, and is yet not of the world; He mingles with publicans and harlots, and is yet "separate from sinners." As the gulf stream passes immediately from its home into the waters of the stormful Atlantic, and, while flowing through them, never mingles with them, but preserves its own course, its own density and color, compressed, inclosed, yet never penetrated, so the Son of Man enters the more treacherous and tempestuous ocean-wastes of life, and though touched on every side, never takes on the moral hue of his surroundings, nor in the least is swerved from the direct line of duty by their variations. Who can tell by what mystery of attraction the blue waters of the Gulf of Mexico are so closely bound, or who explain why the emerald walls through which their way is channeled should never be able to invade their sanctity, every effort to do so only pressing them into a ridge, rising high and sloping both to right and left? and who can account for the fact that this peasant-preacher not only preserves unstained his righteous character in an evil world like this, but even develops a loftier and grander righteousness the more closely he is hemmed in by wickedness and environed by temptation? It will not do to say that His personal exaltation was due to the healing influence of the age in which He lived, or to the surroundings of His youth, or to the training of His parents; for the times were morally malarious, and the community in which His lot was cast was famous for its degradation, and the home education He received was not at the best superior to that which millions have enjoyed. And yet, though His social environments were unfavorable to virtue, He evinces from the first a moral greatness, unequaled in the annals of mankind. Rousseau, alluding to Socrates, exclaims: "What a delusion it is to venture to compare the son of Sophroniskos with the Son of Mary!"

and multiplied endeavors have proved the hopelessness of finding a parallel anywhere. He stands alone among men, the sole perfection. The righteousness of others looks like the travesty of some sublime code, a poor attempt running into caricature, it is so flavored with inconsistencies, so flecked with evil; while that of Christ is so complete that it seems to be the very code itself translating itself into the vernacular of conduct. His purity as far excels that of the purest as the reflection of the sun's luster in the ocean transcends its dim sparkle in the stagnant pool; it is as superior to everything that claims kindred with it as the sun itself is superior to the stars whose mingled light it quenches in its flood of glory. Well, therefore, may it be confessed that He cannot without violence be classed with beings merely human; for while He is allied to them, and while He shares their nature, it is as one who is not of it, but above it.

Attention has frequently been directed to this particular trait of His character, and doubtless much more could be added; but there are others which have not been as fully considered, and which very strongly point toward the superhuman. Stress should be laid on His independence— an independence that marked alike His thought and His action. This, taken by itself, would hardly warrant the supposition of even preternatural manhood, for it is not an uncommon virtue; but, taken in connection with all the circumstances which surrounded Jesus, it forms a link in the chain of reasoning that apparently necessitates divinity. It is, to say the least of it, remarkable that a youthful member of a conquered race, who must have seen that his people were doing their utmost to conserve the good will of their masters, should have pursued his way in perfect indifference to their opinion. If it is suggested that He is but one of many heroes who have championed the cause of their distressed country, it should be remembered that these chosen leaders have always sympathized with the spirit and institutions of the land for whose sufferings they felt so deeply. This, however, is not true of Christ. He not only treads the earth as though there were no Romans, but He pursues His way as though there were no Jews. He antagonizes with the ideas, customs, rites, of His own people far more than He opposes the invader. In one sense, He seems to live in an atmosphere of oblivion, to speak and act from a deep realization of duty, unconscious and heedless of those whom He might offend. Of course, events made Him fully sensible of the enemies He was creating, but it worked no change in His manner or conduct. To the end He stood by His convictions, calmly listened to the revilings of His foes, and with the shadow of the cross on His path, continued to denounce their bigotry, their ceremonialism and self-righteousness. Having shocked his generation by proclaiming the equality of man, the spirituality of worship, the sacredness of charity, and the universal need of a Redeemer, He quietly surrenders His life, and in His last moments startles all who contemplate His sufferings by breathing the then unheard-of prayer: "Father, forgive them, they know not what they do." Such independence as this cannot be classed with that of the patriot, for the intense love of country which makes a hero mighty against his enemies also blinds him to its faults, and leads him to extenuate, not expose, them. Neither can it be accounted for by the spirit of the age, which was servile and calculating; nor can it be traced to the influence of royalty, as it might be in the case of Buddha, for Jesus was a peasant born, and had only a peasant's inspirations. Under these circumstances it is difficult to divest oneself of the impression that it is the sign of a superior nature, and possibly of a nature outranking in dignity every degree of creaturehood.

The ancient Egyptians rendered divine honors to the

Nile. Unlike other rivers, that sacred stream derives no addition to its fullness from humbler profluent tributaries, but is fed by hidden sources and by rains from heaven. It gives to the land through which it flows, and receives not in return. Unsustained, unsupplied, and unincreased by waters from the heart of Egypt, it proudly pursues its journey to the sea, enriching but not enriched. Its stately independence aroused the admiration of the millions who in olden times dwelt along its banks, and to their faith it assumed the sanctity of a god. On the verge of the glacier, planted among sterile rocks, surrounded by inhospitable snows, confronting defiantly ten long months of rigorous winter, the arolla lives, strives, and conquers. The hurricane cannot subdue it, the searching icy wind cannot penetrate it, the might of the avalanche cannot overwhelm it, and the fierce frost that rends the granite cannot cleave its sinewy trunk. Upon what does it feed? from what does it derive its strength? by what is it supported in a region where other plants find only death? Light! the rays of the sun nourish and comfort it in its deary solitude. Not from the earth but from the heavens it receives its aliment, which it appropriates to itself, incorporating the subtle power of sunbeams into its own vitality. And why may not this lonely Jesus, this solitary man, who poured the wealth of his love on an unappreciating and unresponsive world, who streamed through its barren wastes bearing spiritual healing and plenty to its desolate millions, and who received nothing in return and who sought nothing, have descended from heights grander than those in which the origin of the Nile is hidden, and have sustained a closer relation to the Everlasting Father than that sacred river to the rain-dispensing clouds? And why may not He, fittingly called by the inspired prophet "a root out of dry ground," whose barren and wintry surroundings threatened to crush and to destroy, but who amid the human tempest lifted high His head, and dauntlessly spoke His message, have been upheld and rendered free of fear through the indwelling of a Light surpassing the sun in power and radiance, and why may not His affinity for that Light — which here shall not be named — proclaim a nature more deeply allied to the inner glory of the heavens than to the weakness and shame of earth?

If we associate with the independence of Jesus His infallibility, these conjectures will gather additional force, and may lead us to the truth. As His biography is studied, His profound insight into men and things and His foresight of particular and general movements cannot be overlooked. The reader hardly knows which to admire most, His spirit of penetration or His spirit of prophecy; His vision that discerns the hidden thoughts of His contemporaries, or that which sees through the vista of ages the end from the beginning. But from whatever side it is contemplated, His infallibility is undeniable. He made no mistakes. It cannot be shown that on any occasion He fell into errors of speech or of conduct. He was always accurate, always correct, always right. No necessity has arisen in the course of eighteen centuries to revise His teachings or to apologize for His predictions. They have both vindicated themselves; the first, by their adaptation to man's spiritual needs; the second, whether relating to the fall of Jerusalem, the progress of Christianity, or to the march of empire by their fulfillment in history. Other men have been inspired, and have uttered truths concerning the present and the future, but none who, in every respect, in conduct as well as in preaching, in personal as well as in public affairs, has been absolutely unerring. Your Johns, your Pauls and Peters were not exempt from infirmities, or saved from the commission of serious blunders. It would seem as though the Infinite Spirit had painted faithfully their career, that all might see that even inspired men are not infallible men, and that the only infallible man known to the world is Jesus — and such being the case, that it is very questionable whether it is admissible to speak of Him as man at all.

The wonderful influence of our Savior is calculated to aid us in arriving at a reliable conclusion on this point. Christ in subsequent history is more marvelous than Christ in Galilee. Since the removal of His human presence He has wrought more stupendous miracles than He performed in Syria. There and then he simply opened the eyes of a few blind men, restored to health some who were sick, fed occasionally a hungry crowd, and raised an inconsiderable number from the dead; but since His ascension He has removed from nations the veil of mental darkness, has imparted moral health to entire communities, has satisfied the longings of millions for the imperishable bread, and has rescued tribes, races and peoples from the dreariness of spiritual death. For some eighteen hundred years He has been the real leader of the world's progress. Its majestic movements, surprising revolutions, startling reformations, upheavals, convulsions and transformations are traceable to the power of His name. And for what yet grander results may we not hope from this apparently exhaustless source? Plato said that "beauty is the reflection of truth," and it is equally safe to say that truth is the reflection of God. In Christ it shone supremely, and before His presence the night of nights could not endure. As the Scriptures represent Him, like the sun He rose upon the world and began His triumphant journey, "rejoicing as a strong man to run a race." But the zenith has not been reached; it is not high noon yet. Already His celestial rays, falling on the horrible brood of superstitions engendered by weary years of mud and slime, have inflicted on them a mortal wound, as in the legend the burning shafts of the god of day destroyed the pernicious offspring of many-folded Python. Already the mists and vapors, born of the turbid seas of human error, and which once obscured the heavens, He has dispersed, and faintly at least the gates of the Holy City can be seen. Already the clouds of suffering are transfused by His love, and the silver lining can be discovered, prophetic of the hour when every shadow shall cease to fall on human lives. Even now His burning splendor melts the sunless heart, gently opens the sleeping eyes of childhood to the high concerns of an eternal scene, and calls the weary pilgrim to the blessed song of hope; but by and by He who is shining more and more shall bring the perfect day, and then the weeping that endures for the night shall cease, and joy, endless, world-wide joy, shall come with the eternal morning. Lecky, in his *History of European Morals*, calls attention to this potent and boundless influence in these vigorous words: "It was reserved for Christianity to present to the world an ideal character, which through all the changes of eighteen centuries has inspired the hearts of men with an impassioned love, has shown itself capable of acting on all ages, nations, temperaments and conditions, has been not only the highest pattern of virtue, but the strongest incentive to its practice, and has exercised so deep an influence that it may be truly said that the simple record of these three short years of active life has done more to regenerate and soften mankind than all the disquisitions of philosophers and all the exhortations of moralists. This has been the well-spring of whatever is best and purest in the Christian life." But who is this Being of whom an avowed rationalist is constrained to speak in these unmeasured terms? Surely not a mere creature like himself; surely not an empty ideal, a beautiful fiction. And who or what is He who in so brief an earthly ministry acquired such tremendous, lasting and beneficent power over the destinies of mankind?

Before I undertake to formulate the answer you already anticipate, permit me to emphasize the significant fact that the most diverse, not to say adverse, schools of thought have conceded the inscrutableness of Christ's manhood. Rugged Carlyle, who, whatever may have been his faults, could appreciate nobility of soul, and who protested all his life against shams, acknowledged the impenetrableness of Jesus. He studied Him; he tried to fathom the depth of His mystery, and concluded that He would ever remain unfathomed and unfathomable. Hear him in his chapter on *Symbols:* "Highest of all symbols are those wherein the artist or poet has risen into prophet. . . . I mean religious symbols. Various enough have been such religious symbols, what we call *religious*. . . . If thou ask to what height man has carried it in this matter look on our divinest symbol,— on Jesus of Nazareth, and His life and His biography, and what followed therefrom. Higher has the human thought not yet reached; this is Christianity and Christendom; a symbol of quite perennial, infinite character, whose significance will ever demand to be anew inquired into, and anew made manifest." Speaking of heroes he says: "Hero worship, heartfelt, prostrate admiration, submissive, burning, boundless, for a noblest godlike form of man: is not that the germ of Christianity itself? *The greatest of all heroes is one whom we do not name here.* Let sacred silence meditate that sacred truth; you will find it the *ultimate perfection* of a principle extant throughout man's whole history on earth." Dr. Channing maintained that "such a character utterly surpasses human comprehension." Napoleon is credited by Abbott with this thoughtful expression: "The nature of Christ is, I grant it, from one end to another a web of mysteries; but this mysteriousness does not correspond to the difficulties which all existence contains." That is, in it he sees something more perplexing than is offered to the mind by all other orders of being. John Stuart Mill, who explicitly denies Christ's Divinity, yet in his posthumous book on the *Utility of Religion and Theism* writes of Him in the following glowing terms: "The most valuable part of the effect on the character which Christianity has produced by holding up in a divine person a standard of excellence and a model for imitation, is available even to the absolute unbeliever, and can never more be lost to humanity. For it is Christ rather than God whom Christianity has held up to believers as the pattern of perfection for humanity. It is the God incarnate, more than the God of the Jews, or of nature, who, being idealized, has taken so great and salutary a hold on the modern mind. And whatever else may be taken away by rational criticism Christ is still left, a unique figure, not more unlike His precursors than all His followers, even those who had the direct benefit of His personal teaching. It is of no use to say that Christ, as exhibited in the gospels, is not historical, and that we know not how much of what is admirable has been superadded by the tradition of His followers. The tradition of followers suffices to insert any number of marvels, and may have inserted all the miracles which He is reputed to have wrought. But who among His disciples, or among their proselytes, was capable of inventing the sayings ascribed to Jesus, or of imagining the life and character revealed in the gospels? Certainly not the fishermen of Galilee; as certainly not St. Paul, whose character and idiosyncrasies were of a totally different sort; still less the early Christian writers, in whom nothing is more evident than that the good which was in them was all derived, as they always professed that it was derived, from the highest source." Evidently Mr. Mill is perplexed. This Jesus is not an invention, He is a grand reality; but how He ever came to be what He is Mr. Mill cannot tell. The problem is too intricate for him. He stammers and falls dumb before it. And Theodore Parker, equally bewildered, when referring to the labors of the primitive disciples, asks: "But eighteen centuries have passed since the sun of humanity rose so high in Jesus; what man, what sect, has mastered His thought, comprehended His method, and so fully applied it to life?" Unquestionably they are right. He is the puzzle and problem of ages, before whom all tongues are mute. As man never spake like Him, so man never lived like Him. The geodetics of philosophy, and the surveyings and weighings of rationalism, fail to give us His true figure and His moral dimensions. His spiritual stature defies our yard-sticks and other instruments of human measurement; and when we have done our best to dwarf Him to the narrow range of our understanding, which is attempted by subtracting from Him in the interest of some poor earthly hypothesis certain graces and powers usually attributed to Him,— we find ourselves still uttering words similar to those written by Renan, when having undertaken this herculean task he exclaims: "Repose now in thy glory, noble founder! Thy work is finished, thy divinity is established. . . . Whatever may be the surprises of the future, Jesus will never be surpassed."

But is there no explanation? Are all inquiries to be baffled, all efforts to unravel the riddle to be unavailing? Are we perpetually to feel the wondrous presence of this mighty Being, and never be able to decide whether He is merely human or essentially Divine? It is incredible that the All-Father should have destined us to this uncertainty and that there should be no clew to the mystery. I for one am compelled to believe otherwise, and cannot resist the logical force of the testimonies borne by reluctant witnesses to this amazing manhood. When Celsus sneers at Christ's predictions regarding the universal spread of His religion, which, however, have been fulfilled; when Chubb acknowledges that we have in Him "an example of a quiet and peaceable spirit, of a becoming modesty and sobriety, just, honest, upright, and sincere," qualities, mark you, that this wicked world of ours does not evince any strong liking for; when Goethe says to Eckermann, "I look upon all the Four Gospels as thoroughly genuine, for there is in them the reflection of a greatness which emanated from the person of Jesus and which was of as divine a kind as ever was seen upon earth," and when Strauss declares that "Christ remains the highest model of religion within the reach of our thought," and "that no perfect piety is possible without His presence in the heart," representations wholly inexplicable on the Unitarian hypothesis, I am constrained to inquire, exclaim, and conclude with Rousseau: "Is it possible that the sacred personage, whose history the Bible contains, should be Himself a mere man? What sweetness, what purity in His manner! What an affecting gracefulness in His instructions! What sublimity in His maxims! What profound wisdom in His discourses! If the life and the death of Socrates are those of a sage, the life and death of Jesus are those of a God." And in view of these concessions, uttered by Unitarians or by those who sympathize with their doctrine concerning the merely human nature of our Lord, I cannot but subscribe to the essentially orthodox statement of James Martineau, the prince of Unitarians, albeit his beautiful words may suggest to my thought a higher meaning than he intended to convey: "Not more clearly does the worship of the saintly soul, breathing through its windows opened to the midnight, betray the secrets of its affections, than the mind of Jesus of Nazareth reveals the perfect thought and inmost love of the all-ruling God. Were He the only born—the solitary self-revelation—of the creative Spirit, He could not more purely open the mind of heaven; being the very Logos—the apprehensible nature of God—which, long unuttered to the world, and abiding in the beginning with Him, has now come forth and dwelt among us, full of grace and truth." Thus all these varied writers, starting from different points of view and pursuing widely divergent routes, arrive at conclusions which are plainly irreconcilable with what they profess to hold. Nor is it possible if they are rejected to make of Christianity a consistent system, or consistently to account for Christ Himself; but, as the great Napoleon is reported by Abbott to have said, "If once the divine character of Christ is admitted, Christian doctrine"—including that of His manhood as well—"exhibits the precision and clearness of algebra, so that we are struck with admiration of its scientific connection and unity."

It is no small source of satisfaction that faith in His Godhood seems to be fully sustained by Holy Writ. Our Lord Himself sanctions it and the apostles confirm it. It is true that the title "Son of Man" is that by which He specifically designates Himself. In the Gospels it occurs sixty times, once in the Acts, and never in the Epistles. But why does He not call Himself "Son of Joseph," or "Son of Mary," or "Son of Israel"? A merely human being desiring to impose on the world might insist on his divinity, but he would hardly feel it needful to remind the people of his humanity. That would be the first thing credited. But Jesus seems to be conscious of a nature broader and grander than this term describes, and is apprehensive that His manifest Godhood will obscure His manhood, and consequently He draws attention specially to the latter. But in doing so He rejects the limitations of tribe, family, and nation, and adopts the title "Son of Man," as expressive of His identity with the race and of His representative character and mission. He does not, however, ignore His divinity. In Matthew xvi, when He inquires of His disciples, "Whom do men say that I, the Son of Man, am?" he accepts the answer of Peter as correct: "Thou art the Christ, the Son of the living God." He constantly affirms His preëxistence (John iii, 13; vi, 58; viii and xvi); He claims to have life in Himself, and to be one with the Father (John v, 26; x, 30, 38; xvii), and, moreover, asserts that He is Himself the very presence of the Highest: "He that hath seen me hath seen the Father."

These startling assumptions appear to have met with uniform acceptance in the apostolic period. In the Old Testament also there is a frequent association of the human with the divine. The marvelous vision seen by Ezekiel of wheels within wheels, of the living creatures, and of the sapphire throne above the firmament of crystal, was pervaded with this union throughout. The prevailing form of the celestial beings was that of man; they had the face of a man in conjunction with the faces of a lion, eagle and ox; and on their four sides were seen the hands of a man, while "upon the throne was the likeness as the appearance of a man above it." Whatever may be the total import of such pictures, they evidently suggested the incarnation and the exaltation of the Incarnate One to supreme dominion. Such hieroglyphical intimations must have prepared the religious world for the reception of Christ's claims, and I am not, therefore, surprised to find the apostles advocating them very earnestly. In the epistles, especially in those addressed to the Philippians, Colossians, and Ephesians, the Savior is presented as the One Being in whom all things in grace, in redemption, and in glory are infolded. He is exalted as the source of all worlds visible and invisible, and of all creatures, earthly and heavenly; He is also "head over all things," "because in Him all the fullness of the Godhead dwells."

"Henceforth he is known no more after the flesh"; and He is approached in prayer and praise as God (Acts vii, 59; Rev. xxii, 20), the worship by which, in subsequent times, according to Pliny and Eusebius, the disciples were distinguished. Nor has their faith failed of justification at the hands of philosophers, who are not fairly chargeable either with the credulity of superstition or the weakness of enthusiasm. I do not profess to interpret Hegel, but that profound thinker evidently means to teach something akin to the Christian doctrine of the Incarnation when in his *Philosophy of History* he says: "Christ has appeared—a man who is God—God who is man; and thereby peace and reconciliation have accrued to the world." To this he adds, "The appearance of the Christian God involves further its being unique in its kind; it can occur only once." And Schelling, claiming that the incarnation beginning with the Savior is to be continued in His followers, yet insists that God truly manifested Himself first in Christ. For, as another German has testified, "the incarnation was complete in Him, and He has therefore the significance of a personal moral creator of the world."

If anything more is needed to confirm this sublime doctrine to our faith, it is furnished by the light which it sheds on the otherwise enigmatical phases of our religion. For instance it shows why, as Schelling has it, "the chief matter of Christianity is Christ Himself, not what He said, but what He is, what He did." Were He only man, it would ever remain a mystery why the apostles should "desire to know nothing but Him," why they should reject every other foundation, why they should magnify Him as the "All and in All" to the race, and why they should exalt Him as the being in whom supreme trust should be reposed. Yet this they do continually and unhesitatingly, as though nothing were more reasonable and nothing more natural. When discoursing on worship they enthrone Christ as its glorious object; when dealing with sin and guilt they turn to Christ as atonement and as interceding priest; when seeking a rule of conduct they find it in Christ's teachings and example; and when feeling after signs of immortality they lay hold on Christ's resurrection both as the pledge of its certainty and the pattern of its beauty. He is presented by them as the "Bread of Life," as the "Water of Life," as the "Dayspring from on High," as the "Morning Star," as the "Sun of Righteousness," as the "Light of the World," as the "Ransom," "Mediator," "Advocate," "Deliverer," as the "Lord of Lords" and "King of Kings," expressions and descriptions which we try in vain to reconcile with creaturehood; but which when divine honors are ascribed to His name we can understand, and, in doing so, clearly perceive why the disciples, like Zinzendorf, "made this Supreme Power in heaven and on earth the only theme they announced, taught in their writings, and treated at length."

Moreover, this view of our Lord's nature throws light on the meaning of the Cross. An old chronicler relates that a Jew in the sixth century fled for refuge from night and storm to an abandoned temple of Apollo. But at midnight the building was filled with ghastly, gigantic shapes. They moved to and fro in the somber darkness, taking counsel of each other, and relating their achievements against the Christians. These were the shadows of the former gods, the pagan deities whose altars had been forsaken. The poor Jew trembled as he beheld them, and in his despair, hardly knowing what he did, made the sign of the cross. Before its sacred and mysterious potency in their turn the demons shuddered, whirled about in maddened fear, and hastily vanished in the gloom. This, of course, is but a fable; and yet it has a spiritual counterpart. The real temple seen by the musty scribe is the soul, within whose sacred but polluted courts conscience, awe-stricken at the foul thoughts, appetites and lusts which revive when we think them dead, and rage when we suppose them bound, trembles and cries for swift deliverance. It is obtained through the cross. When that is embraced, when it is sacred to the soul, then the sense of sin is purged away, and the spectral shapes of evil are dispersed. This has been the experience of millions. But to what does the tragedy of Calvary owe this wondrous power? Nail to the tree the body of a man — only a man, though the best and purest — and the problem is unsolved. He could only die for himself, and none other; and his death could have no more influence than that of others like himself. But let the human sacrifice be sanctified by the divine presence, let it be the earthly expression of God's devotion to the moral order of the universe and to the redemption of the guilty, and it acquires a new meaning, and an explicable moral force.

Christ's Divinity also accounts for His exaltation to the right hand of God, justifies the worship of angels and the confidence of mankind. It makes clear His right to the throne of the universe, and enables the mind to understand why He is exalted in providence, in grace, and in judgment. It is the unifying truth that harmonizes all other teachings of Christianity and renders the entire system symmetrical and complete. And, finally, it is the truth of all others that renders the obligation of the sinner distinct and solemn. In dealing with Christ he is dealing with God. It is not a mere human being that stands at the door of the heart, gently pleading for admission. He that is seeking entrance, who has been seeking through long, weary years, and to whom cold ingratitude has repeatedly said "to-morrow," is not a mere earth-born creature, but the Lord of all. To reject Him is to reject God, and to reject God is to accept despair. Then, how clear our duty! Were He but a man we might reasonably pause, question His claims, and hesitate to admit Him to the inner sanctuary of our being; but, as He is "God over all, blessed forevermore," every obstacle should yield, every hindrance be removed, and the King of Glory be welcomed to His own. Let this duty be performed. Cry to thy soul: "Lift up thy heads, O ye gates! and the King of glory shall enter in;" and with that Divine incoming, righteousness and peace, joy and hope, yea, heaven upon earth, shall be sweetly realized.

It is with reluctance that I bring this inquiry to a close. The portrait drawn is too faulty and imperfect for it to afford me entire satisfaction. Yet such as it is I can invoke God's blessing on it; for it was undertaken in His fear, and, however inadequate, is in accordance with His Word. Tradition records many interesting stories regarding the magnificent masterpiece of the sculptor Phidias. Out of the solid marble he shaped a wondrous image of the mighty Jupiter. The brow of the god was so noble, so fate-deciding seemed "the ambrosial locks" that clustered round it, so majestic his mien, and so commanding his presence, that they who beheld the work of the artist were lightened of care, were relieved of sorrow, and were so enchanted that they were willing to make long pilgrimages for the pleasure of viewing it again. Among other legends is found one of surpassing beauty touching the creator of this famous statue. It is said that when he had finished his labors and thoughtfully contemplated the result, he raised his hands in prayer to Jupiter and sought for an approving sign if what he had done was acceptable to him. The "Thunderer" replied. As Phidias stood with uplifted hands a gleam of lightning flashed suddenly through the roof of the temple, and for a moment played upon the sacred floor. Then he knew his toil had not been in vain. Thus do I meditate, though not with the exultant satisfaction of the sculptor, the unworthy counterpart of Christ which these rude words of mine have fashioned. I know the likeness is sadly inferior to the sublime original; yet such as it is, I implore some token that it is not displeasing to Him whose name is dear to my poor heart, and will be so forever. And if from His holy throne the fire that descended on the apostles when Pentecost was fully come shall rest on you, my reader, irradiating the temple of the soul, and from its altar flash in flame of righteousness, the response I seek will be vouchsafed and my reward will be complete.

SPIRITUALISM.

"If they hear not Moses and the prophets, neither will they be persuaded, though one rose from the dead." *Luke xvi, 31.*

"The oracles are dumb;
No voice of hideous hum
Runs through the arched roof in words deceiving.
Apollo from his shrine
Can no more divine,
With hollow shriek, the steep of Delphos leaving.
No nightly trance or breathed spell
Inspires the pale-eyed priests from the prophetic cell."
Milton.

WHETHER history or parable, this Scripture inforces a very solemn and salutary lesson. Dives, the representative of Godless affluence, when reaping the fiery whirlwind of his folly, calls on Father Abraham to mitigate his terrible agony, and to send Lazarus, if not to himself, at least to his five surviving brothers, that they may be dissuaded from coming to the place of torment. The sufferer is reminded that they who live on earth have Moses and the prophets for their guidance; or, in other words, enjoy the light of a heavenly revelation, and should give heed to its influence and instruction. But to this suggestion the rich man replies: "If one went unto them from the dead they would repent." He seems to feel that a little special supernaturalism judiciously displayed in the interest of his brethren, a few ghosts effectively materialized and sent from the spirit realm, would arrest attention and would necessarily promote reformation. Spectral appearances, he doubtless thought, would overawe and alarm the indifferent, and a message from their phantom lips would decide them to embrace religion. In "the visions of the night, when deep sleep falleth on men," had not a spirit passed before the face of Eliphaz, the Temanite, and did not fear come on him, and his bones shake, as the solemn silence was broken by the strange voice inquiring: "Shall mortal man be more just than God? Shall a man be more pure than his Maker?" If so, why might not other shadowy messengers be sent to earth with profit, and be equally successful in impressing mortals with the reality of things eternal? Some such line of argument probably occurred to Dives; but instead of its soundness being recognized in Hades, he is answered: "If they hear not Moses and the prophets, neither will they be persuaded though one rose from the dead;" words that express clearly and explicitly the absolute sufficiency of the Inspired Books for life and godliness.

It is, however, to be observed that the Savior in this declaration does not deny the possibility of the dead returning, under certain circumstances, to influence the living; neither does the Bible commit itself to any such denial. Indeed, its stringent laws against invoking their presence, and its wide-sweeping condemnation of all who attempt to bring them back, or who, impelled by idle curiosity, seek intercourse with them, seem to imply that those who have gone before may revisit and minister to friends on earth under conditions determined solely by the Almighty. We know that Moses and Elias were with Christ on the Mount of Transfiguration, and that, when He arose from the tomb, many of the saints came with Him, and were seen in Jerusalem. Moreover, the apostle Paul, having described the faith of God's heroes, assures the Hebrews that they are surrounded by a great cloud of witnesses, evidently referring to those of whom he has been writing so eloquently, and who, though dead, are thus represented as feeling an interest in the career of all who are following on to know the Lord. Nor is it altogether incredible that such exalted beings, freed from the trammels of earthly life, should sometimes mingle with mortals whom they love, and who are yet exposed to sin and danger. Why may not the mother, through the misty veil that hides the seen from the unseen, find a way to direct the footsteps of her friendless child? Why may not lamented dear ones, whose visible forms have crumbled into dust, still in spirit linger with us here, and, though unrecognized, assist us in our progress to the skies? Of course, much can be said against this view, but much, also, can be said in its favor, though probably not enough on either side to establish a positive conviction. Our Savior, in the parable, gives no information on the subject. He neither affirms nor denies, just as He expresses no opinion at this time on the kindred doctrine of angelic and demoniac influences. On this latter topic, however, on other occasions He speaks clearly; and from the tenor of His ministry, as well as from the testimony of the apostles, we learn that angels and devils stream into our world, and bring to bear on humanity the beneficence of heaven or the maleficence of hell.

Lavater, as cited by Kurtz, declares "that all known material elements enter into the composition of the body, and all discernible spiritual faculties manifest themselves in the constitution of the soul, so that man is thus necessarily related to the visible and the invisible, to all things and all beings, not even excepting God himself." Constellations and galaxies transmit their fires to his thought, and magnetic currents from earth and sky flash along the nerve-wires of his wondrous organism. Suns, planets, and all the elemental material of this restless globe, are held in solution in his blood as it surges on its ministry of life and health. Atmospheres are the exhaustless fountains which slake his thirst, that support him with their might, and that carry to him on their tireless energies the beneficence of remotest spheres, and waft from him the asphyxial malaria which perpetually threatens his existence. Man is as it were the meeting-place of waters, the bay toward which all tides, physical and spiritual, incline, the recipient and exponent of the universe, the exotery of its esoterics, the crown of its greatness, and the shekinah of its glory. And if, therefore, we may believe with Bulwer-Lytton that, as "millions and myriads" of lives "dwell in the rivers of man's blood, and inhabit his frame as he inhabits earth," so "the circumfluent, infinite and boundless impalpable which we call space" must be "filled with its corresponding and appropriate life," "creatures of surpassing wisdom, or of horrible malignity, some of whom are hostile as fiends to men, and others as gentle as messengers between earth and heaven," we cannot deny the possibility of what Swedenborg taught, and what unimpassioned and inexcitable thousands among the devout have credited, "that man may be instructed by spirits and angels, may be in company with them, and converse with them face to face." The possibility of such mysterious intercourse I would not for a moment presume to question. Man being what he is, and the universe being what it is, I think this commerce highly probable, and it may be necessary to explain many things in our personal experience, and in that of others, such as is recorded in Owen's *Footfalls on the Boundaries of Other Worlds* and Howitt's *History of the Supernatural*. But our Savior, in the parable which gives character to our present study, does not touch on these marvelous matters; nor does it come within the scope of my proposed inquiry to discuss them. He passes by them as irrelevant and extraneous, His immediate object being to emphasize the practical sufficiency of the Holy Scriptures. He teaches clearly and specifically that, having God's Word, the race has everything that it really needs for moral and religious guidance, and that all the sleepers in the sepulcher, and all the shades in Hades, could they by any process be recalled to earth, whatever they might do for human comfort and human progress would not bring with them either increase of knowledge or of spiritual power. This is my own conviction, and its reasonableness will, I think, appear in the course of this discussion.

The human mind has not always been favorably disposed toward so conservative a belief. From time immemorial it has not been entirely willing that God's supreme wisdom should decide how far, if at all, the spectral world should hold communion with this mundane sphere; neither has it been content to leave unexplored the mysterious continent, which He has veiled from mortal sight, and which he has fortified against irreverent curiosity. The boundaries of the undiscovered country have repeatedly been trodden by restless inquisitiveness, anxious to catch the sound of supernatural footfalls, and to learn from spirit tongues what shall be in the future here, or what makes up the wonders of the never-changing hereafter. To go no farther back than the palmy days of Greece, we meet with instances innumerable of attempted intercourse with the dead. Among the people of that cultivated nation, temples, called Plutonia, were consecrated to this object. Within their walls it was professedly maintained between the souls of former and existing generations. Rites conducive to such interchange of thought and influence were established and scrupulously observed; but by what theurgy, sortilege, or incantatory hocus-pocus the deception succeeded as it did we have now no means of determining. Maximus Tyrius throws a little light on the ceremonies connected with Grecian necromancy where he writes: "There was a place near Lake Avernus called the prophetic cavern. Persons were in attendance there who called up ghosts. Anyone desiring it came thither, and, having killed a victim and poured out libations, summoned whatever ghost he wanted. The ghost came very faint and doubtful to the sight, but vocal and prophetic; and, having answered the questions, went off." Considerable sums of money were also spent in obtaining the spectral ear, and the profits of those who engaged in the business—the professional go-betweens—were simply enormous. In Israel this species of superstition was not unpracticed. Saul sought an interview with the shade of Samuel; and some writers, among whom may be named Sir Henry More, believe that his desire was really gratified. But be that as it may, the rigid enactments against every kind of divination go to prove how strong a hold it had upon certain classes, and how difficult it was to convince them of its sinfulness and folly.

One of the poets has the thought:

> "If ancestry can be in aught believed,
> Descending spirits have conversed with man
> And told him secrets of the world unknown."

Unfortunately they have been too implicitly credited, beyond even the warrant of facts, and hence many of our contemporaries clamor at the gates of the Invisible for fresh communications and new revelations. Unwilling to receive merely what graciously may be conferred, they imagine they have the power to wring from spirit-hearts the secret of their dwelling-place. And this, too, in an age that assumes to be remarkably free from bondage to superstition; and what is even more singular, they who most greedily swallow every marvelous story about ghosts are least disposed to recognize the divine origin of the Bible. In the name of reason they reject a supernaturally given book, and at the next moment, with a credulity becoming a Weddah of Ceylon, they surrender their judgment captive to some contemptible school of magic.

As Dr. Carpenter says, "The greatest skeptics in religion are the most credulous in other matters." They are generally like the lady to whom he refers, ready to receive anything that is not in the Bible. Not a few among our Roman Catholic friends believe that they are authorized to pray to the sainted dead, and that the Virgin Mary is especially accessible to their supplications. I have great respect for many who cherish this conviction; but, after all,. the line that separates it from ancient necromancy is very indistinct. It is the old black art baptised and rechristened, in which spiritual solicitations are substituted for spells and sorceries. That departed friends may be made by God the medium of blessings to the living is not the objectionable feature of the doctrine, for the possibility of this is candidly conceded; it is the underlying assumption that mortal entreaties can determine the movements of immortal beings, causing them to reappear among the faithful, that is so repugnant to the higher reason, and irreconcilable with the Inspired Word. It makes the dead servants to the living. It converts the Virgin into a very restless, busy soul, wandering from place to place for the sake of rewarding her devotees with a sight of her pale and hazy person; it changes the beatified into phantom tramps, peripatetic shades, spectral gossips, whose earthly peregrinations are controlled exclusively by the church and her members, and for their benefit.

Spiritualism is the latest and most pronounced development of this morbid and mortuary superstition. Its multiplied adherents regard its rejection by Christians, who believe in the supernatural, as inexplicable and indefensible. They affect not to understand the reasons which influence these disciples, and they generally fail to account fairly for their alleged inconsistency. If I may be permitted to speak for these misapprehended, not to say maligned, skeptics, I venture the assertion that they are not actuated by doubt as to the reality of the supernatural, and neither are they swayed by devotion to mere materialistic theories. The wonderful results which have been brought about in the name of this Ism they are not disposed to ignore; they are willing to admit that they cannot explain them all by laws or forces fully known at present; but they insist that the explanations of those who constantly resort to the marvelous are equally unsubstantial and unsatisfactory. They likewise object to this apparitional hypothesis, that it is an endeavor to organize a sect or religion, a science or philosophy, on a principle condemned alike by Scripture and the sober judgment of mankind. The principle, if in reality it deserves the name, is that human action is only the reflex of spiritual action, and that by a species of legerdemain and of cheap wizardry the relation which the one sustains to the other can be ascertained, and the dead be invoked and governed by shrewd manipulators in the interests of the living. Christians cannot but look on such a system as essentially deceptive, as a kind of charlatanism, as the residuum of former attempts at worthless magic, and as the black art scantily disguised and slightly modernized. As a philosophy they find it proclaiming the crudest metaphysics, consisting of cloudy notions and easily corrigible errors; as a science they perceive that it is little better than a farrago of ghoulish stories, accepted on the slimmest evidence, and wrought out fancifully and vaguely; and as a religion it is to them a mixture of puerility and stolidity, a superficial, superfluous and superstitious speculation. To embody their criticisms in the form of propositions, they maintain, what I shall attempt to make good,—

First, That the alleged marvels of Spiritualism are unverifiable, and, therefore, are unentitled to confidence.

Second, That the so-called revelations of Spiritualism

are unimportant, and, therefore, are undeserving of consideration.

Third, That the practical bearings of Spiritualism are unbeneficial, and, therefore, are unworthy of countenance.

In discussing the first of these propositions, let it not be forgotten that the extraordinary occurrences which distinguish this phantasmal Ism are not without parallels in the past. They are not new. Many of them were witnessed in other ages, and have been chronicled for our instruction. According to Ammianus Marcellinus, as quoted by Mr. D. D. Home, the ancients employed a small table for purposes of divination; and Planchettes, with their attendant phenomena, are no novelty among the Chinese. The reported transfiguration of Imblichus was just as wonderful and just as credible as modern materializations. Among the Greeks and Romans the black art was surrounded with what appeared to the credulous miraculous attestations; and even at this remote period we find it difficult to account for them on any other hypothesis. And yet, thoughtful men who lived in those times did not hesitate to ascribe them to fraud and trickery, or to natural means, the secret of which was confined to a few initiated individuals. Juvenal satirized all superhuman communications, and argued that belief in their reality was really due to ignorance of the nervous principle, which enabled the practiced fortune-teller to gain a knowledge of the thought in the mind of those who consulted him. Horace ridiculed those who gave heed to spiritual manifestations, and characterized them as diseased and fanatical. The Cumæan sibyl tells the Trojan Æneas as much about his family as any modern medium could; and from the shade of his father, Anchises, he receives responses as remarkable as any that have ever purported to come from the dead in our day; and yet the poet Virgil, who describes it all, does not seem to have confidence in this kind of supernaturalism; for he calls the maiden possessed of prophetic frenzy "deranged in intellect." Pliny, the naturalist, is also instructive on these points, for, while he admits some shade of truth in the mystic art, he attributes its phenomena mainly to physical causes. At last even the common people abandoned pagan temple and necromancer's cavern, satisfied that, while they could not explain the strange things enacted, there was more of imposture connected with them than could be reconciled with their superhuman claims. Nearer to our own times we have the witchcraft craze, which was attended by marvels, traceable, according to the testimony of such men as Lord Bacon, Sir Matthew Hale, Bishop Jewell and Addison to occult agencies. Among the wonders that marked this excitement we have unaccountable movements of various objects, such as chests, beds, and smaller articles; rappings, scratchings, and drummings; sounds as of steps on the floor, or of clattering chairs and stools, and the transportation of possessed persons, supposed to be on their way to demoniacal festivities. Ignorant people and people of small mental capacity were suddenly qualified to speak with grace and intelligence; others exhibited mysterious knowledge, similar to that which is often met with in modern clairvoyants; and yet others confessed to having seen specters with their eyes shut as well as open. Fuller information than can be given here on this interesting subject may be obtained from Lecky's *History of Rationalism*, Mather's *Magnalia*, Chamberline's *Stone-throwing Devil*, Bancroft's *United States*, and from a curious book published in 1852, entitled *To Daimonion*. That this entire movement was marked by astounding events no one familiar with it will deny, but that it can only be explained by recourse to the supernatural very few will admit. Self-deception, nervous disorder, the operation of unknown physical forces, even a measure of fraud, can more readily be believed than that. There is something so inherently incredible in the supposition that all these eccentric and useless occurrences were the work of devils or of ghosts that the mind hesitates to give it entertainment. And if it is obliged to reject such an account as untenable, is it not reasonable to conclude that similar wonders in our own day may be explicable on some other hypothesis than that of spirit agency?

That such an origin is at least unverifiable is proven by the impostures which continually are being perpetrated in the name of this Ism. Even the very elect are deceived. The trickery employed is so cunningly devised and cleverly executed that the most devout sympathizers hardly know how to separate the wheat from the chaff. The materializations which took place in Philadelphia some years since will readily be recalled. Hands which shone like phosphorus appeared, and did not seem to be attached to any body; and the alleged spirit who came most frequently from the cabinet was clothed in shining raiment that reminded Mr. Owen of the Savior's transfiguration. Before all eyes this phantom faded away, or was seen to float in the air. During many sittings Mr. Owen and Dr. Childs applied every test to determine the real character of the phenomenon. Yet this most remarkable Katie King affair turned out to be a fraud. The gentlemen referred to admitted the deception, and when the means were produced by which it was effected they were found to be very simple. In 1844 a similar exposure took place in London. A clairvoyant from Paris, called Alexis, carried on his trade for a little time with singular success, until he fell into the hands of Drs. Carpenter and Forbes, who penetrated his wiles and revealed his occult arts. The former gentleman has contributed considerable information regarding the methods by which the public are gulled and cheated, and what he has written in *Fraser's*

Magazine (February and March, 1877) and in his *Mental Physiology* is worthy serious consideration. Mr. D. D. Home, himself a Spiritualist, has also rendered good service in exposing the clever manœuvres of Machiavelian prophets, who in a peculiar sense profess to stand "between the living and the dead." In his valuable work entitled *Lights and Shadows of Spiritualism* he expresses the liveliest contempt for *séances* held in the dark, for "materializations," "cabinet" jugglery, and other profane "manifestations." He relates many instances of deception, and among them one that shows the extreme credulity of our modern wonder-monger. It seems he was present when an adept held up a mask at the window of a cabinet. "I called," he says, "the attention of an ardent Spiritualist beside me to the empty and eyeless sockets. His reply came promptly and with a certain degree of triumph: 'The dear spirits have not had time to materialize the eyes.'" There's simplicity for you, ingenuous faith, and guileless trust! Can it be that we are to be censured for not receiving the testimony of individuals who thus invite imposture, and who seem utterly unfitted to discriminate between truth and error? These dreary illustrations of folly I have no desire to multiply, and consequently I will not refer to the familiar instances of mendacious empiricism associated with the Davenports, Sunderlands, and Maxwells. The examples given are all-sufficient to make good the position that we cannot hope to prove the supernatural source of any spiritualistic marvels when so many of them are impostures. If there are any true they are so much like the counterfeit that even experts cannot with certainty distinguish the one from the other, and novices may therefore be excused if they reject them all as alike unverifiable.

According to the *London Spiritualist* (March 2, 1877), Mr. W. Stainton Moses criticised Spiritualism, in which he is a firm believer, in these terms: "It does very little in the way of scientific verification. Moreover, exoteric Spiritualism is, to a large extent, devoted to presumed communion with personal friends, or to the gratification of curiosity, or to a mere evolution of marvels. . . . Spiritualists start with a fallacy, namely, that all phenomena are caused by the action of departed human spirits. They have not looked into the powers of the human spirit; they do not know the extent to which spirit acts, how far it reaches, what it underlies." This is precisely the weakness of the whole system. It takes for granted that human agency is inadequate, and yet it has no just measurement of what such agency can accomplish. Most of the startling effects produced by its adherents have been duplicated by skillful persons who disavow all connection with the preternatural. A remarkable illustration of this was furnished recently by Rev. Arthur A. Waite, who, having been a medium, claimed that he would duplicate any feat that the friends of this Ism could succeed in accomplishing. His challenge was accepted, and the trial came off in Tremont Temple, Boston. President Washburn gave a very interesting account of the contest in the *Independent*, and from it we learn that Mr. Waite met the medium and actually repeated and explained every one of his tricks, and that his adversary was compelled to retreat in confusion.

Now, I am persuaded by what was done by Mr. Waite at Tremont Temple that an inventive and skilled prestidigitateur, such as Robert Houdin, could with a little study re-enact the mysteries that perplexed the involved intellect of Joseph Cook, or the other misty marvels which have excited so much comment of late among the *savants* of Leipsic. As for the simpler and more commonplace wonders, they have been repeated so frequently that they have ceased to attract attention, and are readily understood by the merest tyro. For instance, no one now is startled by the writing phenomenon, in which the medium reads what is being written with the point of the pen entirely concealed from his sight. This performance once occasioned considerable surprise, but it does so no longer; for it is not difficult to explain. The top of the pen is not hidden, and the educated eye, following its motions, can tell what letters the point is forming. Mind-reading also has lost its marvelous aspect since such demonstrators as Mr. Browne have illustrated how it is done. In the case of this well-known lecturer, he will think of an object in any place you may think of it; he will lead you to the spot where you have concealed any article, and he will follow the course of a watch through half a dozen hands to the right person. If he can do so without ghosts, who shall say that ghosts are ever necessary?

Dr. Carpenter tells us that many persons agree in stating that a Mr. Home was seen sailing in the air out of one window and in at another; and that a Mrs. Guppy was conveyed in a trance through the air from Highbury Park to Lambs' Conduit street. Here, assuredly, we have a miracle that natural causes cannot explain! So it would seem. Yet, admitting that the feat was really accomplished, we learn from Madam Blavatsky, in *Isis Unveiled* (vol. i, p. 495), that levitation can be produced without the interposition of spirit agencies. She says the fakir effects it by the power of his aspiration and will. "So does the priest of Siam, when, in the sacred pagoda, he mounts fifty feet in the air with taper in hand and flits from idol to idol, lighting up the niches, self-supported, and stepping as confidently as though he were upon solid ground. . . . The officers of the Russian squadron in Japanese waters relate the fact that, besides many other marvels, they saw jugglers walk in mid-air from tree-top to tree-top without the slightest support." Of course I do not know how this is done, but it is clear that it does not necessarily involve the supernatural. I might refer to other wonders, but it would be only to match them with others which the ingenuity of man has paralleled. These are certainly sufficient to indicate that human resources transcend the limits placed on them by Spiritualists, and that, were they understood, most of these mysteries would be cleared up entirely. We know that mind acts on mind sometimes without the medium of the body; and it is not improbable that mind also can act directly upon matter, as has recently been maintained in England and Germany, thus making it subject to the supremacy of unfettered volition. As a German scientist has surmised, most likely there are undiscovered properties of matter, and that many of these phenomena may be the result of their activities, or, as Joseph Cook argued, of an unknown force, called the psychic force, which asserts itself under peculiar conditions. Who knows? We concede our ignorance; but as long as we see spiritualistic marvels duplicated, and as long as the probability is as strong as it is that there are resources in humanity adequate to their production, we shall feel that their claim to supernatural origin is as yet unverified.

Nor is this conclusion unreasonable. When Descartes, long before the triumphs of this materialistic age, wrote these memorable sentences: "The experience which I have in physics teaches me that it is possible to arrive at a knowledge of many things which will be very useful to life; and that we may yet discover methods by which man, comprehending the force and the action of fire, water, air, stars, skies, and all the other bodies which environ us, as distinctly as we comprehend the different trades of our artisans, shall be able to employ them in the same fashion for all the uses to which they are appropriate, and thus shall render himself master and possessor of nature," he seems to have anticipated a deeper insight into the heart of things than had been attained in his day. His prophecy has been more than fulfilled; and yet even now those who are most profoundly versed in science will, to adopt the subsequent words of Descartes, "confess that all they know is almost nothing in comparison with what remains to be known." No statement more fully commands, or more readily receives, assent than this. We are all prompt enough to adopt it; and yet when we are brought face to face with some inexplicable sleight-of-hand performance, it is expected that we shall immediately set up the cry of "ghost, ghost!" Now I see no necessity for any such thing. The telegraph, the phonograph, the microphone, the telephone, and a score of other inventions, remind us that we have only crossed the threshold of nature, and that there are deep hidden in its courts secrets as extraordinary as any that have been conquered, and which in time must yield their treasures. Until we have carried our explorations much farther than we have at present, and have fixed more definitely the boundaries of the natural, I for one will not abandon my firm conviction that neither demons nor ghosts, angels nor devils, are necessary to account for the strange signs which are paraded in the name of a magic-loving hypothesis.

Nor is our confidence strengthened in the super-mundane character of this Ism when we judge it by its revelations. We have said that they are unimportant; they are satisfactory neither to skeptics nor believers. Blavatsky admits that "The great majority of spiritual communications are calculated to disgust investigators of even moderate intelligence. Even when genuine they are trivial, commonplace, and often vulgar. During the past twenty years we have received, through various mediums, messages purporting to be from Shakspeare, Byron, Franklin,

Peter the Great, Napoleon and Josephine, and even from Voltaire. The general impression made upon us was that the French conqueror and his consort seemed to have forgotten how to spell words correctly; Shakspeare and Byron had become chronic inebriates, and Voltaire had turned an imbecile." Mr. Home gravely relates various stories concerning the subjects which engage the attention of super-mundane beings, and which are not of a very exalted character. He says that the shade of an old lady in gray silk complained to a medium that a coffin had been placed upon the top of the one which contained her mortal remains. This weighty affair seems to have occasioned her great solicitude. He also pathetically tells how a little phantom girl, Stella, comforted her mother by writing her own name on her boots, "the light summer ones." What consolation there may have been to the afflicted parent in this boot-marking performance I cannot perceive, but to my way of thinking it is absolutely grotesque. It would seem from such cases that death makes sad havoc with common sense, and that it leads the departed to do what they never would have undertaken when in the flesh. Dr. Felton, once president of Harvard, in his *Lowell Institute Lectures*, having written about Pericles, says he invoked his ghost in a Boston circle, and that the famous Greek favored him by taking possession of the medium. "I put to him a series of questions about Athens in his time; but he had not only lost the knowledge of all that he had ever done during the forty years of his administration, but he had even forgotten his mother tongue. I could only exclaim with Hamlet: 'Alas! poor ghost!' and turn again to my books." Gerald Massey, in his tractate on this subject, does not give a very encouraging view of these revelations. He writes: "A large number of impostors have left our world to go somewhere, and possibly they still find us more easily imposed on than their new acquaintance, who are able to see through them, whereas we are so often left in the dark." "The spirits can say what they like, assume to be what they please." If we can rely on the testimony of this author, we can never be sure that the so-called phantom that addresses us is not an impostor, and even when it claims to be mother, daughter, friend, it may be willfully misleading us. Such communications, then, must be absolutely worthless. Gerald Massey also says that "there is a mind-realm in the invisible world, and that the ignorant and trifling may return to delude." On this point Mr. Wallace, the scientist to whom I have referred in a previous discourse, has written some noteworthy words. In *The Fortnightly Review*, during the summer of 1874, he published a very able paper, from which we give a few extracts: "Many scientific men deny the spiritual source of the manifestations on the ground that real, genuine spirits might reasonably be supposed not to indulge in the commonplace trivialities which do undoubtedly form the staple of ordinary spiritual communications. . . . And if a very large majority of those who daily depart this life are persons addicted to twaddle, persons who spend most of their time in low or trivial pursuits, persons whose pleasures are sensual rather than intellectual, whence is to come the transforming power which is suddenly, at the mere throwing off of the physical body, to change these into beings able to appreciate and delight in high intellectual pursuits?" He says such a change would be a miracle; but are not the very communications themselves miracles? If the first is incredible on this ground, the second is fairly objectionable for the same reason. He also suggests that these inferior beings visit earth because the circles are generally "a miscellaneous assemblage of believers of various grades and tastes, but most in search of an evening's amusement, and of skeptics who look upon all the others as either fools or knaves"; and he argues that such companies are not apt to attract "the more elevated and refined denizens of the higher spheres." If he is correct in his estimate of the phantoms who reveal themselves, as wise men always avoid such people when living, they may be excused if they prefer not to associate with them after they are dead. But surely Mr Wallace overlooks the fact that, in a large number of instances, the spirits of Washington, Poe, Newton, Plato, Cicero, grace the *séances* with their presence, and that any of them may be invoked. Should he say that most likely they are counterfeited, then we are again confronted with deception, and under such circumstances may well choose to have nothing to do with these knavish apparitions. One other passage from Mr. Wallace: "Nothing is more common than for religious people at *séances* to ask questions about God and Christ. In reply they never get more than opinions, or more frequently the statement that they, the spirits, have no more knowledge of these subjects than they had while on earth." On the united testimony, then, of these disinterested witnesses we may form a just estimate of the value to be attached to spiritual communications. They are not reliable; they are trivial; they are twaddle; from this source no addition has been made to the world's stock of knowledge; religiously, scientifically, it has contributed no facts, no information, no explanations,— only gossip, garrulity, guesses,— and we cannot but regard such revelations as eminently unsatisfactory; indeed, so unsatisfactory that Pythagorean silence would be preferable, and we need have no hesitation in attributing them to earth, not to heaven.

And yet many intelligent people insist on the importance of this Ism to society. It is urged that to its influence may be traced the survival of faith in the immortality of the soul. Were it not for the constant intercourse between this world and the beyond, it is argued, present

Materialism would smother and extinguish hope of a future eternal life. I am of the opposite opinion. If that future existence may be judged by the disclosures made of it by its representatives — if we are to judge of it by Bacon, who is credited with recent essays which are unworthy a child, or by Clay and Webster, whose speeches from the shades would not have secured them the approval of their fellow-citizens if they had been delivered here on earth — we may conclude, with Hamilton, "that they are souls in the process of losing their mental powers, souls fading away, souls destined soon to become extinct," and under such circumstances certainly eternity is not attractive enough to elicit desire for its possession, or to convince a skeptic that it is deserving any effort to obtain. It rather makes against the dignity and the reality of immortality, and so rather disposes men to live for the present than for the future.

Its influence is further objectionable on other grounds. It will hardly be denied that in many extreme cases it has weakened domestic ties, sympathized with the doctrine of elective affinity, spiritual marriages, and other abominations. Like a remorseless cataract, thundering and howling, it has not only beat violently and destructively against many sacred interests of society, but it has enveloped others in mist, and blinded many eyes to the distinction between right and wrong. An intelligent committee of Spiritualists, reporting at Cleveland, 1867, on certain excesses, said: "Many, if not all, of the disorderly manifestations your committee deem wholly unspiritual, having their origin in half-controlled nervous diseases, poor digestion, torpid liver, and general discord of mind and body." Very likely this is a true account of the matter. Bodily convulsions also distinguished witchcraft. Pliny, Galen, and others of the ancients, regarded the magical art as physically injurious; and we are certainly warranted in characterizing a system as pernicious which undermines bodily vigor, and fatally deranges the courses of nature. I admit that there are many holding to Spiritualism who are not involved in these evils; but were their number greater, still the terrible effects of the system on the few may well justify our doubt of its wholesomeness. Moreover, its drift is undesirable considered from another standpoint. It is radically anti-Christian. By many of its advocates Christ is represented simply as a medium; the inspiration of the Scriptures is denied, and its essential doctrines rejected. Perhaps the famous, or rather the infamous, Rutland Convention may be taken as a fair sample of this antagonism. Mr. Wallace, alluding to this solecism, asks, "How is it that the usual orthodox ideas of heaven are never confirmed through these mediums? There is no more startling a radical opposition to be found among the diverse religious creeds than that which the majority of mediums have been brought up in, and the doctrines as to a future life which have been delivered through them." And we may add the inquiry: How comes it that they so continuously deny other matters of revelation, such as the fall of man, the incarnation of Christ, His divinity, the efficacy of His sacrifice, and human regeneration? Their influence is against Christianity. Why? If it is suggested that the spirits, having been admitted into eternity, know whereof they testify, I must be allowed to reply that, according to their earthly representatives and friends, they are generally a good-for-nothing set, given to twaddle and deception, whose word, consequently, is not deserving of confidence. We cannot think that very many of our fellow-beings are shallow enough to yield to such questionable testimony; but it should never be overlooked in judging the system that its drift is in opposition to all that we hold most real and true.

It has already been intimated during this discussion that the Scriptures recognize the existence of a vast spiritual empire, whose borders lie near to our own world, but forbid all efforts on our part to pry into its secrets, or by our devices to bring its inhabitants hither. "We are not to seek those who have familiar spirits, and unto wizards that peep and mutter." (Isaiah vii; Deut. xviii.) For such prohibition there must be sufficient reasons. The first doubtless is, that God knows best how much of supernatural influence we can bear, and would regulate it in harmony with our capacity, our weakness, and necessities. He has no desire to convert the earth into a mad-house, to unseat the reason, or to shatter our poor understanding. We are not only overawed by many of the terrific exhibitions of nature's forces, but sometimes feel utterly crushed before them. How, then, could we hope to stand before a lawless, uncontrollable influx of spirits, with their bewildering revelations, and their sublime manifestations? Even the belief that they are near, the imaginary communion with them, and the allusion that they can be summoned, have proven too much for ordinary intellects. The strain of such wild fancies has unsettled the mind; what, then, would the reality be? Spiritualism not only disregards this divine prohibition, and in doing so attempts to usurp God's prerogative, but in its profane recklessness fills the soul with damaging fancies. On this ground, also, it is pernicious. Another reason, doubtless, that sanctions this restriction on restless curiosity is to be found in the importance which God has attached to the development of man's own resources. Having given sufficient light in the Bible for all necessary purposes, enough to serve as an impulse to thought, man is left to investigate, to train his native powers in the domain of inquiry, and to rise through his own endeavors. If angels are sent to strengthen, or sainted friends to comfort, their ministry is so ordered as to harmonize with this fundamental idea. They help without superseding; and they direct so gently that they never divert the creature from his own responsibility. Spiritualism, in reality, ignores this arrangement. It is a short, convenient road to knowledge. It tends to paralyze effort, and hence the large number of dreamy, visionary individuals who make up its circles and compose its conventions, who ramble in their talk, and by their general incoherence create the impression that they are nerveless and aimless. This emasculating, debilitating and prostrating influence, this weakness, languor and effeminacy, are among the most striking signs of its inability to bless the race, and of its purely mundane origin and character. And on this account, if on no other, it should be set aside by thoughtful people as unworthy their attention and their countenance.

But if not to this spectral superstition, to whom or to what shall we go that we may obtain the words of eternal life? Permit a Russian idyl to fashion a reply. There were three brothers who lived near the Black Sea. Not satisfied with their own country, they proposed to go in search of happiness. They said behind the forest there is a mountain, behind the mountain there is a great blue sea, and beyond the sea there are wealthy cities, and doubtless there the birds sing more sweetly, and there are treasures of joy known not in our land. So they saddled their horses, their good black horses, took their lances, and set off on their journey. The eldest brother and the one next in age wandered over the hills, and maybe are wandering still, but happiness they have never found. The youngest did not go far when his heart failed him and he retraced his steps. As his horse's head was homeward turned all nature seemed to say, "Thou hast done well;" and when he arrived at the door of his house he beheld a maiden at the threshold spinning, and he asked the maiden with the golden hair, "Who art thou?" and she answered, as smiles stole from her brown eyes, "I am happiness!" Ye restless ones, ye who would penetrate worlds unknown to satisfy your souls, ye who are weary of earth, and the wonders of a gracious providence, hear this: cross the phantom mountains and seek the ghostly cities, but your quest will only multiply sorrow and increase your gloom. Return! There, sitting at thy door, is one fairer than woman, more radiant than angels; her benign aspect is assuring; her hands are filled with works of beneficence; and in her eyes is the deep azure of heaven's love. "Who art thou?" "Christianity," she answers, "the daughter of eternity, the sister of humanity, the mother of hope. I am happiness, peace and joy." Sit thou at her feet, and within the influence of her all-composing calmness thine all-disturbing activity shall be gently soothed into quietness and peace; there shall thy weary soul find rest and bliss.

SKEPTICISM

"Ever learning, and never able to come to the knowledge of the truth." 2 *Timothy iii, 7.*

> "Rent from the startled gaze the veil of Night,
> O'er old delusions streams the dawning light;
> Man breaks his bonds — ah, blest could he refrain,
> Free from the curb, to scorn alike the rein!
> 'Freedom!' shouts Reason, 'Freedom!' wild Desire —
> And light to Wisdom is to Passion fire.
> From Nature's cheek bursts forth one hurtling swarm —
> Ah, snaps the anchor, as descends the storm!
> The sea runs mountains — vanishes the shore,
> The mastless wreck drifts endless ocean o'er;
> Lost — Faith — man's polar star!"
> *Lytton's Schiller.*

LAPLACE, the brilliant author of *The Mécanique Céleste*, whose thought eagle-winged and eagle-eyed surveyed the pathless immensity of the universe, is a sad example of that unhappy inability so tersely described by the apostle in our text. Born in an age of religious doubt, he lived in a state of mental unquiet and unrest. He seemed incapable of arriving at any settled conclusions regarding God and immortality. The spirit of the infinitesimal calculus, which Napoleon said he carried into business, also inspired and influenced him in his dealings with invisible realities. At times he gravitated toward Atheism, criticised what he was pleased to consider imperfections in the structure and order of earth and heaven, and ascribed faith and worship to ignorant credulity or to cruel imposture. At other times he expressed dissatisfaction with these opinions; and when approaching death, with gloomy discontent, confessed the enormousness of human ignorance, and in effect retracted what he had previously advocated. In a curious little book entitled *Things Not Generally Known* there is recorded an interview which occurred during his last days, between himself and an English philosopher, Prof. Sedgwick, in which the dying astronomer, having spoken of the religious endowments of England, said: "On this point I deprecate any great organic changes in your system; for I have lived long enough to know what at one time I did not believe — that no society can be upheld in happiness and honor without the sentiments of religion." And yet there is no evidence that even then he perceived clearly or grasped firmly the verities of theology, or esteemed them otherwise than as useful measures of effective government, or, at the most, as vague shadows of obscure ideas, the twilight of an indefinite, awful something in the universe, back of its phenomena, which had eluded the searching tests of his mathematics. Ever learning and ever oscillating, his mind in a constant state of unquiet itching and of troubled flux, fluctuating and floundering, he seems to have passed away without having come to the knowledge of the truth on those subjects, which of all others are most intimately related to the well-being and progress of humanity. And many, like Laplace, remain in suspense all their days, vacillating between theories, unsettled in faith, at times half persuaded, then utterly rejecting; and, at last, dying unresolved, carry their doubts with them into that eternity where the interrogatory mark is never found darkening the punctuation of spirit-speech.

Skepticism exists under two forms: the permanent and the transient. The former is termed "systematic," "dogmatic," or "speculative;" the latter "experimental," or "practical;" and the first is more subtle and dangerous, though not more distressing and depressing, than the second. Systematic or philosophic skepticism is the apotheosis of incertitude, the canonization of doubt, the beatification of ignorance. Its world is a combination of mirage and phantasmagoria, inhabited by a dim-visioned, short-sighted, color-blind race, who are being constantly befooled by their senses, and by the varying phenomena which surround them. Such a conception as this I have no desire to discuss; neither would I again undertake the thankless task of vindicating the trustworthiness of nature and the reliableness of man's faculties from the aspersions of this Ism. This has already been done in the discourse on Agnosticism, and need not be repeated. But it may not be amiss to remember, if the universe cannot but defy our explorations, and if there is no key fitted to the sinuosities of the soul, and if, as is assumed, everything is uncertain but uncertainty, no conceivable argument could hope to prevail against such a theory, and time would only be wasted in attempting to frame one.

The other form of skepticism is more tangible, more general, and more deserving of thoughtful and immediate attention. Unlike the first, it is not a system, nor a philosophy, but a mood, temper, or state of the intellect — a suspense of judgment, a sense of confusion and perplexity, a feeling of hesitancy, and a lack of conviction on the particular subject in debate. These are its elements; and they are supposed usually to exist in connection with a deep and earnest spirit of inquiry; and hence, according to the radical import of the name, a skeptic is one who has not found truth, but who is diligently seeking its discovery. It does not, however, always follow that the unsatisfied, questioning mind is at the same time faithful in its search for light, especially for the light needed to dissipate the darkness which enshrouds the grave problems of theology. Unhappily, when doubt invades the soul, and the doctrines of religion are looked upon as chimerical, it too frequently becomes chronic, and the labor of investigation is abandoned. Sir Walter Raleigh, it is reported, burnt the second part of his *World's History* in a moment of excitement caused by his inability to verify a little incident that occurred under his very eyes while a prisoner in the Tower of London. On which occasion he is credited with these reflections: "How many falsehoods must this work contain. If I cannot assure myself of an event which happened in my presence, how can I venture to describe those which occurred thousands of years before I was born, or those which have passed at a distance since my birth? Truth! truth! this is a sacrifice that I owe thee." Whereupon he threw the manuscript into the fire. It is believed by some people that the nebular hypothesis of Herschel was due to the want of power in his forty-feet reflector, rather than to ascertained data. When his magnificent instrument, which had resolved the milky way into stellar millions, brought to view other milky ways in the depths of the universe which it could not thus resolve, the astronomer fell to theorizing, and concluded that these new nebulæ were masses of formless matter, the raw material out of which solar systems are fashioned. Instead of recognizing the limitations of the reflector he straightway started a hypothesis, and took for granted what he could not prove. Whether the story about Raleigh is true, or this representation of Herschel's theory is just, they both illustrate the too common course pursued by those who entertain suspicions regarding the teachings of Christianity. Feeling how difficult it is to decide on the character of events taking place around them, and realizing how frequently they fall into mistakes, they avoid investigations which, they have prejudged, would yield no satisfactory results. They sneer at their childhood's faith as semi-mythical, surrender it hastily to the flames, and obstinately walk on in darkness to the grave. Or, failing to take the measure of their own mind, and overlooking the limitations which rest on thought, because they cannot resolve the nebulæ of revelation into suns and stars, and fancying that they are severely scientific, when, in fact, they are diffusively sentimental, they impetuously adopt some unproved and unprovable theory of Godless materialism.

Shakspeare has called "modest doubt the beacon of the wise," and when it preserves this character it is certainly deserving of sympathy. The harshness with which it has at times been treated seems to me unwarranted. He who has fallen beneath its shadow is not to be thoughtlessly derided, for it may cause him as much pain to doubt as it gives Christians to have him doubt. If he is honest he suffers enough without additional pangs being heedlessly inflicted by those who have never tasted his cup of bitterness. Only the most stolid and unreflecting will deny that there is much in the world to perplex, that its mysteries multiply as they are touched, like the loaves and fishes in the Savior's hands, or that there is much in Christianity as it exists among us to impair confidence in its divine origin. Very few thoughtful people are to be found whose faith at some period has not been temporarily eclipsed; and their own experience should teach them to bear patiently with the unbelief of others. He who has never questioned the truth of the things that are urged upon his acceptance in the name of religion, who has never felt the very foundations departing beneath his feet, and who has never agonized in the grasp of giant and overwhelming difficulties, may be congratulated on the strength of his faith, but he cannot be complimented on the depth of his intellect. Moreover, it should be remembered that doubt has its office and function, and has a mission to accomplish, as truly as belief. Schiller lays stress upon this thought in his *Philosophical Letters,* and shows in the following passage how that which we deplore becomes a minister of good: "Skepticism and free-thinking are the feverish paroxysms of the human mind, and must needs at length confirm the health of well organized souls by the unnatural convulsion which they occasion. In proportion to the dazzling and seducing nature of error will be the greatness of the triumphs of truth: the demand for conviction and firm belief will be strong and pressing in proportion to the torment occasioned by the pangs of doubt. But doubt was necessary to elicit these errors; the knowledge of the disease had to precede its cure. Truth suffers no loss if a vehement youth fails in finding it, in the same way that virtue and religion suffer no detriment if a criminal denies them." Hence it is that to the influence of Skepticism we owe our release from bondage to manifold superstitions. Man's ability to question, and his indefeasible right to do so, lies at the root of all progress, whether civil or religious. It has gradually emancipated him from errors and delusions; it has enabled him to sift the true from the false, and it has exalted him above the despotisms of priests and potentates. And unless we can prove that the future has no fresh treasures of knowledge to yield, no clearer and more accurate views of Scripture to discover, we must admit that it has yet a work to accomplish, and is neither to be indiscriminately derided nor rashly denounced. But when it degenerates from an honest suspension of judgment, and abandons its questioning attitude, and settles into blind, rooted, stubborn and uninquiring incredulity, it fails to be reasonable and forfeits its claim to kindly consideration and generous sympathy. When it ceases to be "a tortuous deviation of the wandering reason seeking the straight road to eternal truth," and becomes a disguised or undisguised endeavor to escape from religious obligation, it is guilty of inconsistency, and makes itself a principle of infinite mischief. Into this low state has Skepticism fallen in our times, and from its fatal power every generous, serious soul should desire deliverance. And it may assist all, who are thus sincerely anxious to be freed from its bondage, to look at it thoughtfully from a Christian standpoint.

First, Christian thinkers regard the mental processes of Skepticism as unsatisfactory and inconclusive. They primarily object to the assumption of its advocates that the head is fully qualified to judge the credentials of religion, whatever may be the condition of the heart. No allowance seems to be made for prejudices and prepossessions, or for a low tone of morals. It is taken for granted that spiritual truth can be settled just as mathematical truth is decided, by a purely intellectual method. Such, however, is not the case. Herbert Spencer has shown very clearly in his *Study of Sociology* the tremendous influence of personal, educational and professional bias on investigations of this character; and Hazlitt has argued that every man is responsible for his belief, on the ground that wishes, inclinations and predilections govern the understanding as irresistibly as logic or evidence. Fichte, the philosopher, has well said, "Our system of thought is often but the history of our heart; conviction arises from inclination, not from reason, and the improvement of the heart leads to true wisdom"; and he adds in another place: "If, then, the will be steadfastly and sincerely fixed upon what is good, the understanding will of itself discover what is true"; or, in other words, "men do not will according to their reason, but reason according to their will." Goethe expresses a similar sentiment, and it may be accepted as axiomatic. Instinctively we feel that a man of mere intellect, cold and abstruse, in whom the rational absolutely predominates over and excludes the emotional, and who is an incarnation of mind, and only mind, is far from being completely and harmoniously developed. We shrink from these unnatural and portentous individuals, and find ourselves reluctant to commit our lives to their guidance. Something is lacking in them, and when they report adversely to the Faith we feel that if they had possessed a heart to speak their testimony would have been different. When Skepticism, therefore, approaches, proudly announcing its incertitude in the name of reason, and of reason only, we hesitate to receive its conclusion, as the process by which it has been reached is radically defective.

We also know that most of its supporters are not careful to scrutinize their likes and dislikes, their prejudices and passions, for according to their assumption these have no bearing on the issue, and as long as they thus think must their ratiocination be open to question. There is much in Christianity to excite antagonism. It declares the awful facts of sin, responsibility and penalty, and building its house of mercy on these foundations it invites all to accept its saving hospitality as an unmerited gift and favor. These representations are not agreeable to those who incline toward iniquity, nor hardly more so to those who pride themselves on their morality. Naturally they feel indignant with a system that overwhelms their guilt and overturns their vanity, and are in a favorable mood to be captivated by any bewildering sophistry that chimes harmoniously with their predilections. Likewise professional pursuits may exert a warping influence on the judgment; for when the attention is directed exclusively to physical phenomena, as in the case of naturalists, or to the animal side of humanity, as in the case of physicians, it is not improbable that they will fail to see anything beyond the particular objects in which they are personally interested. As the surgeon's scalpel lays bare no soul, and the astronomer's glass discovers no God, they are in danger of inferring that there is nothing grander or more wonderful in the universe than the dull material with which they are familiar, and with which they have exclusively to do. Until Skepticism makes due and adequate allowance for the mental obscurity and obliquity which these prepossessions may occasion, and until it takes counsel of the deeper longings of the heart, its doubts will fail to carry conviction; and when it does this, in my opinion, few doubts will remain for it to cherish and express.

Christians also question the validity of an argument that exaggerates the uncertainties of religion, and that overlooks the vagueness of science. It is well known that this form of unbelief owes much of its influence to the impression, which it has industriously cultivated, that religion is too indefinite, changeful and mysterious for it to inspire confidence. This is its favorite position, and by far its strongest; and yet it is a long way from being impregnable. The mystery that rests on spiritual subjects must be admitted; for, as Goethe says, "the farther we advance in research, the nearer we approach the unsearchable"; but this is no more prejudicial to the authority of Christianity than it is to the trustworthiness of nature. William Wirt, who clearly discerned this fact, in a letter now in the possession of a prominent citizen of Chicago, expresses his opinion regarding the worth of this objection in these terms: "Would to God you could believe with me that the Bible is true, the revealed will of God, and offers to us the only terms of salvation. Human reason may revolt at it, and what is poor human reason, unable to explain how a blade of grass grows? Surrounded every moment with realities which it admits to be inexplicable mysteries, and yet presuming to measure and pronounce upon the counsels of Omniscience, and rejecting the Christian religion because it is a mystery.

Can anything be more mysterious than the union of soul and body, unless it be the still greater mystery, which some profess to believe, that matter can be so organized as to produce the amazing intellectual results which we witness in man? In believing our own existence we believe a mystery as great as any that the Christian religion presents, for there are no degrees in mystery. Pass the sphere of reason, and all is mystery of equal degree; all the works of the Almighty are mysterious to our poor limited faculties. What a series of magnificent mysteries does astronomy present! Philosophers resolve the motion of the planets into gravitation, and what is gravitation? Let reason answer the question. It cannot do it. She finds herself involved in a world of mysteries, and yet she rejects the Christian religion because it is a mystery. Is not God himself a mystery? or if the solar system is believed to be uncreated and eternal, is not that a mystery? Would I have a man renounce his reason? No. I ask only that he will confine it to its proper sphere, and not pronounce the ocean without a bottom because it cannot touch it with an inch of line." Likewise, may we not with equal propriety inquire, who is able to solve the problems of medicine, or accurately define the relations and properties with which geometry has to do? The physician talks learnedly about a principle of life which eludes his touch and defies his analysis, and the mathematician uses terms in his discourse with a freedom that suggests a refreshing unconsciousness of their inexplicableness. What does he mean by "space," "properties," and "relations" with which his geometry deals? It would puzzle him to answer, especially so unobjectionably as to command the assent of every other thinker. And what about the solution of Euclid's Postulate, the squaring of the circle, and the geometrical axioms which we accept but cannot demonstrate? Then as to fickleness, what has been more mutable than the interpretations of nature, which have been put forth by its zealous explorers and expounders? For instance, concerning the age of the earth, how various and contradictory are the opinions of eminent men who enjoy the same opportunities for investigation. Sir Charles Lyell held that two hundred and forty millions of years have elapsed since the beginning of the Cambrian period, while Mr. Darwin indulges in calculations that would date its origin a billion of years ago. On the contrary, Sir William Thomson is satisfied with less bewildering figures; he limits the existing state of things on the earth to about a hundred millions; but Prof. Tait is even more modest, and argues that physical considerations render it impossible for life to have been here for more than ten or fifteen millions of years. You perceive that millions, more or less, make very little difference with these gentlemen; and the same uncertainty appears in other departments of inquiry. The theory of emission has been supplanted by that of undulations; caloric has been driven from heat by atomic motion; phlogiston and protoplasm have both succumbed to electric and magnetic forces; and it is impossible to foretell how light will reach us in the future, or what elements our scientists will permit to compose the atmosphere we breathe, and the world we inhabit. Now is it not a curious instance of inconsistency when a man challenges the credibility of Christianity on account of the variable and conflicting views to which it has given rise, and yet remains an ardent believer in the trustworthiness of nature, concerning whose operations so many giant battles have been fought? The changing aspects of religion, and the differences of opinion which exist among its disciples the Christian does not deny, though he claims that there is greater unity and permanence in the interpretations of its doctrinal and ethical teachings than is generally recognized; and he argues that its certitude is no more impeachable on these grounds than is that of the material universe. He claims that it is God's plan that man should search for truth in the spiritual and physical domains; that the privilege of investigating involves the possibility of error, and that it is no more than reasonable, therefore, to expect diversity of thought about both, on account of which to reject either would be folly.

The failure of Skepticism to attach a proper value to the testimony of religious experience, and to discover a suitable sphere for the exercise of the faith-faculty, is regarded by Christians as fatal to its pretensions. Its attacks are directed almost entirely against historical evidences and alleged Scripture discrepancies. In these it earnestly seeks for flaws, but pays no attention to the statements made by the vast body of living witnesses, who testify to what "they have seen, and heard, and handled." The well-known lines of Horace, condensed by Tennyson, express the thought,

"Things seen are weightier than things heard";

but things felt carry even greater weight; for there is nothing more real and certain than our heart experiences. Well, here are thousands of worthy people, among them the most cultivated, sober and blameless members of society, who assure us that they have been favored with visitations from God's Spirit; that they are now conscious of His indwelling; that their prayers have been answered, and that in suffering and tribulation they have enjoyed a deep sense of the Divine presence and sympathy. Here are also other thousands who are going down to death radiant with triumph, contemplated by weeping friends whose tears gleam strangely with the iris hues of hope, and who to the last ascribe their victory to "the Lamb of God, who taketh away the sin of the world." These are not fanatics; many of them are very commonplace persons, not given to sentimental emotions, and in all other relations of life their word would be taken and relied on. Why should they be doubted when they testify to what they experience of God's goodness and grace? Unless we are warranted in treating with disdain the inner world of thought and feeling, we cannot refuse to listen to its voices. And as these voices assure us of the substantial reality of religion, only the exigencies of a desperate cause will ignore their testimony, or sneer at it as vain and meaningless. Nor have infidels always been able to bear consistent testimony against them; for at times their own conduct has indicated the existence of deeper spiritual necessities than their systems countenance. Rochester turned to Christ in his closing hours, and like Julian acknowledged that the Galilean had conquered; David Hume was not a stranger to the house of God, but in Scotland sometimes joined with the people in solemn worship; Voltaire reared a church at Ferney; Collins, it is said, insisted that his servants should be faithful to the claims of the Sanctuary; Robespierre decreed the extraordinary festival of the Supreme Being; Huxley has plead for the retention of the Bible in education; and Tyndall has waxed indignant over the imputations cast on his belief in Deity; and M. Littre, in the shadow of the grave, has confessed, "They are happy who have faith"; and it is natural to conclude that this amiable disregard of the logic of their views is due to a dim consciousness of something in their own hearts which cries out against their truth.

Reason, conscience and volition have received from thinkers considerable attention, but the faith-faculty has never yet been exhaustively discussed. Within our necessarily circumscribed limits, and dealing with a different subject, it is impossible to do more than allude to its significance. We find in man capacity for faith, and, as Goethe has shown, the ages in which it has been in active exercise have been the most brilliant in the annals of time. It bears "a heaven-storming character," and intuitively seeks an Infinite Being, and is as dissatisfied with any other as reason is with sophistry. Religion appeals to it, strengthens, feeds it, and where it is nourished the entire character feels its benignant influence. It can no more be neglected in the harmonious development of a man than conscience or volition. But what kind of training does it receive from Skepticism? None at all, or, if any, simply mistraining. Skepticism does not know what to do with it. If the normal attitude of the mind toward spiritual subjects is doubt, how comes it that instinctively it trusts? Why should faith be so natural if it is unreasonable? What is its place, what its function, what its object? To these questions this Ism has no answer to return. All it attempts to do is to blight, wither and destroy, root and branch, this faculty, and in its place plant the seeds that may at last grow into the colorless and perfumeless weed of unbelief. According to Goethe, even "natural religion, properly speaking, requires no faith," and if so, where every kind of religion is rejected its operations must be entirely superfluous. Goethe says: "The persuasion that a great producing, regulating and conducting Being conceals himself, as it were, behind Nature, to make himself comprehensible to us,— such a conviction forces itself upon everyone. Nay, if we for a moment let drop this thread, which conducts us through life, it may be immediately and everywhere resumed. But it is different with a special religion, which announces to us that this Great Being distinctly and preëminently interests himself for one individual, one family, one people, one country. This religion is founded on faith, which must be immovable if it would not be instantly destroyed." Then a special revelation is indispensable to the training of this faculty, just as specific and diversified objects are indispensable to the development of vision; and if it is to be preserved at all its wants must be adequately supplied. The difficulty, not to say impossibility, of Skepticism affording nourishment to faith, taken in connection with its disregard of the testimony borne to religion by experience, completes the dissatisfaction which its mental processes produce, and increases the conviction that they should be as little trusted as "adders fang'd."

Secondly, reflecting Christians consider the moral qualities of Skepticism as unattractive and reprehensible. They object to its intolerance. It is an erroneous notion, though one widely spread, that belief in holy things leads to narrowness, exclusiveness, and cruel bigotry. Unquestionably it has served as a pretext for this unlovely spirit; but, as Naville argues, it is in direct contradiction to its essential nature. Christianity fell away from its original character before it began to persecute. In fact, it became skeptical before it became bloody. It doubted the sufficiency of God's arm, and entered into alliance with the civil government; it doubted the adequacy of Revelation, and invented infallible popes and councils; it doubted the efficiency of Christ's mediation, and created interminable intercessors out of dead saints and virgins; and it doubted the power of the gospel to convert the soul, and it went forth to evangelize, sword and torch in hand. Thus its doubts bred intolerance, as they do in every mind where they are cherished; hence the dogmatic manner with which religion is treated by those who profess to be questioning its claims. No pope ever delivered himself more positively than do these devotees at the shrine of uncertainty. They are ready, to use a Shakespearean phrase, "to spurn the sea if it could roar" at them. All who differ from them are set down as fanatics or simpletons.

They are vilified in writings, are caricatured in speeches, and are held up to derision and contempt. The prejudices of society are sedulously excited against them by inflammatory appeals and misrepresentations, and they are described as the victims of idle, cunning priests, whose influence is pernicious and ruinous. They are stretched on the rack of ridicule; they are scorched in the fires of denunciation; they are decapitated by the guillotine of sarcasm; and were it possible, their churches would be closed, and they themselves be ostracised. And all this vituperative intolerance in the interest of doubt! For the sake of conserving the sanctity of negation, and upholding the authority of nothingness, this petty and contemptible, arrogant and tyrannous course is pursued. If some noble and glorious cause were at stake we might find some palliation, under the circumstances, for this bitterness and severity; but when, according to uniform consent, there is nothing but uncertainty to defend, never was passion and anger more unjustifiable and idle.

Heartlessness as well as intolerance is chargeable upon this Ism. It robs and makes no return; it tears from the souls of the young and old ideals that elevate, aims that inspire, hopes that sustain. Careless of the wounds it inflicts, of the desolation it creates, it seeks to undermine confidence in prayer and providence. It is a dull, dumb iconoclast that destroys without building, that smites faith with palsy, and then stands gibbering over the helpless wreck it has wrought. If we are in sorrow it has no comfort, if we are in sin it has no deliverance, if we are in perplexity it has no wisdom, if we are in darkness it has no light. The virtue it preaches is without foundation, the heroism it inculcates is without inducement, and the immortality it whispers is without evidence. Its loftiest sentiments are borrowed from the religion it affects to despise; the liberty which it claims to champion, it has sacrificed but little to secure; and the sweet charities it commends, it has done nothing to establish. The garland of eloquence wherewith it clothes itself is the adornment of a corpse; every flower sheathes a worm in its bosom, and every breath of fragrance is mingled with death. Its oratory smells of the tomb, and the symbol of its hope is an eyeless, tongueless skull, grinning in mocking insolence at everything that dignifies and ennobles life. It brings no benefaction, it pronounces no benediction; but casts its baleful shadow on all that is fair and sacred. From its cold lips there comes no grand and full rounded "Yea," to match its piercing, blighting and destroying "Nay." It is simply a huge Negation, seeking with one hand to stop the mouth of religion, and with the other to write on human aspirations and beliefs a bitter and derisive "No." It has no gospel of salvation even for this world, but only an evangel of destruction. If it had anything to say, if it had a better message to deliver than Christianity speaks, its zeal would be explicable. But why it should desire to impoverish the heart and life of thousands, why it should labor to deprive the world of the only sun that irradiates its gloomy fields and its deep, dark valleys, and why it should be gratified at the prospect of blotting out suns and stars from the immortal soul, cannot be imagined, and requires the malicious ingenuity of fiends to parallel. Do you recall these words of Tennyson? —

> "Oh, thou that after toil and storm
> Mays't seem to have reached a purer air,
> Whose faith has center everywhere,
> Nor cares to fix itself to form.
>
> "Leave thou thy sister when she prays,
> Her early heaven, her happy views;
> Nor thou with shadowed hints confuse
> A life that leads melodious days.

> "Her faith through form is pure as thine,
> Her hands are quicker unto good;
> Oh, sacred be the flesh and blood
> To which she links a truth divine."

If such a faith should be tenderly and thoughtfully dealt with by one who rejoices in emancipation from "form," how much more deeply should it be reverenced by him who unhappily has no faith at all. His own dreariness and loneliness should touch his heart with compassion and restrain him from saying or doing what would carry the sense of solitariness and sadness to others. Indifference to this duty betrays a heartlessness and recklessness which augurs ill for the world should Skepticism ever triumph. If so heedless of the pain it inflicts now, who can foresee where it would stop were it exalted and enthroned?

The injury that is wrought to souls by this cruel thoughtlessness, or deliberate cruelty, is faithfully portrayed by Schiller. He represents (*Philosophical Letters*) a certain Julius as writing to Raphael in the following strain: "You have robbed me of the thought that gave me peace. You have taught me to despise where I prayed before. A thousand things were venerable in my sight till your dismal wisdom stripped off the veil from them. I saw a crowd of people streaming to church. I heard their enthusiastic devotion poured forth in a common act of prayer and praise. Twice did I stand beside a death-bed and saw — wonderful power of religion! — the hope of heaven triumph over the terror of annihilation, and the serene light of joy beaming from the eyes of those departing." But faith in the reality of this worship, and confidence in the certainty of immortality, had alike been destroyed by the sneers of his friend; and unhappy Julius was left with his rationalism and his cynicism a poorer, and not a wiser, man. No wonder that the honest growler, Carlyle, treats with contempt the men who lend themselves to this pitiable and despicable business. "Cease, my much-respected Herr von Voltaire," he says. "Shut thy sweet voice, for the task appointed thee seems finished. Sufficiently hast thou demonstrated this proposition, considerable or otherwise: that the Mythus of the Christian Religion looks not in the eighteenth century as it did in the eighth." . . . "But what next? Wilt thou help us to embody the divine Spirit of that religion in a new Mythus, in a new vehicle and vesture, that our Souls, otherwise too like perishing, may live? What! Thou hast no faculty in that kind? Only a torch for burning, no hammer for building? Take our thanks, then, and — thyself away." Evidently Carlyle felt that it might offend ears polite for him to write all that was in his heart when thinking of such melodious faith-murderers as Voltaire. With them he had no sympathy; neither have we, and we feel their bigotry and heartlessness so keenly that we turn from them with horror and deplore the condition of every man who falls a prey to their insidious wiles.

Whether this aversion is justifiable or not, you, my readers, must decide. I leave you to ponder the serious matter in your souls; but being satisfied in my own that it is, and feeling interested in your spiritual well-being, permit me to press home the duty incumbent on you if you would be free from the entangling meshes of Skepticism. The Country Parson gives this good advice to persons in your condition: "Don't turn your back upon your doctrinal doubts and difficulties. Go up to them and examine them. Perhaps the ghastly object which looks to you in the twilight like a sheeted ghost may prove to be no more than a tablecloth hanging upon a hedge; but if you were to pass it distantly without ascertaining what it is, you might carry the shuddering belief that you had seen a disembodied spirit all your days. Some people (very wrongly as I think) would have you turn the key upon your skeptical difficulties and look away from the pig-sty altogether."

I do not belong to this class. I think it is the duty of every man to confront boldly and investigate fearlessly all kinds of objections that may obscure the truth of Christianity. As a rule, the more thoroughly they are sifted and the more closely they are scrutinized, the less real and weighty will they appear. Have the courage to grasp them, to clutch them firmly and look them squarely in the face, and you shall find their seeming solidity to be nothing but vapor, and their pretentious speech to be but empty gasconade and windy rodomontade. Take the claims of Christianity and all the difficulties in the way of their reception, apply yourself to understand, examine, and judge them, and if the task is undertaken in the right spirit the result need not be apprehended. Search diligently, for this is no child's play for sluggard brains and fitful, spasmodic efforts; search impartially, for this is too grave a work for purblind prejudice, obstinate onesidedness, and nutsheil narrow-mindedness; search systematically, for this is too deep and profound a theme for irregular, immethodical, and indiscriminate thinking; search exhaustively, for the problems involved are too intricate and abstruse for shallow-headed, dull-witted, shoaly superficialness; and search reverently, for the issues are too solemn and wide-reaching for quip and quirk, conceits and comicalities, showy smartness, buffooneries, and idle farcicalities. Thus search, reverencing God, reverencing truth, and reverencing self, and then shall it be found that reason and faith coalesce in lucid union, that Christianity is not a phantom, but the one reality mocked by gibing ghosts, and that Skepticism is not unconquerable, but vulnerable to earnest and exacting thought. But even if it should resist laborious meditation and refuse entirely to surrender, if faith should continue to be darkened by great shadows and grow faint and cold before the breath of drear despondency, nevertheless, though struggling to see in the imperfect light, and failing to rise above the murky atmosphere, the knowledge mastered and the evidence tested would not be useless. At least they will bring a certain confidence in the reality of religion, a profound conviction of the utter folly of unbelief, and if they do nothing more, they will constrain the troubled and unsatisfied soul with the sad, bereaved one in Tennyson's *In Memoriam* to exclaim:

"I falter where I firmly trod,
 And falling with my weight of cares
 Upon the great world's altar-stairs
That slope thro' darkness up to God,
I stretch lame hands of faith and grope,
 And gather dust and chaff, and call
 To what I feel is Lord of all,
And faintly trust the larger hope."

LIBERALISM.

"Him that is weak in the faith receive ye, but not to doubtful disputations." *Rom. xiv, 1.*

"Why is my liberty judged of another man's conscience?" *1 Cor. x, 29.*

"O love-destroying, cursed Bigotry!
. . . Of ignorance
Begot, her daughter, Persecution, walked
The earth, from age to age, and drank the blood
Of saints; with horrid relish drank the blood
Of God's peculiar children, and was drunk,
And in her drunkenness dreamed of doing good.
The supplicating hand of innocence,
That made the tiger mild, and in his wrath
The lion pause, the groans of suffering most
Severe, were naught to her; she laughed at groans;
No music pleased her more, and no repast
So sweet to her as blood of men redeemed
By blood of Christ." *Pollok.*

THANKS be to God, all this is changed! But the greatness of this revolution is more vividly realized in Europe than in America. There the eye frequently rests on the now useless weapons of persecuting ages, and on the monuments which the modern spirit has reared to murdered saints. The hypocritical pharisees of Christ's time, who garnished the tombs of the righteous, were accustomed to say, with what degree of sincerity you who have studied their character can judge, "If we had lived in the days of our fathers we would not have been partakers with them in the blood of the prophets." And many of those who have been instrumental in quenching the fires of martyrdom, and in commemorating the grandeur of suffering goodness, may have been equally insincere; but if they were, this fact shows only more clearly the strength of the liberalistic movement, before which even their bigotry was compelled to succumb. In the Tower of London the now harmless thumb-screws and the now edgeless ax are exhibited to the curious, and recall to thoughtful souls the terrors of secret tortures, and of public or private executions. How innocent they seem, and yet what a story they could relate of undeserved pain inflicted, of piteous shrieks and groans unheeded, and of hearts sobbing in helpless anguish beneath the iron rule of tyrant kings and priests, who recognized no conscience but their own. Their tragic work is ended forevermore, and now the red republican can mock the ax, and the despised heretic can smile at the cruel thumb-screw, while they give free expression to their political or theological dissent.

In Venice there are three buildings significantly joined together, and each bears its own peculiar testimony to the decline of oppression. The first is the basilica of St. Mark, that noble creation of Byzantine art on which Ruskin has lavished so much praise. The next is the palace of the Doges, so closely connected with it that the chief of the government could pass from his regal home to the place of worship without exposing himself to the public view; and the third is the prison bound to the palace by the ever-famous Bridge of Sighs. Here we have in stone the suggestive symbol of the hated alliance which wrought so much mischief to society. Whenever the church and state are banded together, the darkness and horror of the prison are inevitable. But in our times the Italian hierarchy is practically dissevered from the Italian government, and St. Mark's attracts the curious tourist more than it does the devout worshiper. The palace of the Doges and of the mysterious Council of Ten is converted into a picture gallery and museum, and the prison is devoted to criminals, not to saints; while from their hinges the doors have been torn by the outraged people from the dungeons beneath the palace, in which so many noble men and women suffered unjustly, and in whose dampness and gloominess so many foul deeds were perpetrated.

Florence rejoices in its sacred temple of St. Croce, enriched with memorials to departed greatness. Among the monuments are two which mutely, but distinctly, proclaim the revolution that has taken place in human sentiment regarding the rights of conscience. They are reared to the memory of Dante, who was banished to Ravenna, and there died, and Galileo Galilei, who was hounded mercilessly by the Inquisition. The tomb of the astronomer, who was execrated by the church, represents him with a telescope in one hand, and with a diagram of the earth in the other; a ladder above him reaches to the heavens, denoting his aspiring intellect; and two burning vases symbolize the immortality of his fame. Who would have been mad enough to predict, when he tremblingly bowed before the authority of the haughty Roman church, that he would ever be honored with such a tribute within the walls of one of her most stately edifices? Nevertheless, what would then have been considered a wild dream has been accomplished; and between the lines of his epitaph may be read the undeniable fact that freedom of thought and of speech has gloriously triumphed.

While it is a cause of congratulation that the victory is thus pronounced, it is not yet possible to claim that it is absolutely complete. The old spirit of persecution is not yet quite dead. It asserts itself still, as occasion serves, in the decrees and deeds of the Papacy, and sometimes peers forth undisguised in the words and works of Protestantism. Bigotry, intellectual narrowness, and ignorant prejudice, if not as common as in the past, are altogether too frequent for unalloyed satisfaction to be felt in the present. Although it is readily conceded that no church is infallible, and that no body of men have mastered the *omne scibile*, as a *Princeton Review* writer phrases it, and although it is expected that new light will be evolved from the Holy Scriptures, it is a very hazardous undertaking for an adventurous teacher to run counter to the received opinions of the majority, or to advocate what the fathers failed to formulate. There is enough intolerance in the religious world to make the position of such a man exceedingly uncomfortable. Supposing that he is not guilty of heresy, and that his presentation of truth differs more in form than in substance from what is generally received, or that it is simply a development and a carrying to a higher plane the doctrines that are currently accepted, nevertheless, his boldness and progressiveness will alarm conservatives and arouse their antagonism. Even questions of a lower order, which pertain to the domain of expediency, and which confessedly must be decided by the individual, are dealt with by some Christians acrimoniously and dogmatically. If their brethren exercise their liberty in these things the law of charity is quite forgotten, and they are denounced and derided in a manner that suggests the harsh, rough ages when no ill-usage was considered too severe for the wicked wretches who presumed to think and act according to the dictates of their conscience. But it is not necessary to point out the various ways, or to chronicle the miserable and mean methods, by which the attenuated bigotry of modern times seeks to maintain itself; it is enough simply to notice the tenacity with which it holds to life without exposing any further its ghastly deformities.

Professors of religion, however, are not the only ones in this liberalistic age who are guilty of illiberality. Outside of the church, among those who claim to be the special champions of free thought, and who are constantly sneering at the narrowness of Christ's disciples, dogmatism in its worst form reveals itself. Infidel lecturers, who admit that they have nothing particularly definite or valuable to communicate, breathe out their anathemas in a manner worthy the Vatican. Even men of science are sometimes impatient and violent when the soundness of their theories is called in question. It is a matter of common notoriety that Virchow, because he has had the moral courage to say that the descent of man from the ape has not been substantiated, is hooted and howled at by the advanced evolutionists of Germany. And his experience is identical with that of others who have had the temerity to challenge the claims of an hypothesis, whose facts are very largely fancies, and whose fancies are pretty generally fatuities. The lamented Mr. James T. Fields describes an impressive scene that was enacted at a meeting of the French Institute in 1798. St. Pierre, the author of that delightful book, *Paul and Virginia*, was requested to present a paper on the question "What institutions are the most proper to form a basis for public morals?" He undertook the work, and embodied in it his own deep convictions regarding the indispensableness of piety. His colleagues were avowedly skeptical and atheistical, and were not prepared to welcome an expression of religious sentiment. When he read his essay the Institute became violently agitated, and on the mention of God's name the entire body seemed to lose its composure and self-control. St. Pierre was mocked, insulted, threatened. One member sneeringly inquired when had he seen God. Others offered to fight him, that the sword might decide whether or not such a Being existed; while others derided his advanced years, insinuating that he had come to his second childhood; and yet another, more furious than the rest, threateningly cried out,

"I swear that there is no God, and I demand that his name never again be pronounced within these walls." Just think of a company of scholars, pledged to the cause of liberty, unable to restrain their fanatical hatred of Christianity, and betrayed by it into a course of conduct as indecent as it is intolerant. In the presence of such a humiliating spectacle, it is only fair to conclude that bigotry is not peculiar to the church, but is possible and frequent in every other department of thought and life, and that even the profession of extreme charitableness is far from being an assurance of its possession or consistent exercise.

But, while this vice should be condemned wherever it is found, it is not to be concluded that Liberalism in its theories and practical workings is entitled to unqualified praise. It is far from being an unmixed good. Bishop Ken said of it, many years ago: "It is the common sewer of all heresies imaginable;" and his Grace of London, in 1850, declared it to be a sea without a shore, having no polar star to guide those who embark on it but the uncertain light of reason. Mr. Mallock, who has thoroughly studied its various phases, in his *New Republic* gives a not very flattering account of its character. He makes Leslie say, when criticising Dr. Jenkinson's sermon: "You forget that Dr. J's Christianity is really a new firm trading under an old name, and trying to purchase the good will of the former establishment;" to which Herbert responds: "It is simply our modern Atheism trying to hide its own nakedness for the benefit of the more prudish part of the public in the cast-off grave-clothes of a Christ who, whether He be risen or no, is very certainly not here." Possibly this is an extreme view of the situation; but no one can read the amiable latitudinarian sentiments of Dean Stanley, or the beautiful indefiniteness of Matthew Arnold, or the yet graver looseness of a London divine, who recently proposed the formation of a Christian fraternity with Christianity left out, and not perceive that the drift is toward a charity that disregards principle, that imperils truth, and that threatens to substitute license for liberty. From the writings of these brilliant men, and from other works in circulation that treat the question more or less completely, it seems legitimate to infer that Liberalism regards itself as the only estimable thing in the universe, and as the only thing having rights which everyone should respect. Faithfulness to God's truth, conscientious convictions, devotion to law and order, it esteems as of secondary moment, and not to be brought into comparison with its own more vital interests. They who differ from its teachings it stigmatizes as bigots, and they who decline to give aid and comfort to its hazy notions, because they believe them to be pernicious, it characterizes as persecutors; and then becomes as blind, obstinate, and ungenerous in its own assumptions and defense as it conceives its adversaries to be in their resistance to its encroachments. Evidently there is something wrong in all this. Exaggeration and perversion exist somewhere. If this is the animus of modern Liberalism, it is as unattractive as ancient bigotry; and one could hardly have a choice between them. They are both fatal to religious growth and influence. If bigotry may be likened to a rifle that murders with a single bullet the spiritual susceptibilities of our nature, Liberalism may be compared to a shot-gun, which, with its numerous leaden pellets, can hardly fail to hit, tear, and slaughter. The only discernible choice between them is the preference one may have between being pierced or riddled.

In the New Testament, and particularly in the chapters from which the texts introducing this study are derived, the law of charity, as binding on churches and individuals, is very clearly stated and very fully discussed. "He that is weak in the faith is to be received"—received into fellowship, but not to "doubtful disputations," or not to the impugning of motives and criticism of doctrines. Judged by what follows, the apostle has special reference to ritual and traditional observances, which Jewish Christians esteemed very highly, and desired their fellow-disciples to honor. The principle involved, however, seems to me susceptible of a wider application. Their attitude toward the ceremonial must have been occasioned by their view, or their conception of Christianity as a system. That it was a faulty view the entire argument of the apostle implies, and yet he is prepared to fraternize with those who held it. If their divergence from the Faith is not perfectly analogous, it is fairly comparable to that which is not infrequently met with in our times. In every congregation there are those who entertain grave doubts regarding some rules governing the administration of ordinances, or some interpretations of important Scriptures. Nevertheless, because they are not in full accord with the majority they are not to be treated as the enemies of truth. They are to be received, but not to any kind of disputation or wrangling. While they are entitled to respect, they, in their turn, are not to despise others. Toward each other they are to exercise mutual toleration; and here is brought to light what toleration always presupposes— namely, differences. It is an impossible grace where there is no disagreement. Is it not a solecism to speak of tolerating the presence or the opinions of one with whom we have no controversy? And yet professors of religion frequently use the term in this meaningless manner. They claim to be tolerant, and would wax indignant at any intimation to the contrary; and yet when an actual case of dissidence occurs, even on points, such as amusements, over which, in general, the church has no control, or on moot-doctrines, such as the degree and nature of inspiration, the philosophy and limits of atonement, and the precise character and extent of retribution, they are censorious in their judgments, and are prepared to adopt the extremest measures. This is not charity. While charity "rejoiceth in the truth," it "beareth all things, believeth all things, hopeth all things, endureth all things"; but that which beareth nothing, whatever else it may be, certainly is not charity. To call it by so sacred a name is like denominating that quality courage which parades itself in the season of safety but cowers and trembles on the approach of danger.

Nor should it be overlooked that this grace ever leads its possessor to sacrifice his own liberty for the good of others. He will be careful not to put a stumbling-block or an occasion to fall in his brother's way. The man who has an appetite for strong drink may have no right to demand that the temperate shall abstain, and he may be very dictatorial and absurd in his reasoning; nevertheless, charity will constrain the Christian, if his example may cause another to offend, quietly and unostentatiously to refrain. A disciple of Christ will realize deeply that it is not his special business to care for himself, or proudly to stand for his own rights, but to aid his fellow-beings; and if such service can be better rendered by avoiding antagonism with what his broader vision sees to be ignorant prejudice, he will rather in the spirit of toleration yield to the unreasonable than diminish his power for good. "For meat" he will not "destroy the work of God;" but "will seek the profit of many, that they may be saved."

But the exercise of this grace is not without limitations. On the one side the individual, remembering what Paul has said regarding his supreme responsibility to God, will not allow himself to be coerced by the conscience of other people into conformity with ideas and practices which are unauthorized by clear Scripture warrant, even though, as a matter of expediency and in the enjoyment of liberty, he may be willing to adopt them. Here he finds the limit to his toleration; as Coleridge puts it, it is limited by the intolerance of others. And, on the other side, the church as a body, recalling the stress everywhere laid by the sacred writers on the importance of truth, on the duty of contending earnestly for the faith, on the obligation to walk in holiness and in every way worthy of the Christian vocation; and remembering the exhortation of the apostle "to give none offense," or, rather, to cause none to offend, the church itself being included, and "to follow after the things which make for peace, and things wherewith one may edify another," may not without guilt permit such radical divergence from the precepts, doctrines, and ordinances of the gospel as would set at naught these obligations. While she has no warrant to insist on subscription to man-made definitions, or to demand a strict adherence to the letter of her creed if its spirit is honestly maintained, or to exact such slavish submission to her teachings as would render investigation a crime, she is bound to forbid such departure from them as would wreck her unity, undermine her vitality and overthrow her authority. Liberality is here hedged in by the higher law of faithfulness. It is always easier to be liberal than it is to be true. When that which the church represents, and which she is set to defend, is imperiled by the disloyalty of members, either in faith or in practice, toleration becomes a crime against the Headship of Christ and the welfare of humanity. Its limits have been reached. The church must clear herself of all complicity with the evil-doers. Charity to them means cruelty to the world. Up to this point she should bear and forbear; up to the promulgating of doctrines subversive of her essential nature, and destructive of her unity, she should patiently endure; but when that point is passed, the only recourse left is — separation. "How can two walk together unless they be agreed?"

This, as I understand it, taken in connection with the more general and fully accepted principle that the civil government has no authority to regulate religious belief, is New Testament Liberalism. But that which sails under this flag in our day is something very different, and something whose influence cannot but be regarded as prejudicial to Christianity.

Its questionable tendency may be inferred from its antagonism to definite statements of truth. Among its advocates the opinion prevails that Christ's teachings are fluid, susceptible of various meanings, and comparable more to music than to doctrine. Hear Stopford Brooke on this point: "Neither you nor I can say of that air of Mozart's that it means this or that. It means one thing to me, another thing to you. It leaves, however, an indefinite but similar impression upon us both, — a sense of exquisite melody which soothes life, a love of a life in harmony with the impressions made, and an affection for the man who gave us so delicate an emotion. So it is with the words of Christ. The understanding cannot define them; the spirit received them, and each man receives them in accordance with the state of his spirit." This, of course, is meant to be complimentary to "Him who spake as never man spake;" but in my judgment it is just the reverse. If it means anything it means either that Jesus had no truths to make known and hid the emptiness of His message beneath glittering generalities, or that He was not skillful enough to embody His thoughts in language. I am not willing to accept either reflection on His fitness to be the world's prophet, especially when it is evident that they who accuse Him of indefiniteness are seeking, at His expense, to justify their own rejection of the cardinal doctrines of Christianity. If it could for one moment be admitted, it would follow that religion has no specific faith, and consequently its claims to be an intelligible system would be absurd.

Is it not possible for every clear idea to be accurately stated? and, if it is to be communicated, must it not be stated? and if it is thus stated, does it not become a doctrine? Now, what objection can there be to such an expression of what is really believed? Scientists, philosophers and legislators would never expect to enrich the race with practical knowledge if they were to adopt a gushing, loose, sentimental style. They aim at exactness, dogmatic exactness, and we would not have it otherwise. How can it be hoped that religious knowledge can be successfully imparted in any other way? Indeed, I do not suppose that anyone really thinks that it can. However liberal a teacher may be, he does not hesitate to affirm his faith in God, and it is only when he comes to doctrines which he cannot accept that he begins to talk his vague nonsense about "slavish, arrogant, and barren dogma." But we are not deceived; it is not the verbal proposition he dislikes, it is the idea it conveys. Then let him just say so. Let him say, I reject such or such a doctrine, because I am convinced it is false, not because it is wrong to define it accurately. Were he to do this the world would see that the difference between him and other Christians is not in the breadth of their generousness, but in the range of their belief. But as it is, his unguarded denunciation of dogma is calculated to leave on the mind of the people the impression that there is no such thing as Christian truth, or, at least, nothing specific enough to be of any particular value.

Such an effect, surely, is to be deplored. Modern Liberalism claims that it is more interested in conduct than in creed. So is orthodoxy. But can it be proven that the one is independent of the other? I venture to say that it cannot. Back of every noble life there are principles which have fashioned it. I am not going to say that these principles must be identical with the evangelical faith, though I think it would be better if they were; but only that they must be adequate. Every worthy character has its basis in truth, as the most enduring structure has its foundation in the rock. Now my objection to Liberalism is, not that it cannot subscribe to evangelical teachings, but that its antagonism to definitions, consistently followed, involves all that it may suggest for the guidance of life in such indistinctness and doubt that principles of any kind must be impossible. That this is its influence may be inferred from the lax morality which is developing on every side. Every religious community feels the presence of this Ism more or less potently, and in proportion as it is felt indifference to obligation is painfully manifest. And never may we hope for a change until truth is restored to its lawful place in the life, and its dogmatic specificness, as well as its authority, is candidly acknowledged.

The questionable tendency of genial laxity may also be inferred from its incompatibility with order. God evidently dislikes confusion, fitfulness, and irregularity; for everywhere in the universe we discover their opposite. Southey has said, "Order is the sanity of the mind, the health of the body, the peace of the city, the security of the state;" and Carlyle has declared that "disorder veracious created nature, even because it is not chaos and a waste-whirling fantasm, rejects and disowns." When carelessness prevails in the home there will be boisterous tongues, fretfulness, neglect, and general untidiness and unthriftiness; when it obtains in the state there will be distrust, oppression, insurrections, and hourly danger to life and property; and when it is transferred to the church there will be contentions, impatience, grumbling; inconsistency in life and indefiniteness in aim; or having repudiated government, doctrines and ordinances, there may be sweetness and sentimentality, but there will be little consecration or concentration in religious work. Verily, as Hooker said many years ago, "Of law there can be no less acknowledged than that her seat is the bosom of God, her voice the harmony of the world: all things in heaven and earth do her homage, the very least as feeling her care, and the greatest as not exempt from her power."

The primary assumption of latitudinarians that the church should be a common receptacle for all kinds of contradictory teachings and speculations is utterly destructive of everything like order. It may read beautifully in theory; but what does it actually mean in practice? To realize such an ideal one of two conditions must be complied with— either the members must consent to have no ideas or they must agree never to express them. But if they have none, an organization is superfluous, for there is nothing of sufficient interest to draw them together; and if they have some, and fail to avow them, it is still difficult to see how, without either object or motive, they could effect anything like an organic union. Then supposing that they have convictions, differing as radically as those which now separate various denominations of Christians, and honestly express them, and conscientiously believe that religious effort should be determined by them, how can strife, contention, and the consequent paralysis of endeavor be avoided? If it shall be suggested that every member of the church, with those who may sympathize with him, would work as his conscience dictates, and others could do the same, no possible advantage, but only disadvantage, would accrue to the whole body from the arrangement. It would simply be another form of existing sectarianism, with this difference, that the sects would all be represented in one single community, and the closeness of their intimacy, and the antagonisms to which their conflicting interests would give rise, would render anything like government impracticable. Thus, there seems to be an insurmountable difficulty in the way of attaining to order on the basis of Liberalism. Now, what the world requires to-day is something more than diffusive and sentimental good nature. It needs philanthropic effort, concentrated and well-directed endeavor, which can only proceed from bodies — bodies complete and in substantial harmony. Sin is in earnest, crime is intensely so, and they both strengthen their hold on humanity by evil confederacies, and at least are strong enough to defy the attacks of such undisciplined forces as Liberalism can bring into the field. If Christianity is to succeed, it must be in earnest, too, and if it is, then it must build up organizations on a definite faith, having a common aim, and a united heart. Only through such means can it expect to prevail against the foes which swarm around it, seeking its utter overthrow.

Believe me, we shall attain more speedily the harmony of views, and the victory over evil which we all so long to achieve by faithfulness than by this perversion of charity. So much is now said in praise of this latter grace that we have quite overlooked the higher and nobler one — Faithfulness. And yet it is the heroic quality — that to which we can trace not only the preservation, but the progress of religion; that which sheltered the infant church, defended her purity from tyrants, and guarded her life from corruption. How many volumes have been written to record the victories of freedom, of prayer, of love, and how much has even been ascribed to the unsettling influence of infidelity. Doubtless they all have been potent; but the deeds of Faithfulness will compare with any of them. It was Faithfulness that saved Christianity when threatened by the Empire, that rescued it from Romanism, and that delivered it from Secularism. But for her it would have been exterminated by the one, paganized by the other, and thoroughly corrupted by the third. Faithfulness defied the emperors, sang her song to the accompaniment of growling lions in the arena, wrote her belief on dungeon walls, and shouted it amid the hiss and the roar of martyr-fires. Faithfulness prayed when others cursed, circulated the gospel while others slept, contended for every inch of the ground with error, detected its devices, resisted its encroachments, thrust her bleeding form in the way of its progress, and when crushed, rose again to pluck from its hand the victory it had nearly won. Let this magnificent record assure you that your usefulness will be measured by your loyalty more than by your liberality, and that your success in overcoming the enemies of Christ, and in harmonizing His friends, will depend more on your fidelity to principle than on your tolerance of error. Both graces are of the highest moment; but let it never be overlooked that the beautifying one is charity, while the practical one is faithfulness. So sublime is this virtue that it excites admiration even in its enemies. Frederick Robertson, when illustrating the poetic sentiment in conduct, describes how a company of soldiers were separated from their command among the mountains of India, and how they were butchered by the hill tribes. When their bodies were found, around the wrist of each dead soldier was tied a red thread, a tribute which the savage foe had paid to their valor. It signified that the men fell at their post, and by fidelity had won this red thread of honor. Singular treatment this, but not uncommon. Whenever Faithfulness has shown herself in this feculent world she has been pelted with mud. Literary scullions, reputationless hirelings, the low camp-followers of vice and degradation, have never hesitated to chase her up and down the streets and trample her in the mire. Nor may she ever look for a more kindly reception while society remains the coarse and vulgar and ungenerous thing that it is. But it is not for her to be dismayed. In patience she must possess her soul. The hounds may bay on! The devils may howl! No devil yet has ever been able to stamp out the glory of an angel's plumage; and no breath of slander and no attack of calculating maliciousness shall ever permanently stain the robe of Faithfulness or mar her beauty. Enemies may assault her; they may cast her body into the vale beneath the height on which she dwells; but even in their dastard hearts there will be found a lurking admiration for what they cannot imitate; for while they curse they will twine the red thread of honor round her wrist. They cannot but reverence what they would destroy; and future generations, when these enemies lie ignobly forgotten in the dust, will rise up and call her blessed,— and motive this for every heart to give her loyal entertainment.

FORMALISM.

"The good Lord pardon everyone that prepareth his heart to seek God, the Lord God of his fathers, though he be not cleansed according to the purification of the sanctuary." 2 *Chron. xxx, 19.*

> " Ceremony leads her bigots forth,
> Prepared to fight for shadows of no worth;
> While truths on which eternal things depend
> Find not, or hardly find, a single friend;
> As soldiers watch the signal of command,
> They learn to bow, to kneel, to sit, to stand;
> Happy to fill religion's vacant place
> With hollow form, and gesture, and grimace."
> *Cowper.*

WHEN Goethe was a boy the controversies which agitated religious circles, and which resulted in the secession from the established church of the Separatists, Pietists, and Moravians, impressed his precocious mind very deeply, and led him to devise a worship of his own. The young priest felt that the Almighty should not be approached through ecclesiastical ceremonies, but through the things which He had made; and yet, instead of communing directly with Him through nature, he patterned after the very ritualists from whom he dissented, and reared unto Him an artificial altar. A red-lacquered music-stand, beautifully ornamented, and rising like a four-sided pyramid, was chosen as the foundation of his pious work. This he covered with ores and other natural curiosities, crowning the summit with a fine porcelain saucer, from which he desired a flame to ascend emblematical of the heart's aspirations. How to produce this flame occasioned him some perplexity; but at last his ingenuity suggested the use of fumigating pastiles, which, though they would only sputter and sparkle, would at least emit a pleasant fragrance. The arrangements being perfected, and, kindling his pastiles one fine morning, with the aid of a burning-glass, he performed his devotion in an edifying manner, and to his own entire satisfaction. But the course of worship, like that of true love, is not always smooth, and Goethe found that his experiment was doomed to meet with ignominious disaster. Undertaking to repeat his adorations, he discovered, when too late, that the porcelain dish had been removed, and that his aromatic cones must be placed directly on the upper surface of the music-stand. In that position they were kindled, and the result was that they mercilessly burned into the red lacquer and the gold flowers, sadly and ineffaceably marring the beautiful and valuable work of art. The effect of the mischief, as may easily be imagined, was not conducive to piety. What the youth said on the occasion is not recorded; but in his *Autobiography*, where this narrative in his own words is found, we have the following reflections on the occurrence: "The spirit for new offerings was gone, and the accident might almost be considered a hint and warning of the danger there always is in wishing to approach the Deity in such a way."

Had the boy been content to draw near to God by "the true and living way," in lowliness and simplicity, his ardor would have escaped the chill it experienced on account of this absurd anti-climax, and probably would have saved his manhood from moral blemishes and irremediable mistakes. The old saying, "the child is father to the man," was never more completely verified than in the case of Goethe. He was essentially artistic in his tastes. His religion was æsthetical, not ethical and devotional. In after years we recognize in his writings the spirit of the boy-ritualist. He has passed from altar-building to literature, and yet his literature is a kind of altar, reared, however, more to nature than to God. It seems impossible for him to rise higher than the outward and visible; and when his pages gleam with religious sentiments we find that they are excited by the sublime and beautiful in God's works, and not by any deep discernment of what God is in Himself. His toy-worship is indeed abandoned forever, but he remains in heart to the end a formalist; delighting in creation, his genius thrilling with its wonders, but never, apparently, rejoicing in the Creator, or feeling the influences of His spirit.

Humanity at large in this respect is not very unlike the poet-philosopher. From its infancy to the present it has manifestly tended toward some species of ceremonialism, or mere outwardness; has inclined toward the multiplicity of observances ; and in magnifying their value beyond measure, it has frequently lost sight of the realities and the essence of religion. Herbert Spencer, in one of his latest works, has very amply shown that punctilious courtesy and minute formality in social and national relations do not mark the highest civilization; but that among such savage people as the Ashantees and Loangoes they receive the most scrupulous attention. Thus, "in the kingdom of Uganda, where, directed by the king to try a rifle presented to him by Speke, a page went to the door and shot the first man he saw in the distance; and where, as Stanley tells us, under the last king, Suna, five days were occupied in cutting up thirty thousand prisoners who had surrendered, we find that an officer observed to salute informally is ordered for execution, while another, who, perhaps, exposes an inch of naked leg while squatting, or has his *mbugu* tied contrary to regulations, is condemned to the same fate." This excessive respect for the trivialities of social intercourse, and the heartlessness exhibited in maintaining their authority, indicate that among these people ceremony is substituted for politeness, and the symbols of reverence for its spirit. A similar inversion makes up what we mean by Formalism in religion — the sign is taken for the thing signified, and the soul is satisfied with the name instead of the substance — as one might be content to live on the menu instead of the meal. When the church service is composed of innumerable and unintelligible rites, which burden the conscience without refining the heart; and when its rubric prescribes the precise manner in which devotion shall find expression, we have Formalism. When Brother Martin finds the priests, who have just been conducting mass, laughing and joking at the credulity of their flock, to employ no harsher term, he has an exhibition of Formalism; and when the sacred duties which spring from our relations with the Supreme and with each other are fulfilled as a matter of course and from sheer necessity, or when the simplest worship is performed from worldly motives, and emptied of all sympathy and interest, Formalism is as apparent as it is in him who smiles his congratulations through hyena eyes, snarls his compliments through canine teeth, and commends his love with the serpent's clammy, slimy touch. This is Formalism, and toward it there is an ever-recurring trend.

It is met in connection with, perhaps, every historical faith. The simple cult of the Veda was crushed beneath the weight of Brahminical observances; the primitive freedom of Buddhism fell a prey to Lamaistic superstitions; the pious feelings of the Romans were strangled by the rigid clutch of prosaic divinities; the Greek religion, which was conquered, like their country, in the hands of its new adherents degenerated into endless mummeries and theatrical pomposities; the spirituality of Judaism was at last fatally hampered with the dead body of narrow, literalistic and bigoted pharisaism; while Christianity itself, the most unfettered of all systems, and requiring more heart in its service than any other, has been equally distorted and travestied by ritualists on the one hand, and by nominalists on the other. To-day the empire of faith suffers as much from this cause as from any that can be specified. Romanists announce a salvation which is inseparable from ceremonial observance, and have so interblended and intermixed ritual with ethics that it is next to impossible for an ordinary mind to discriminate between them. While the coherence of this organization is wonderful; for, judged by what is known of it in Europe and America, it is a vast and complicated machine, well oiled with promises of eternal felicity, it affords very little opportunity for the free play of the heart. Indeed, whatever degree of heartiness is in it is there as a foreign element, unprovided for in its arrangements, and unnecessary to their execution. Highchurchism errs in the same direction, if not to the same extent, while the various Protestant bodies, though wisely and rightly discarding the temptation to formality which exists elsewhere, have not altogether escaped from its deadening influence.

It is to be remembered that it is possible, even where the forms are few, bare and unassuming. For instance, when a creed is upheld by one who has no deep, genuine and practical belief in what it teaches, or when the importance of intellectual subscription is exaggerated over soul affiliation, how shall this be justly characterized? Or, if the plainest dress is worn as a badge of distinction, for the empty purpose of asserting unworldliness, and the significance of the garment be forgotten in the transactions of ordinary life, what name ought to be applied to such inconsistency? Or, still further, if ordinances are looked upon as talismans and charms, and substituted for the blessings they denote; if the lips are eloquent with praise while the heart is far from God; and if the service of the sanctuary becomes frigid, stiff, and perfunctory,— the echo from a sepulcher, and the rattle of a fleshless corpse,— how shall such a shoaly, skinny, viscerated piety be described? Each of these questions is answered by a single term, "Formalism;" for evidently we confront in each of these cases what the Savior condemns in the pharisees who paid "tithe of mint, and anise, and cummin, while they neglected the weightier matters of the law, judgment, mercy, and faith."

Against this evil the Scriptures constantly utter their warning. They do so even when urging compliance with all the outward requirements of religion. Certainly they are far from treating contemptuously the ordinances or duties which have been solemnly sanctioned by the Spirit. These externals have their place in the divine economy, and they are neither to be treated with disrespect nor ignored. We are exhorted, at least by implication, to "keep the ordinances as they were delivered" to us, to "maintain the form of sound words," and to be faithful to the profession made before many witnesses. Nor is it practicable altogether to dispense with shadows, symbols, and particular observances. "It is difficult," says the Greek philosopher, "fully to exhibit greater things without the aid of patterns;" and Lord Bacon insists on "the indispensableness of similitudes." Figures in action, as well as of speech, are the means by which our faith reveals itself, asserts and communicates its message to mankind. It is impossible to teach without words, which are the signs of ideas; and it is equally so to sustain an organization without some recognized external order, or to conduct divine worship without some appropriate ceremony. These things give definiteness, shape and expression to beliefs, thoughts and convictions, which, apart from them, would be somewhat indistinct to their possessors, and totally valueless, because intangible, to the world. Consequently the New Testament, as well as the Old, has its laws, rites, and symbols. It describes a church which is not air-built, vague, or phantom-like, but a substantial, well-founded, and visible institution. It is clothed upon with a body, and, though in comparison with the opaque Jewish dispensation it may be a very transparent one, it is yet as real as the texture of the crystal through whose flinty pores the light streams, and in whose rocky heart it delights to dwell. And, to follow this illustration, the church, like the unflawed crystal, while it has a definite form, is permeable with spiritual light, and is to be careful neither to obstruct its incoming, nor its indwelling and outgoing.

This duty was not entirely overlooked among the ancient Jews. Though their religion was eminently ritualistic,— and, remembering the peculiarity of their position, we ought not to be surprised that it was,— their prophets frequently taught, and their most notable men discerned, that the ceremonial, however important, was secondary in value to the spiritual, and subordinate to its culture. The Psalms of David may be taken as fairly exhibiting the recognition of this distinction. There we meet with praises and prayers which have been appropriated by the devout of all ages as the language of their heart's deepest and loftiest experiences.

From the chronicle of which our text is part we have an instance of enlightened discrimination in this direction. Hezekiah summoned the people to Jerusalem to keep the Passover, but many of them had no opportunity to comply with the ceremonial requirements which qualified for participation, and consequently they approached the solemn rite in what is described as an unsanctified condition. But on this account they were not thrust aside. The king realized the vital significance of the celebration to Israel, and, under the circumstances, permitted anyone to come who prepared his heart, though "he had not been cleansed according to the purification of the sanctuary." He did not question the binding authority of the ceremonial law which had been neglected; for he prays that all who are unable to keep it might be pardoned; but he does not exalt it to such a height as to leave the impression that its observance outweighed in value the preparation of the heart. In this estimate he but follows the judgment of Samuel, who said that to "obey is better than sacrifice, and to hearken than the fat of rams;" and anticipated Isaiah, who in ringing words denounced the formal fasting that failed "to loose the bands of wickedness, to undo the heavy burdens, to let the oppressed go free, and to break every yoke." Moses also distinguished between the letter and the spirit; for he urged the people to circumcise the foreskin of the heart, as did Jeremiah in another age; and the promises of God maintained in the nation a distinct recognition of the superior glory of the latter.

Christianity was announced in language such as this: "And it shall come to pass afterward that I will pour out my spirit on all flesh; and your sons and your daughters shall prophesy, your old men shall dream dreams, your young men shall see visions;" "I will pour water upon him that is thirsty, and floods upon the dry ground; I will pour my Spirit upon thy soul, and my blessing upon thine offspring;" and that these predictions might be accomplished the Savior said: "It is expedient for you that I go away, for if I go not away the Comforter will not come unto you; but if I depart I will send Him unto you." Peter, on the day of Pentecost, announced that this sacred pledge had been fulfilled: "Therefore, being by the right hand of God exalted, and having received of the Father the promise of the Holy Ghost, He hath shed forth this, which ye now see and hear;" and Paul, contrasting the Jewish economy with the Christian, and having in view the comparative freedom of the latter from ritual, and its completer possession of the Sanctifier, calls it "the ministration of the Spirit." These representations from both Testaments, combined with our Lord's solemn warnings uttered on the Mount against formality, and Paul's description of it as a "form of godliness, denying the power thereof," are enough to show that this is a tremendous evil; one that is to be resisted, and one from whose influence the Almighty is seeking our deliverance.

Possibly we may be brought into closer sympathy with the Divine mind on this subject by examining the true relations of form to spirit, the limitations governing them, and the reasons why they should be conscientiously recognized and respected.

First, it seems evident that form should adequately express, but never obscure, the spiritual. Just as too many words hide the idea they are designed to convey, and just as excess of light blinds the eyes it is ordained to illuminate, so too numerous ceremonials darken the truth which they are supposed to adumbrate. We know there is a kind of choir music which fails to excite in the heart emotions of praise, because it appeals overwhelmingly to artistic appreciation. Were it less operatic it would be more devotional in its influences. Congregational singing has this to be said in its favor, that as all share in it no one can easily lapse into the position of critic; and however inharmonious and inmelodious it may be, and unfortunately it is generally both, as it is the effort of each individual to worship, it stimulates devoutness in spite of discord. As music may so charm the ear that its religious value is measurably, if not totally, lost, so elaborate rites challenge so powerfully the sense that they fail to penetrate and influence the soul. Hence, it has been observed that in proportion as ceremonial observances are multiplied spirituality declines. Of the truth of this position such countries as Spain, Italy, and Mexico, long subject to the sway of a sacerdotal system, afford abundant proof. With them, for many centuries, religion has been so much a matter of form that they have lost sight of its spiritual aspects, and in doing so have deteriorated in other respects. Victor Hugo, arraigning the church of Rome on the charge of blighting the nations where her superstitious observances have been most intolerantly enforced and most abjectly obeyed, points to the two great Catholic centers, and says: "Look at the first of these lands, Italy, the mother of genius and of nations, which has spread over the world the most brilliant marvels of poetry and art; Italy, which taught mankind to read, knows not how to read. Gaze on Spain, which received from the Romans her first civilization, from the Arabs her second, and from Providence a world, — America! But Rome has robbed her of the secret power which she had from the Romans, the genius of art which she had from the Arabs, and the world which she had from God." Do you remind me that the Frenchman, in this invective, is laying stress on the persecuting spirit of the Papacy? Granted; but this very spirit is the outgrowth of ritualism. Beneath its weight the sense of right and wrong, of conscience and charity, was deadened, and in its place arose that haughty intolerance which, drenching itself in blood, furnishes the best of reasons for restricting outward observances to their God-appointed limits.

Among the Jews, as I have already intimated, types, shadows, symbols, prevailed beyond what is authorized by Christianity. This is to be accounted for by the fact that Judaism was a preparative system. It was God's ordained instrumentality for the introduction of certain fundamental ideas into the world, for which there existed no adequate verbal equivalents, and which had to be revealed through visible institutions and picturesque enactments. The ideas of "holiness," "atonement," "mediation," were thus imported and fixed, and then the ceremonies which had performed this service, like nuggets of gold, were melted and coined into words, which retain the significance derived from them to this day. When the end for which they had been set apart was accomplished they were dispensed with as henceforward unnecessary, and in their place came the written gospel which is given to every man "to profit withal." This corresponds to the truth, as the letter does to the type, and the study of its teachings ministers to holiness. Christianity also has a few expressive signs that appeal to the senses, and through them to the heart. It has symbolical rites, such as baptism and the Lord's supper; and it has ethical and pietistical forms, such as almsgiving, prayer and praise, which may properly be thus characterized, as they have definite visibility. All of these are so closely related to important religious truths that, when properly honored, they become their vehicle and their mirror. Thus praise and prayer suggest the ideas of human dependence and of divine providence; almsgiving, the surrender of self and its possessions to the service of God and man; baptism, the resurrection of Christ with all it imports, and the Supper, the twin mysteries of incarnation and atonement. But when these acts are exaggerated, perverted or degraded, they obscure the system which they were appointed to irradiate. When baptism is administered to adult or child as a means of salvation, how seriously is the grace of God narrowed and impugned; when the Lord's Supper is given with a similar end in view, how is the atonement of Christ caricatured and darkened; or when almsgiving and other excellent works are credited with so much merit that the Almighty may become debtor to the creature, what a grievous misrepresentation of religion is imposed upon the world. Under the circumstances the outward aspects of Christianity become a curse; for generating errors, sanctioning monstrous absurdities, and burdening the conscience, they tend to alienate thoughtful men from its support and to debase those who sustain its authority. These considerations indicate the importance of proportioning aright the symbol to the substance, and of sacredly conserving the design of its institution. Only in this way can it be of service to the truth, and as it is contrary to common sense and Scripture to suppose that it might have been established for any other reason, the obligation to restrict it to its legitimate sphere and office is imperative.

Secondly, it seems equally clear that form should effectively supplement, but never subordinate, the spiritual. We know how the solemnities of public worship intensify devotion, how acts of charity tend to deepen benevolence, how verbal confessions strengthen faith, how ordinances vivify belief, and how religious acts in general, undertaken with genuine heartiness, contribute to growth in grace and to advancement in the life divine. When the outward thus waits upon the soul, ministering to its sanctification, we feel that it is conforming to heaven's plan. But when it rejects this lowly but useful mission, and insists on its claims at the expense of the spiritual, it manifestly transgresses its prerogative. The Scriptures teach that the spirit of the gospel is worth more than the letter; that Christ Himself must henceforward be known "not after the flesh, but after the spirit"; and that the inner motive prompting a sacrifice is of greater value than the measure of the sacrifice itself, as in the case of the widow whose mite outweighed the treasury full of gifts which pride donated from its superabundance. Moreover, the Savior intimates that whenever the interests of the formal and the spiritual come into collision the first must give precedence to the second. Thus, for instance, when He does good on the Sabbath day, His defense is not that the fourth commandment is abrogated, but that ritual is secondary in importance to philanthropy. "The Sabbath was made for man, not man for the Sabbath." It was appointed for his welfare and happiness; but if some regulation regarding the observance must under no circumstances be violated,— if the house that is on fire may not be rescued on the Sabbath, nor the ship that is drifting on the rocks be saved,— then the day ceases to be a boon to humanity. Our Lord protested against this narrow interpretation, as He would against that which could condemn David for eating the shewbread which was ceremonially forbidden him. The hunger of the psalmist was his justification in setting aside a merely ritualistic regulation, and Jesus in sanctioning his conduct develops an important principle.

The principle is, that the external aspect of Christianity should be subordinated to the well-being of the soul. Thus if the manner or method of worship is found to work detrimentally, we may order it in such a way as to promote the end it is designed to secure. A failure to do this, because our fathers cherished it, or because venerable men arranged it, evinces a sentimentalism bordering on superstition, which will parch and wither the religious life. If we confront a positive ordinance, such as baptism, which we have no right to change as we have the man-appointed regulations of worship, it should be received only at a time when the recipient is conscious that it will advance his spirituality. For it to be thrust upon the unbeliever is to exalt it unduly, and to invest it with a rank that does not pertain to it. If one comes to the Lord's supper who has not complied with all the orderly prerequisites, and who is impelled by a hunger of soul to approach uninvited, the church, while she does not approve his irregularity, yet, lest a too rigid enforcement of the ritual may be interpreted adversely to her charity, and may in some way injuriously affect the applicant, is bound to remember that David ate the shewbread, which was ceremonially unlawful for him to eat, and not inderdict the coming of one to the Lord's table whose hunger is even deeper than his. Were this principle generally recognized, and generally accepted as a guiding rule, there would be more freedom and more fervid delight in God's service everywhere, and less danger of falling into listless, perfunctory and exacting ceremonialism. It would deepen the impression that soul preparation is more important than anything else, and then care would be bestowed primarily on that, and everything else being held subordinate, we should approximate in all of our congregations to that worship which is bounded neither by Jerusalem nor Gerizim, but which is as broad as the Savior's love, and which, in its essence, is spirit and truth,—"For God is a Spirit, and they that worship Him must worship Him in spirit and in truth."

Thirdly. It also seems reasonable that form should sufficiently adorn, but never supersede or supplant, the spiritual. Within proper limits, especially those suggested already, it is eminently fitting that we should invest both the Christian church and Christian character with whatever may enhance their beauty. Works of righteousness attractive in themselves may receive an added grace from the manner in which they are wrought. These constitute the ritual of individual daily life, and when they are performed thoughtfully, gently, sweetly, they influence as much by their loveliness as by their worth. There is indeed a kind of moral worth in beauty, to which the conscience instinctively renders homage. No man can afford to be good uncouthly or carelessly. There are types of piety that repel; some that are gunpowderish, sensitive and explosive; others that are tomahawkish, sharp and censorious, and yet others that are edgeless, indefinite and colorless. These specimens, naturally enough, are disliked, and they are but a little in advance of that which, for reasons satisfactory to itself, determines that its good shall never be evil spoken of, by doing no good whatever to call forth remark. As the individual is not to be indifferent to the beautiful, so neither should the church. Her house of worship may be as imposing and attractive as art can make it, as long as the investment yields an adequate profit in spiritual results, and the outlay can be afforded by the congregation. The public offices of worship should be rendered impressive and satisfactory to refined taste as well as to devout impulses, provided always, as has already been argued, that they do not obscure the essentials of Christianity. No other rule upon this point can be laid down. This simple restriction will prove sufficient to guard against excess, and when it is respected, the beauty of holiness will never jeopardize the integrity of holiness.

It is surely unnecessary to add that no perfection of the form will be accepted by God as a substitute for the reality. The one cannot supersede the other; and of the two, the second is preferable and indispensable. If ye fast to be seen of men, if ye pray to be praised of men, if ye give to be honored by men, verily ye have your reward. Ye seek human approval, and "he that soweth to the flesh shall of the flesh reap"; were ye to purpose these things in your heart, and perform them unto God, God would not forget your self-denying labor of love. The service of the lip and the empty sacrifice of the body the Almighty does not regard. As in the days of Samuel, He judges not by the countenance or stature, but by the heart, and if other motive were wanting, this ought to be sufficient to convince us that Formalism is a dreary, worthless piece of theatricality, from which every genuine soul should turn away with scorn and contempt.

Sometimes when near the sea I have been sadly impressed with the dry, stunted, dwarfed and naked trees struggling to preserve their hold on life amid barren wastes and in the chill, brackish air. On the island known as Martha's Vineyard I have frequently wandered among the thin, attenuated oaks,— meager shadows of their giant brotherhood,— and have mourned the bitterness of their heritage. Their wretched branches in one direction bent seem to reveal a desire to break from their rootage and escape the storm; while their ragged foliage, whitened by the flying sand and the dust of pulverized shells, proclaims that their enemy has prevailed against them, imparting to them the visage of death, and shrouding them for the grave before they have quite perished from the earth. Alas! for the poor, miserable, tattered, discolored and faded "cumberers of the ground." Perhaps than themselves there is nothing more pitiable in this pitiable world, unless it is that which they appropriately figure,— a soulless, sapless, shriveled church. Seeking to thrive in a worldly atmosphere, rooted in barren professions, bearing no fruit, and maintaining only the semblance of existence, such a church cannot long survive. It will soon wear the complexion of death; speedily will its gorgeous ritual become as the mummy's rags, and its beauty expire as the moth. Over such a withered, emaciated, undersized representative of Christianity one could weep for very shame, and pray for some good woodman's ax to smite the pigmy, or some burst of Heaven's indignation to level it with the earth. God grant that our unuttered prayer may be answered, and that for every lifeless church destroyed, one may spring up which shall be like the tree described by Daniel,—"whose height reached unto the heaven, and the sight thereof to all the earth; whose leaves were fair, and the fruit thereof much, and in it was meat for all; under which the beasts of the field dwelt, and upon whose branches the fowls of heaven had their habitations."

Hegel assumes that, while "the artist makes for the

expression of his spiritual conceptions stones, colors and sensuous forms," the idea is of paramount importance, and must be in the mind, even though unconsciously, before it can be presented for the contemplation of others. In applying this principle to Greek art he shows "that the human being elaborated his physical being in free, beautiful movements before the attempt was made to give them expression in marbles or paintings." The archetype of all subsequent triumphs with chisel and brush originated in the development of the body, was naturally transferred to the mind, and from thence reproduced itself in plastic stone. Such also is the sublime law of Christ's kingdom. "Ye must be born again," is its primary and supreme requirement. When the moral nature receives the divine image through regeneration, then will it impart the same to the otherwise lifeless material of public worship and of private duty. Then will it mold and fashion the humblest ceremony into a heavenly likeness, and breathe upon the simplest acts a heavenly grace. First, the soul must be spiritual, then it will spiritualize everything about it, and the ideal kingdom be realized. Therefore I close this discussion with one appeal, one representation, one distinct assertion, the echo of our Lord's own words to Nicodemus, and which points the way, not merely to personal peace and usefulness, but to the fundamental condition of spirituality, without which the church is as a whited sepulcher and as a tinkling cymbal:—
"Ye must be born again."

DENOMINATIONALISM.

"But now are they many members, yet but one body." *1 Cor. xii, 20.*

"Here all the rage of controversy ends,
And rival zealots rest like bosom friends;
An Athanasian here in deep repose
Sleeps with the fiercest of his Arian foes;
Socinians here with Calvinists abide,
And thin partitions angry chiefs divide;
Here wily Jesuits, simple Quakers meet,
And Bellarmine has rest at Luther's feet.
Great authors, for the church's glory fired,
Are, for the church's peace, to rest retired;

. . . .

For most she fears the controversial pen,
The holy strife of disputatious men;
Who the blest gospel's peaceful page explore,
Only to fight against its precepts more."
George Crabbe.

THERE is a widespread impression that the denominationalism of Christianity and the conflicts of doctrinal opinion within the limits of its different sects seriously militate against its super-mundane origin and character. On this ground Lord Herbert attempted to justify his Theism; and in the judgment of many did so with remarkable force, if not with entire success. And Voltaire also, in his *Dictionary*, with shrewd skill and sarcastic sharpness, wrote: "There is no sect in geometry, mathematics or experimental philosophy. When truth is evident it is impossible to divide people into parties and factions. Nobody disputes that it is broad day at noon." Both of these writers proceed on the assumption that moral questions should be dealt with as we deal with numbers, triangles, polygons and circles, and that the same kind of certainty is to be looked for in the one case as in the other. But this is unreasonable. There is a broad distinction in kind between these departments of inquiry, which necessarily affects their methods and their conclusions. Truth in the domain of morals and religion is more open to debate than in the physical; for it relates to profounder and more complicated issues; is, in the nature of things, more difficult of proof, and comes into collision with deeper prejudices and intenser antagonisms. These differences being possible in the realm of spiritual inquiry, they easily account for parties in the Christian church without involving the implication of Voltaire that they are contending about that which is radically false.

May it not also be said in answer to this objection that the alleged harmony of experimental philosophers is more fanciful than real? There are sects in science as in religion, and they are just as uncompromising and as uncharitable, and probably more so. Not to weary you with illustrations of this statement, permit me to allude to one which was related to me recently in the city of Berlin. Huxley and Owen quarreled over the brain of the chimpanzee. One of these eminent scientists contended that the upper lobe extended over the lower, and the other denied it. Friendship was broken in consequence of this disagreement, and the rivals would not acknowledge each other courteously. The war between them was stern and pronounced, and even the discovery that both were correct did not end hostilities. Although it was shown that what one gentleman affirmed was true of the male chimpanzee, but not of the female, and that what was affirmed by the other was true of the female but not of the male, concord would not return. They both continued to look askance and defiantly at each other, like the famous servants of the implacable and irreconcilable Capulets and Montagues:

"Do you bite your thumb at me, sir?"

"I bite my thumb."

And in the same spirit of sectarianism Professor Huxley criticises M. Comte: "In so far as my study of what specially characterizes the Positive Philosophy has led me, I find therein little or nothing of any scientific value, and a great deal which is thoroughly antagonistic to the very essence of science as anything in Ultramontane Catholicism. In fact, M. Comte's philosophy in practice might be compendiously described as Catholicism minus Christianity." Ah! Could the dead philosopher revive again most likely he would answer this stinging rebuke with scathing sharpness, and entertain society with a new version of the ancient feud:

"I serve as good a man as you."

"No better?"

"Yes, better, sir."

Alarmed by the damaging inference drawn from their divisions, and half persuaded of its cogency, a large number of disciples insist on the immediate union of all denominations. In their fright they make some singular proposals, suggest the most astounding compromises, and remarkable theories; and may very properly be called the peace-at-any-price party. Some of them are willing that present differences of opinion and belief should continue, if by some happy device a solid front can only be presented to the world. What they seem to desire is that an end should be put to all discord, at least in appearance. Hence they have invented evangelical alliances, great and small; union societies and union movements, big and little; all valuable and desirable in their place, but without as yet accomplishing anything very wonderful. Others of this class are so intensely interested in this cause that they make the impression that conscientious scruples and moral convictions ought to yield to its superior claims; and that it would be better to narrow the circle of truth than consent to perpetuate the evils of separation. From the beginning of the Christian era there have always been worshipers at the altars of uniformity; who have regarded it as the easiest thing imaginable for all persons to square thought and conduct to the requirements of a single standard. These ecclesiastical morphologists have not only demanded that conduct should be conformed to the same pattern, but that belief should be cast in the same mold. They never, however, have succeeded in actualizing their ideal. The decrees they fulminated, the persecutions they employed, and the anathemas they invoked, came short of their aim. Religious people would not think alike, would not act alike, would not fetter the free life in them; but persistently ran into all sorts of irregularity, singularity, and nonconformity. In our time this zeal in behalf of oneness has not abated; but recognizing the difficulty of controlling thought, in some quarters it now pleads for agreement in outward observances and ceremonies, whatever may be the individual belief. However motley, multifarious and heterogeneous faith may be, it is assumed that practical submission to the same forms would impart to the church that union which was contemplated by the Savior, and which for so many reasons is desirable. This is the present attitude of the Roman Catholic church and of the Church of England. A great variety of opinions are tolerated within their communions on condition that the ritual be faithfully maintained. But this spirit of compromise is looked upon as deplorable by a more radical class, who have not yet been convinced of the utter impossibility of actualizing the other half of the old strict conformity theory. They do not understand how any person can arrive at different conclusions, in reading the New

Testament, from their own. Diversity is inexplicable, extraordinary, monstrous. They are ready to ascribe it to eccentricity, aberration, or something worse; and, forgetting that they themselves are not in entire accord with the theology of the past, they are ready, in the interests of union, to cut off from their fellowship the members who offend against what they regard as inspired truth. But however these parties may dissent as to means and measures, they are all intent on the unification of the church in some fashion, more or less complete. This, in their judgment, is the supreme question of the hour, toward whose solution they are struggling along somewhat confusedly and blunderingly.

I am convinced that whatever of error is involved in the views current on this subject is largely due to unacquaintance and unfamiliarity with the real law of unity as it is revealed in nature and revelation, and to the failure to recognize the degree and kind of diversity that is not only compatible with it, but inseparable from it.

If we look upon the sky we find it at times overcast with clouds, which assume the most varied and changing shapes. Now they drift like fleecy snow across the expanse of blue, then wander slowly up and down, like flocks of sheep, seeking pasturage among the stars, and shepherded by the gentle wind; or they are piled up on the horizon's extremest verge, dark with storm and heavy with tempests, resembling some huge citadel frowning on the peaceful vale; or they are spread out beneath the glory of the setting sun, from whose glittering planes majestic forms arise, picturing to the eye the beauty and harmony of the heavenly city, with its streets of gold, its gates of pearl, and its walls of precious stones. Their transitory and fleeting shapes, that now appeal to fear and then to fancy, are but sculpturesque, though unsculptured, figures of that one element that falls in the rain, gleams in the dew, and that sparkles in the ice-particle. Here we meet with unity in diversity, a diversity that magnifies the unity. Schiller, describing natural scenery, writes:

> "Flowers of all hue are struggling into glow
> Along the blooming fields; yet their sweet strife
> Melts into one harmonious concord";

and in his *Philosophical Letters* he adds: "Millions of plants drink from the four elements of nature; a magazine of supplies is open for all; but they mix their sap in a thousand different ways, and return it in a thousand new forms." We cannot, surely, have failed to think of this ourselves, or to have overlooked the kindred but deeper fact that the endless variations of root and leaf in each particular plant are indispensable to the perfect fullness and harmony of the flower. They all spring from unity, and they tend to unity again. And what is true of earth's floral beauty is true of earth itself. Mountains and valleys, deep, dark forests, wide, sweeping prairies, rocky wildernesses and grassy glens, that break the monotony of its surface, are all bound together in the fellowship of matter. Of a common nature, they effect, through their diversity, a common good. As the mutability of clouds is needful to shield the tender crops from heat, and to bedew them with refreshing moisture, so the irregularities of the earth are inseparable from its habitableness. Were it not for these, human beings could not exist upon its bosom, and progress in arts and sciences would be impossible. Believe me, there is not a mountain range too many, nor too long or lofty, not a vale too wide or deep, not a superfluous stream or ocean, nor a single region whose essential character can be changed with entire impunity. So nicely ordered, balanced, measured, are these diversities that on their preservation rests the welfare of the whole. Man, the tenant of this wondrous house, is himself the most notable illustration of this principle. How like, and yet unlike, are the teeming millions that make up the race. No two are identical in body or in soul. They are all similar, yet dissimilar; they are oneness in manifoldness. They possess in common the same nature, faculties and organs, but in degree, quality and aptitude how endlessly diverse! And who can doubt but that this very lack of uniformity has proven the most potent factor in the world's advancement. It has given us our specialists, our statesmen, poets, soldiers, inventors; it has exalted our civilization by multiplying its departments; it has lessened the evils of life by distributing its burdens; it has unified races and nations by demonstrating their independence, and it has stimulated and elevated the individual by bringing him face to face with the competition of the many.

> "See how the iron powers of thoughtful skill
> Are shaped and quickened by the fire of strife."

Scientists are now calling attention to the growing diversity that may be traced throughout the universe. The sidereal system, with its spiral and spherical nebulæ, with its clusters of stars, ranging from two to several thousand in number, they claim has increased in heterogeneity during the long time spaces that have elapsed since the creation. The same fact is urged of the earth in its progress from original chaos. Fossil remains are said to prove that "the more heterogeneous organisms, and groups of organisms, have been evolved from the more homogeneous." Also, in the history of the arts the law of diversity is recognized and pointed out by these writers. But perhaps the most striking illustration of the principle involved is furnished by what Grove and Spencer call the "Correlation of Physical Forces." It is now believed that heat, electricity, chemical force, and every other kind of force, have reciprocal affection and dependence, and that any one of them may be convertible into any of the others. Thus, for instance, heat produces electricity under certain conditions, and electricity produces heat, and either of them or both may be the cause of motion. These elements or energies, therefore, are but forms of some one supreme force,—differentiations, modifications, and transmutations of some ultimate subtle energy. That—whatever it is—tends to diversity of manifestation and of operation, and thus falls in with what appears to be the method of universal progress. For it is to be observed that these changes from the simple to the complex, from the homogeneous to the heterogeneous, result in greater definiteness and distinctness of structure and of organism, and in greater perfectness of form and function. Everywhere the law of diversity is seen to be elaborating a more complete and glorious order of things; as Mr. Spencer says, "is the deepest knowable cause of those modifications which constitute physiological development, as it is the deepest knowable cause of all other evolutions," and is not, therefore, to be lightly esteemed, deprecated or deplored.

Is there not something analogous to this in the domain of the spiritual? I believe that there is. As I read the New Testament I find that there is a sense in which all Christians are really one. Superficially and outwardly they may be separated, but essentially and spiritually they are united. This is our Savior's doctrine. He represents His disciples as partaking of the same life, as being members of the same kingdom, and as engaged in the same work. In the parables of the vine and the mustard seed they are set forth as being vitalized and sustained by the same life-current, and as bearing fruit from the same source. They are one flock, having one shepherd; and they are one family, having one Father. If our Lord prayed for their unification, we are not to conclude that He meant to teach that they are naturally and necessarily separated from each other like the sands of the sea; but that its degree might be intensified until they should come to share with each other and with Christ in that mysterious fellowship which blends His personality with that of the Father. As there is growth in grace, so is there growth in union; and as the first is only possible when grace already exists, so the second is only attainable when the disciples are bound together in Christ by deep, spiritual ties. And just in proportion as it approaches the ideal will it be manifest to the world; not by some dull uniformity, but by the fuller revelation of that which is its cause. All concede that its source is Christ; it is a union in Christ; and as it draws nearer to perfection the Christ-life will be more apparent. His spirit, His purity, the beauties of His character, will become more conspicuous in His followers, and will draw to them the attention and approval of the world. Without referring to the apostles for the confirmation of this view, we may conclude that it is worthy our support, and should be recognized as fundamental to a just conception of Christian union. Whatever differences of doctrine or practice may seem to wall denominations from each other, they are fellow-disciples, brethren and sisters in the Lord, resting in a common Savior, rejoicing in a common hope. They may have fallen into errors of faith, they may have drifted into errors of government, they may have adopted singular ceremonials, and even more singular customs, but if they breathe the spirit of Christ in their words and deeds they are equally His, and equally members of His body. This is being realized to-day, perhaps more distinctly than in the past, and hence, though the number of sects may not have diminished, sectarianism has perceptibly declined.

This unity in the Savior does not prevent diversity,

and the diversity is not destructive of the unity. This seems to be clearly taught in the sacred writings. Such figures as the vine and mustard-tree, which are employed to illustrate it, imply variety; for we know that no two leaves are perfectly alike. Marked differences separate the apostles, not only in character but in their way of looking at the truth. While their teachings are essentially the same, they are distinguishable by a Jewish or a philosophical cast of thought. In the twelfth chapter of second Corinthians we have presented an elaborate account of the diversities that were found in the primitive church. Gifts, administrations or governments, operations and methods, were not alike. They were dissimilar. Some members had the word of wisdom, others the word of knowledge, others divers kinds of tongues, and others yet the interpretation of tongues. But over all and through them all wrought the self-same Spirit. Now, admitting that many of these particular distinctions were peculiar to the apostolic age, and conceding that in Revelation we have an outline of everything to be believed or done to secure even the most complete outward agreement among disciples, are we not taught by this chapter that diversities are not destructive of essential unity; that their continuance in some form is always not only possible but probable, and that as they were in the Corinthian church overruled for good, so in all after-times they would be made subservient to the well-being of Christ's kingdom? This, at least, is the inference I draw from the chapter.

As the genius and other mental and spiritual qualities of the apostles colored their presentation of truth, it is not unnatural to suppose that similar qualities would influence those who interpret it, in subsequent periods. And as disciples were gifted by the Spirit, doubtless in harmony with their natural endowments, to fulfill certain offices and ministries, and as there was evidently a disposition to magnify their special work at the expense of that which was being wrought by their brethren, how reasonable to expect that in the future similar preferences would be shown, and that out of them denominations would even develop. This is just what has taken place. Different interpretations, various views of doctrine or of church government, combined with predilections for this or that mode of doing Christian work, have resulted in the formation of religious bodies. As the vital principle in nature takes to itself varied but appropriate forms, and as the primary force asserts itself as magnetism, heat or electricity, so the spirit of grace, which permeates the entire company of the saved, being modified by their personality, reveals itself in various creeds and various organizations. Unity is no more sacrificed in the one case than in the other; and more than this, as we have seen that diversity in the physical ministers to the highest good of the universe, to its progress as well as to its stability, we are warranted in believing that diversity in the spiritual promotes its development, its advancement and its triumph.

We generally assume, when the subject is under consideration, that Christianity would have accomplished more for the world than it has if it had remained a stranger to disruptions and discords. This is the prevailing opinion. It is repeated without any sort of misgiving on all occasions where the limited triumphs of the Cross form the theme of conversation or discussion. But it is very questionable whether, in the sense usually intended, the position is sound and trustworthy. Of course there must be some explanation of the failure to fulfill the fair promise which the new religion gave at the beginning of its history, and for want of a better it is not unnatural that it should be sought in the rise and perpetuity of variances and factions. Undoubtedly little can ever be effected in the spirit of sectarianism, or alienation; and so far as the inner and vital union between God's people has come short of the beautiful ideal, every agency for good has been weakened and impeded. This may be conceded, and yet what we mean by denominationalism not be responsible for the comparatively unsuccessful endeavors of the church. Whether she would have succeeded better had uniformity distinguished her is, in my judgment, open to debate; and whether she would have exerted a greater power if monotony had been the rule is not altogether clear and certain. I think as much can be said on one side as the other, and at least enough to occasion hesitancy in subscribing unreservedly to the common view. A Moslem proverb has it, "The leaves of God's book are the religious persuasions"; and I am not convinced that the variety of readings, practically as unimportant as the multiplied differences between the several versions of the Scriptures, have proved in the least detrimental to the establishment and progress of Christianity. Standing by the Falls of Niagara, the spectator must be impressed with the fact that the rapid sweep and concentrated solidity of the waters do not prevent them from breaking into eddies and currents and separate streams. Rolling impetuously onward they are divided by rocky beds rising in their course, by inequalities in the channel, and by huge boulders that seem to have been placed in their path to torment them and to excite their wrath. And yet these impediments, around which they swirl and at which they growl with foamy lips, only intensify their strength and add momentum to their fury, so that when they leap restrainless from the giddy height they carry everything before them, and slowly, but surely, grind the rocks on which they beat to powder. Eugene Thayer tells us that in listening to the mighty voice of these floods he detected in its awful roar the various tones of a great organ and the sweet harmony of mysterious sounds. Souls in whom the richness of melody dwells not may never recognize in the beat of the waters anything like music, only crash and discord and the reverberations of stridulous monotone, but music dwells there nevertheless. And music dwells in Christianity. Beneath the chatter, clatter and prattle, and lying deep below the noisy loquaciousness of wrangling sects, the psalmody of redeeming love may be heard by those who have "ears to hear," and the different parts of the song of grace, in divinest unison blending, making glad the city of our God on earth, as it shall at last make glad the new Jerusalem in heaven. As it moves forward with outward clash and discord, but with inner harmonies, like Niagara, our religion, divided into many streams and by dissensions rent, has still been one, and has seemed to gather power and velocity from its schisms, so that it has swept before it hoary superstitions and given the assurance that every form of evil on which it falls shall at last be ground to powder.

Denominational distinctions have not been without advantages to the cause of truth. This has been noted by the poet Schiller. In one of his letters he says: "All tortuous deviations of the wandering reason at length strike into the straight road of everlasting truth; all diverging arms and currents ultimately meet in the main stream." Experience has abundantly verified this position. Theological dissent necessitates and facilitates investigation; it sets independent seekers to work, and insures an increase of light on the question in dispute. The advocate on either side, zealous in behalf of his view, abundant in labors to demonstrate its correctness, and unsparing in his criticism of opposing views, prepares the way for an enlightened judgment. By this process error is eliminated, and truth is not only discovered, but is vindicated as well. This result has been brought about by denominational antagonisms. Watching each other, jealous of each other, anxious to justify their own existence, they have unweariedly labored and brought together such a mass of information that it is now comparatively easy to decide what was really taught by Christ and His apostles. Mutually they have contributed to make clear the real doctrines of the Scriptures, and in so doing their divergences have proven eminently advantageous. And it is to be further observed that they have actually tended to bring the warring churches closer together, as it were, in spite of themselves. The search has shown that they are not as wide apart as they supposed, that they are more in harmony than they suspected, and that what they had once regarded as fatally erroneous is, after all, not irreconcilable with truth. They have also demonstrated that God's Word has nothing to fear from investigation; that the path of safety lies in the utmost freedom of thought and of inquiry; and that, while at times this liberty may lead to mistakes, it must at last end in some fresh and some more definite conception of the teachings of Revelation.

Diversity has also ministered to Christian efficiency. Were the members of a single church alike, how narrowed would its sphere of usefulness become. If they were all gifted with executive abilities, and were destitute of devotional qualities, how little they would accomplish apart from governing. If they were enriched in knowledge, but poor in sympathy and charity, how pedantic and uninteresting they would be. If zeal was not checked by wisdom, and activity by meditation, into what extremes they would run. In every church there is needed faith, the gifts of healing, of prophecy, and of tongues. Not one alone, but all. "If the whole body were an eye, where were the hearing? If the whole were hearing, where were the smelling?" And if the whole were talking,— as is frequently the case,— where were the doing?

The fact that we meet with these diversities is one cause of the success which attends the labors of Christ's people. The aggressiveness of one rebukes the sluggishness of others; enthusiasm startles apathy, earnestness rouses indifference; while, on the other hand, conservatism restrains radicalism, gentleness tempers impetuosity, and common sense curbs the impatience of fiery zeal. And in a similar way the various denominations act and react upon each other. Their existence is the occasion for generous rivalries and noble emulations. If one is more enterprising than the rest, its example cannot be lost; if it is more liberal and spiritual, others will feel the power of its influence. I confess, unless Christian human nature were to undergo a radical change, I should look with grave solicitude on the dawning of undenominationalism. Were we all one body we should lose the tremendous stimulation that comes from the present arrangement, and I fear that our uniformity would become the uniformity of death and the tomb. Let us not then decry or undervalue the good that accrues to the cause of Christ from what many consider an unmitigated evil.

Nor should we hide from ourselves the fact that these diversities seem to facilitate the work of the churches in drawing men to the Savior. There are marked varieties on the outside that demand those on the inside. Many persons can be influenced by Methodism who would never be reached by Presbyterianism, and there are some who will cheerfully attend to preaching from an undenominational pulpit who would refuse to hear the message from a denominational one. A supremely intellectual ministry, a ministry of light, proves effective in some cases, while in others a spiritually magnetic or electrical ministry is alone successful, and yet in others a correlation of these forces is indispensable. They all have their value, and the world as at present constituted would be infinitely poorer, and immeasurably more helpless, for the destruction of any one of them.

From these thoughts you will infer that I do not attach much importance to uniformity. Certainly I am not disposed to idolize it. I am not clear that it is at all desirable, and I am sure that it would not be at the cost of mental liberty. As I view the case, the last thing to be attempted is an artificial and constrained union of churches. Instead of talking a great deal about it, and proposing impossible schemes for its realization, we had better simply study to be right in faith and practice, and leave to God and to His providence the ultimate solution of the problem. He knows what is best for His people and the world, and He will doubtless, in His own way and time, bring about whatever of structural union is necessary for the final triumph of His kingdom. In the meanwhile let the heart be kept clear of bitterness and discord, and let the hand place no stumbling-block in a brother's way because his creed in some of its articles is different. Let good feeling and true fellowship be cultivated, and we shall then not be unprepared and unfitted to coöperate with God, who is, I am persuaded, working out by these diversities a grander and sublimer union in the spiritual than He has already effected, and by similar processes, in the physical.

Somewhere I have read of two monks who had never quarreled or disagreed, but had lived for years in sweetest amity and peace. At last one suggested that they should have a falling out after the pattern of the world. But the other replied that he knew not how to quarrel, and that he did not understand how to perform his part. "Well," said the first monk, "we will put this brick between us, and you shall say, 'It is mine,' and I will say, 'It is mine,' and so we will gradually grow heated contending." With smiling faces the simple-hearted brethren prepared to enter the arena of debate. "It is mine," said the first, sternly; "It is mine," said the second, falteringly; "Yea, again I declare it is mine," responded the first, solemnly; "*Then take it,*" lovingly answered the second. Brethren, I do not say that this spirit is always possible; but something kindred to it is what God expects. It is not for Christian denominations to wrangle and contend, each madly alive to its own little interests, and careless of the interests of the others. "Mine and thine" should lose their significance with them, and they should be ready with loving accord to yield to each other, and to bear each other's burdens. We shall never recognize what is grand and good in our neighbors, and we shall be blind to their claims on our fellowship, if we fail to cultivate this spirit of gentle amity. Ruskin shows very eloquently the sad effects of anarchy and competition in a piece of common mud. The elements which compose it "are at helpless war with each other, and destroy reciprocally each other's nature and power; competing and fighting for place at every tread of your foot; sand squeezing out clay, and clay squeezing out water, and soot meddling everywhere, and defiling the whole." Such, also, is the dreary outcome of sectarian jealousies, rivalries and contentions. They present the members of the warring, fermenting sects in the most unlovely of lights; they are offensive to each other, and their touch is regarded as somewhat contaminating. Ruskin proceeds to describe the glorious results that would follow if his piece of humble mud were left for sufficient time in perfect rest. Beginning with the clay in the compound, he traces its progress to the consistency of finest porcelain, and then upward until it becomes clear, white and hard, and gathering to its heart "the loveliest rays only," it is known to us as a sapphire. He then takes the sand, and assuming a "similar permission of quiet," he shows how it attains "the power of reflecting, not merely the blue rays, but the blue, green, purple and red rays, in the greatest beauty in which they can be seen through any hard material whatsoever. We call it then an opal." Next the soot is taken in hand, and its efforts to become a diamond vividly depicted; for even this worthless element can "exchange its blackness for the power of reflecting all the rays of the sun at once." "Last of all, the water purifies, or unites itself; contented enough if it only reach the form of a dewdrop; but if we insist on its proceeding to a more perfect consistence, it crystallizes into the shape of a star." And in like manner, if the various sects will only fully cease from criticism, sarcasm, and railings at each other's expense, and will strangle their dull-eyed bigotry and smother their stupid self-esteem, and if they will seek peace and follow "brotherly love," they will furnish the condition needed for each to develop its peculiar "fruit of the Spirit," and its individual perfections. Then it will be seen that there is "faith" in the Catholic, to remind us of the precious and highly painted porcelain; "gentleness" in the Episcopal, to remind us of the rare and softly gleaming sapphire; "knowledge" in Presbyterians, and "diligence" in Methodists, to remind us of the beautiful and many-hued opal; "charity" in the Unitarian, to remind us of the pure and lustrous diamond; and "longsuffering" in the Baptist, to remind us of the fresh and pearly water, symbol of bitter but wholesome tears of sorrow, which hope transforms into the never-fading stars of "joy." The Master of the treasure-house will not despise any of these jewels, but will find a place for each one in His radiant crown; and if so, we should remove every obstacle from the way of their flashing from His footstool; and the more we realize their worthiness to shine, the more fully will we blend our rays together, and when this consummation shall be reached, then will the greatest obstacle be removed from the way of final unification; and then, though diversities may still exist in doctrine and practice, the world will no longer be able to say with scornful lips: "See how these Christians love each other."

It would be well for the unconverted, before they articulate this sneer, to consider how much of the present diversity is permitted in condescension to their own weakness and waywardness. The manifoldness of sin, as I have already intimated, cries out for manifoldness in religion, and the differences that reign in the natural most likely can only be met by differences in the supernatural. If God allows us to remain Methodist, Baptist or Episcopalian, it may be on your account, that you may be without excuse; that every type of man may be confronted with a corresponding type of doctrine and of method. Instead of these varieties lessening your responsibility, they rather heighten it, and instead of extenuating your indifference, they only condemn it. Surely somewhere you can find a faith and a church to suit you; surely there are means adapted to your state, and ministries fitted to your peculiar temperament. Think of this, remember this, and instead of jeering at what is tolerated for your good, earnestly seek those aids which a merciful God will bless to your soul's salvation.

> "Thro' all life's thousand-fold entangled maze,
> One Godlike bourne your gifted sight surveys,—
> Thro' countless means one solemn end, foreshown,
> The labyrinth closes at a single throne."

MAMMONISM.

"Ye cannot serve God and mammon."—*Matthew vi, 24.*

"Gold! gold! gold! gold!
Bright and yellow, hard and cold,
Molten, graven, hammered and rolled;
Heavy to get, and light to hold;
Hoarded, bartered, bought and sold;
Stolen, borrowed, squandered, doled:
Spurned by the young, but hugged by the old
To the very verge of the church-yard mold;
Price of many a crime untold,—
Gold! gold! gold! gold!" *Hood.*

THERE is a picture by Wertz in an art collection at Brussels which must profoundly impress the thoughtful student of our times. It represents one of those unfortunate French women who played so prominent a part in the tragedy of the Paris Commune, with her back to a wall and her hands tied before her, flashing scorn and contempt from eyes glistening beneath thick shadows of raven hair partly fallen over the face, and a squad of Versailles soldiers, who are mechanically preparing for her summary execution. The story is easily understood, and hardly needs an interpreter. Sympathizing with the enemies of Thiers' new republic, the poor creature has been taken in the act of firing some public building, or in filling her dead husband's place at the barricades, and must meet the consequences at the mouth of a score of muskets. There she stands, life-like, on the canvas, pale but defiant, and there the uniformed assassins with their guns leveled at her defenseless breast. So painfully realistic is the composition that the beholder expects to hear the sharp word of command from the officer, the swift-answering report of the death-dealing weapons, the half-suppressed cry of the wretched prisoner, and to see the flashing fire, the blinding smoke, and then the unsightly heap of bleeding clay. Instinctively he holds his breath, shuts his eyes, and turns away.

But he cannot exclude from his mind the terrible scene, or escape the somber reflections to which it gives rise. These will continue to haunt him for some time, and may not be altogether unprofitable. Realizing that the picture represents a passage in the history of this enlightened century, he will most likely regard it as illustrating to some degree its spirit. Possibly he will find himself propounding curious questions and arriving at very unsatisfactory conclusions. Here, in a civilized nation,—perhaps the most highly civilized in the world,—the people abandon themselves to wholesale butchering, and with the torch of the vandal destroy their grandest edifices and slaughter their prisoners and hostages like beasts. Refinement, education, the finer feelings, indeed everything that makes them Frenchmen, are powerless to restrain their passions when excited by the frenzy of revolution. Naturally the query arises, Were these men and women, who act like human devils, ever really civilized? Were they ever in advance of the furious Huns? and wherein do they really differ from their savage ancestry? Outwardly, in dress, in houses, in pursuits, and customs, they are manifestly far removed from their uncouth sires, but in heart the distance between them does not seem very marked. Of Alaric it is written that, when he sat down with his army before the gates of Rome, he promised to leave its citizens their lives, if nothing else. M. Thiers was not as humane as Alaric; he made no promise, or, if he did, he certainly failed to keep it. In what particular, then, was Thiers more fully civilized than Alaric? The Cimbrian women acted as priestesses in a barbarous age, and delighted to cut the throat of prisoners taken in war, draining the blood of their victims into brass vessels and offering it to their deities. But in what particular were these women worse than their Parisian sisters? Was life less sacred to the one class than to the other? or were the dignity and gentleness of their sex properly appreciated and exhibited by either?

Let us not, however, suppose that such questions are suggested exclusively by the atrocities of the Commune and its antagonists, for in every nation, and equally in our own, there are many things which prompt them. Much is being written and said in praise of our era. Poets, orators and editors never grow weary extolling its achievements and triumphs, its material and social advancement, and its educational and philanthropical enterprises. Windy speeches, double-leaded editorials, eagle-soaring verses, set forth with doubtful modesty the superiority of this century over its less fortunate predecessors. There never was such a century before,—possibly never will be again,—never such enlightenment enjoyed, such liberty attained, such prosperity realized, and such elevation achieved. And yet, without controverting these extravagant representations sharply, there are uneasy suspicions abroad that modern progress is not just what it ought to be. While we travel faster, fly higher, plow deeper, see clearer, grow richer, communicate easier, and in general thrive more than our forefathers, nevertheless there is a skeleton in our social structure having the huge proportions of Leviathan. Civilization unquestionably excels in various repects, and, perhaps, as a whole, every former effort in the same direction, and yet it seems far from deserving the unqualified encomiums which are lavished on it so unstintedly. I have no desire to detract from it, but at the same time praise should not outstrip merit or congratulations overstep the boundary of justice. Wordsworth starts a very serious and important doubt in the following expressive lines:

> "Man now presides
> In power where once he trembled in his weakness;
> Science advances with gigantic strides,
> But are we aught enriched in love and meekness?
> Aught dost thou see, bright star! of pure and wise
> More than in humbler times graced human story;
> That makes our hearts more apt to sympathize
> With heaven, our souls more fit for future glory,
> When earth shall vanish from our closing eyes,
> And we lie down in our last dormitory?"

That is, in other words, are we as highly civilized as we think we are? Has morality kept pace with material progress? Has the elevation of humanity been proportionate to the development of physical resources? Has the race, under the most favorable circumstances, been entirely purged of its old barbarities and savage tendencies? Are we really what we seem, or are we at best but the prophecy and promise of what we ought to be and shall be.

I am afraid these questions are not susceptible to the answer our vanity would dictate. But if there is truth in the saying of Edmund Burke, that "adulation is not of more service to people than to kings," then it is much wiser to look at the facts as they are, however humiliating, than to be deceived by fancies. These facts point to the mortifying conclusion that the history of the Paris Commune is a too faithful portraiture of the age in which we live; an outbreak of its spirit, a revelation of its innermost heart. As we meditate on its terrible record, its insane cruelty, and the bloodshed of which it was the occasion, and remember the pretensions of the French capital, we cannot avoid the apprehension that under similar circumstances the horrors of its brief career might be repeated among other peoples, if they are not being enacted in ways not less striking and appalling, though not one whit less shocking, every day and in almost every city.

That this is the case,—that to an alarming extent oppression overrides justice, and wrong overreaches right, that our wonderful civilization is yet cursed by the cruel and degraded spirit of ancient savagery,—a brief induction of facts I think will fully establish.

It seems to be proven by what remains among us of the man-eating propensities which have disgraced many tribes and nations. Cannibalism does not flourish, of course, in its old form, but it would be premature to affirm that the sanguinary Mexican has no successor, and the ferocious Fijian no imitator. Some wild races have devoured their enemies, that they might in this way appropriate to themselves the special qualities for which they were distinguished. Thus, for example,—according to Herbert Spencer, whose *Synthetic Philosophy* has furnished me much lively information regarding the habitudes of primitive races,—the Dakota used to eat the heart of a fallen antagonist to increase his own courage, and a New Zealander would swallow the eyes of a slain foe that he might see the farther. These interesting practices are not altogether unknown to this civilized age of ours. Not as grossly, it is true, but quite as really, men prey upon each other, and strive to make good their deficiencies at each other's expense. When a cunning manipulator of stocks, by "ways that are dark and tricks that are *not* vain," appropriates to himself the money of his less wily and astute fellow-citizens, he is assuredly following in the footsteps of the Dakota and New Zealander. They simply rob their victims of eyes and heart, but the conscienceless speculator plunders even his friends, for his own advantage, of that which is sight to their age and as strength to their helplessness. Moreover, large classes of work-people suffer a silent martyrdom, and are annually sacrificed by the thousands to sustain useless pomp and idle extravagance.

"Beneath the sun
The many still must labor for the one:
'Tis nature's doom."

So says the poet; but I am inclined to the opinion that man has more to do with this arrangement than nature. Not satisfied with his own share of this world and a trifle over, he clutches at the share of others. Availing himself of the necessities which poverty, disease and failures have created, he burdens his dependents with excessive toil, prates pathetically about political economy, and piously of "nature," too, and continues to underpay them. Steadily they sink into more abject pauperism, until they shiver in the ghost of a garment and for shelter are forced to herd together, where decency, much less dignity, is hardly possible. Are not such unhappy creatures devoured by our civilized cannibals?

Take as an illustration of the wrongs of labor some facts gleaned from an intelligent article in *The Examiner and Chronicle*, published in New York, concerning the working girls of that city. Doubtless they can be duplicated in every other great center of population. These girls are represented as earning the "munificent sum of thirty-five cents" for making the best and heaviest of overcoats; twenty-eight cents for handsome spring overcoats; six to ten cents a pair for pants; seventy-five cents a dozen for calico wrappers, and about a dollar and a half for complete suits for ladies. "Cash girls get from seventy-five cents to a dollar and a half per week. 'Must come neatly dressed' is in the advertisement of 'cash girls wanted.'" Then, in addition to such meager wages, it seems they are outrageously cheated. "They have to contribute to presents for the foreman and bookkeepers." "A little girl in a tobacco factory who earns a dollar and a half per week had fifty cents deducted to buy the 'boss' a present." "The men were invited to give; the girls were openly robbed." Well does the writer ask, "When a girl earns three dollars and a half in six days, and pays three dollars for board and lodging, thirty cents of it for car fares, does her own washing at night, seldom irons at all, how long before she must be looking for clothing? Where *can* she find it?" Is it not true that their employers feed upon their skill and strength, grow fat and haughty on their suffering toil, and merry on their misery, yea, and vampire-like, greedily suck their life's blood to renew their own vigor, and to minister to their own social importance? And possibly when their elastic conscience occasionally bids them pause, some gentle poet sings in their ear the deceitful strain "'Tis nature's doom." Deceitful I call it, because nature has never ordained that a few men should grow immeasurably rich at the expense of suffering millions; or that the least among them should be deprived of all that makes life desirable for the benefit of the already affluent. She is too kind a mother to countenance such unjust discrimination. The decree attributed to her is a fiction, a forgery, not a verity. She ordains equality, not inequality; judgment, not oppression; righteousness, not a cry.

Wild, lawless races are generally reported indifferent to the value of human life. With the Bhils assassination is a pastime; with the Fans cruelty is a delight; while the Bushmen are brutal in their ferocity, and the Fijians malignant in their revenge. Among some tribes the least breach of savage etiquette is visited with instant death, and among others the aged and sick are helped out of the world by appropriate tortures. This indifference, however, is not confined to the swamp and the jungle; it manifests itself in other quarters, in the centers of culture and refinement. Witness the great armies of Europe, the immense fighting-machines organized to destroy those to whom they bear no enmity, with whom they have no quarrel, and in whose "violent taking off" they have not the least personal interest. Or, witness the daily chronicle of murders committed by drunken ruffians in saloons, or by idle scoundrels on the highway or by the fireside. Murders by disreputable loungers in defense of an imaginary quality called "honor," generally not worth the powder exploded on its behalf; wife-murders, child-murders, murders for money, murders for revenge, murders for licentiousness, and murders in sheer recklessness, make up the frightful catalogue which blackens the pages of our newspapers, and on which we every morning breakfast "full of horrors." And yet so little is life prized among us that the reeking stews and drinking dens which are responsible for most of these barbarities are not only tolerated, but are allowed with impunity to violate the law. Aye, and so lightly does the community seem to regard their crimes against life that their shambles are not even closed on the Sabbath; and so highly are the efforts of boozy ruffians to diminish population esteemed that they are actually made the fountain of political honor and preferment. The rum-shop governs the primary meetings, and the primaries the elections, so that the still of moral death becomes the spring of political life to our successful parties.

Not satisfied with destroying the body, our civilization is ingeniously contrived to slaughter the moral qualities of manhood, such as honesty, industry, frugality, and faithfulness. Material interests are more highly prized than the spiritual. Supremacy in commerce, political sovereignty, and social aggrandizement, are the idols of the hour, and to their welfare everything else is subordinated. The innocence of childhood, the gentle graces of maidenhood, the sterner virtues of manhood, are all counted of secondary importance, and are deliberately imperiled or sacrificed at the shrine of what we are pleased to term "modern progress." Consequently "wealth accumulates, but men decay." Carlyle sums up the situation when, concerning the children of toil, he writes: "It is to live miserable, we know not why; to work sore and yet gain nothing; to be heartworn, weary, yet isolated, unrelated, girt in with a cold, universal *laizzez-faire;* it is to die slowly all our life long, imprisoned in a deaf, dead, infinite injustice, as in the accursed belly of Phalaris' bull! This is, and remains forever, intolerable to all men whom God has made." If this is a fair description, we can readily understand how such a state of things must undermine the moral life. To be deprived of hope, to subsist from hand to mouth, to be sunless, restless, joyless, is in the large majority of cases to be careless of manhood and callous to its loss. Much is being said of over-population. Europe ships as many thousands as possible to these hospitable shores, and even here at times we feel uncomfortably crowded. "There must be something wrong," writes Carlyle; "a full-formed man is not only worth nothing to the world, but the world could afford him a round sum would he simply engage to go and hang himself." There is indeed something wrong. It means that civilization has so blundered during the past fifty years in organizing its industries and in developing its material resources that it has cursed the earth with an inferior manhood, which now cannot care for itself, and which cannot be gotten rid of at pleasure.

Savages are not tenderly solicitous for the welfare of their offspring. Their children are pretty much left to grow up as they please. According to facts collated from various sources by Herbert Spencer, the Fuegians, though manifesting some paternal fondness, sell their little ones to the Patagonians for slaves; and New Guinea people cheerfully barter theirs for articles of merchandise. While all this confessedly is very inhuman, and has no exact parallel in decent communities, it is questionable whether something similar is not discernible in the neglect, and worse than neglect, in which multiplied children of civilization are reared. Many of them are not only deprived of home influence, but the community being indifferent to their future, they grow up on the streets uninstructed in right and wrong, immoral, vicious, precocious in sin and ready for evil. Every man's hand seems to be against them. The Romans once gathered the children of the Goths into cities and there massacred them; and society, by its cruel neglect of children, whose parents may be stigmatized as modern Goths, is justly chargeable with the extinction of their moral life. What a revelation on this subject is furnished by the recent reports of Bridewell and of the Cook County Sunday School Convention. According to the latter, 85,694 children in Chicago, out of a population, between the ages of 6 and 21, of 135,694, do not attend any place of religious instruction, and in one district of about 20,000 people not 10 per cent attend church or Sunday-school; and according to the former, during the last twelve months 6,755 persons were committed, of whom 1,454 were 21 years old and under, including children of 7 years, 8 years, 9 and 10 years of age. Picture to yourselves these infants immured with hardened criminals in close cells,—for as the prison accommodations were not adequate they had to be crowded together;—picture also solemn judges committing two seven-year-old villains to the safety of stone walls, and then picture your own selves, sitting meekly worshiping in silks and satins, and then ask yourselves the profoundly interesting question, How much better are we than the Fuegians? They sell their children to the Patagonians; we sell those of our worthless neighbor to the devil. Before God, of the two, of the civilized and uncivilized, are they or we the least culpable? Better answer the question at once, for if we do not we shall not be prompt to mend our ways, and if we do not mend our ways in this and in other matters to which attention has already been directed, we shall speedily be confronted by social convulsions and earthquakes, whose violence will cover our foolish boasting with contempt and scorn.

The more I reflect on the present state of society the more fully am I convinced that the evils of which I have complained are to be traced to that particular sin which is condemned by Jesus in the text—"Ye cannot serve God and mammon."

In warning the people against evils into which they were liable to fall he admonishes them not to lay up treasures on earth, but in heaven, as their heart would certainly be with their treasures, and they ought to desire that to be in the holiest and safest place. This naturally leads him to the question of divided allegiance. Can a man have two masters? Can two beings or things be equally supreme in the affections and the life? If we are devoted to Republicanism, can we be equally devoted to Royalty, and if we are zealously attached to the Protestant idea, can we at the same time be enthusiastically enlisted in behalf of the Catholic? Evidently not; for if our allegiance is divided between two, neither one nor the other is really lord, and the sovereignty of one always and necessarily implies the subordination of the other. There can be but one master. Various interests may claim and probably should receive attention, but they must inevitably pay tribute to the ruling ideal. "Ye cannot serve God and Mammon." Either, but not both. If the Almighty is chosen to be your king, then your aims and endeavors must be regulated in harmony with His supreme will, and your relations to money and business must be determined by His law. He does not condemn, but rather encourages frugality and the spirit of accumulation, and He has never declared Himself an enemy to affluence. What He protests against, what the Savior in our text seems to denounce, is the possibility of Mammon usurping in the soul the throne of God. Such a contingency the Scriptures in the strongest terms deplore. When the inspired writer exclaims: "If I have made gold my hope, or have said to the fine gold 'Thou art my confidence;' if I rejoiced because my wealth was great, and because mine hand had gotten much,—this were an iniquity to be punished by the judge, for I should have denied the God that is above;" and when the apostle warns: "Be not deceived, for neither fornicators, nor idolators, nor thieves, nor *covetous*, nor drunkards, nor revilers, nor extortioners, shall inherit the kingdom of God;" and adds: "No *covetous* man who is an idolator hath any inheritance in the kingdom of Christ," we perceive not only the reality, but also the imminency of the peril; and when we read such passages as "the wicked hath swallowed down riches, but he shall vomit them up again; God shall cast them out of his belly; though he heap up silver as the dust, and prepare raiment as the clay, he may prepare it, but the just shall put it on, and the innocent shall divide the silver:" "They that trust in their wealth and boast themselves in the multitude of their riches cannot, by any means, redeem his brother, or give to God a ransom for him;" "Their silver and their gold shall not be able to deliver them in the day of the wrath of the Lord, they shall not satisfy their souls, because they are the stumbling-block of their iniquity," we discern the corrupting and debasing influence of Mammonism, and the reasons why its reign should be detested and denounced.

Thomas Carlyle thinks that modern society has gone over as never in the past to the service of this "The meanest and least erect of spirits that fell from heaven."

In the *Latter-Day Pamphlets* he says: "The Universe is a huge, dull Cattle-stall and St. Catherine's Wharf; with a few pleasant apartments up-stairs for those that can make money. Make money and don't bother about the universe! That is M. Crowdy's notion; reckoned a quiet, innocent and rather wholesome notion just now; yet clearly fitter for a reflective pig than for a man." To which he adds that "Property is our god at present," and lawyers "our pontiffs, the highest priests we have." Unfortunately this representation is not without color of truth, and yet the shadows are altogether too deep and dark. Unquestionably we find the money plague everywhere, and tainting everything. Society, literature, morality, and religion have not escaped; and it is more than suspected that justice, patriotism, virtue, genius and piety are bought and sold in the market-place; and that were some modern Jugurtha to view the general venality he would cry out as that ancient Numidian did against Rome: "Rome itself is to sell, if anybody wants to buy it." But while it is true that the lust of gold distorts and deforms our civilization, it is hardly fair to speak of it as exceptionally Mammonized. I know of hardly an age in which the thirst for gain has not been intense and has not displayed itself, if not in mercantile pursuits, at least in militant aggressiveness. For the sake of gain barbarians have plundered monarchies and dismembered kingdoms, heartless soldiers have ravaged empires and blotted out nationalities, wild adventurers have braved unknown seas and explored savage continents; for the sake of gain the sanctities of the Jewish temple were invaded by the Babylonians, and the territory of the Greeks by the Persians; for the sake of gain Alexander rioted in blood and his successors in murderous deeds, the Romans in butchery, and the Goths, Vandals, and Arabs in cruel slaughter; for the sake of gain, after the self-denying labors of Columbus, the new world was visited with inhumanity and atrocities, and its unoffending inhabitants reduced to slavery or foully slain; and, for the sake of gain, ecclesiastics employed sacrilegious means, frauds, and abuses, their mercenary conduct reaching its climax in the sale of indulgences, and their degradation its completion in the farcical procession of relics, whose charms were at least sufficient to magnetize the money of the people into the coffers of the priests. No age can claim a monopoly of sordid meanness. Covetousness, greediness, avariciousness, rapaciousness, and mercenariness display themselves continuously in the chronicles of history. Only a diseased mind will invest the warriors, chieftains, kings, and rulers of antiquity with heroic virtues, and insist on imputing exclusively to modern representatives of power the vices of cupidity and parsimoniousness. The old leaders and sovereigns of the people were just as base as any in the new era, the only difference being that they were more openly and ruggedly freebooters than their successors, and took with the strong, mail-clad hand what is now filched in a gentler, kid-gloved fashion. Unaccountably blind is he who fails to recognize these facts, and who likewise overlooks the bountiful hospitality, the generous philanthropy, the free-hearted, open-handed munificence, that fosters educational and religious institutions of our times, which exalt the present age beyond its predecessors, and which vindicate it from the charge of exceptional, preëminent, and unmitigated Mammonism, brought against it by such writers as the cynical sage of Chelsea and the over-critical Ruskin.

Nevertheless, while I utter this word of extenuation I realize that the vice complained of is sufficiently vigorous and widespread to occasion painful solicitude, and that it cannot but be advantageous for thoughtful souls to meditate on its Cimmerian darkness and abysmal depths.

IS POVERTY A CRIME?

Mammonism perverts the judgment. When it obtains mastery it beclouds the intellect, suggests strange distinctions, and leads to the most absurd conclusions. This is especially discernible in its estimate of the relative virtue of affluence and poverty. While it is tolerant of evils and coquettes with notorious iniquities, it is particularly severe on indigence, and, indeed, regards it as a deeply-dyed sin, a sin that is mortal and unpardonable. For this it has no charity and no commiseration. Rarely is this opinion expressed in words, but it asserts itself in what speaks louder,— actions. The deference and respect shown by the rich to successful men, even when they are more than suspected of business irregularities, is an indication of the confusion of moral judgments which devotion to money breeds. Such questionable characters are feasted, consulted on grave occasions, and are invariably treated with a consideration far beyond their merits. If a poor man had not more sense and more personal worth he would not be tolerated even in a servile employment, and as for his views, they would not receive a moment's attention. What is it that makes the difference between them? Not knowledge necessarily, for the affluent may be as stupidly ignorant as the indigent; nor virtue, for as we have intimated, one may be as vicious as the other. Evidently it is money. To the eye of Mammom bonds, stocks, acres, possessions of every kind, are inseparable from the individual who owns them, are part of himself, are incorporated with his personality, and when his worthiness is to be weighed ought to be placed alongside of him in the scale. But when honest poverty comes to be valued, lacking these things it lacks everything; and it is censured, criticised, condemned, in such tones and in such a manner as to leave the impression that it is more of a crime than a misfortune. Carlyle, referring to American society, speaks of our "anomalous dukes," "overgrown monsters of wealth," "who have made money by dealing in cotton, dealing in bacon, jobbing scrip, revered by surrounding flunkies, invested with real powers of sovereignty, and placidly admitted by all men, as if nature and heaven had so appointed it, to be in a sense godlike, to be royal and fit to shine in the firmament, though their real worth is — what?" His cynical language is as applicable to England as to America; and, unhappily, in both countries it is true that the coarsest piece of human crockery, "not worth five shillings of anybody's money," if stuffed, like the earthen idol of Somnauth, with "half a wagon load of gold coins," is looked upon by Mammon as a veritable deity entitled to the tremulous homage of mankind.

That money sheds a kind of saintly aureole around the head of its possessor, in the judgment of those who have gained it in abundance, or who are seeking it unweariedly, may be inferred from the pleas that are invented to extenuate his wrong-doings and the praises that are lavished on his good deeds. If a rich man is a faithless husband, reckless gambler, or a confirmed sot, such persons are ready to apologize that, considering his surroundings and temptations, it is quite remarkable that he behaves as well as he does. But the same rule is scarcely ever applied to the poor. The wretched beggar who abuses his wife, or who drowns his conscience in dram-drinking, is at once pronounced dangerous and worthless, and, if possible, is shut up in some penal institution or reformatory. Poor people are blamed for mingling with the vicious, when no other society is probably open to them, and they are condemned for vices which the peculiarities of their position have generated. Then, rich men can purchase a reputation for piety and generousness at a very small cost, and, however limited may be its extent, generally it is broad enough to cover a multitude of sins. If they hire pews, which they rarely occupy, they are model disciples; if they serve on the board of a Theological Seminary or on a Hospital committee, they are exemplary saints, and if they give two or three per cent of their income, duly advertised, they are public benefactors. But it is different with the poor. If they do not attend church, even where they are made to feel that they are not wanted, they are spoken of by the clergyman, in the saddest of tones, as the unevangelized and unreachable masses. Were they to take him at his word and come to the sanctuary, in some instances he would not be overjoyed to see them, and unquestionably his "beloved flock" would be shocked, and would stay at home. If they stint themselves to forward the interests of Christ's kingdom, or go down among the sick, and for the love of souls sacrifice ease and comfort, they are set down as fanatical folk or as not altogether sound in mind; and, as for their self-denying gifts, they are rarely appreciated at their true value, and cut no figure in newspaper reports. Different by far is it with the sordid affluent who give of their "superflux," and at best give only what is to them a *bagatelle*. Their donations are oftentimes mere attempts to purchase exemption from punishment due their iniquitous course in amassing wealth. The two proverbs quoted by Timothy Titcomb, somewhat similar in character, describe them accurately: "They steal a pig and give away the trotters for God's sake"; and "What the abbot of Bamba cannot eat he gives away for the good of his soul." This aptly pictures those who are committed to the worship of the money-god, and the purblind money-god mumbles an unconditional approval of a liberality so much to its liking.

Mammonism corrupts the conscience. This is a serious evil; for God gave the moral sense to be our guide, and if that is debased there is no sufficient barrier anywhere against the triumph of evil. Woe to the nation or individual in whom this monitor is debauched; doomsday is not far off. The great Greek historian presents as a sign of the degradation of his own times that men spake of vices as though they were virtues, altering, as he says, "at their will and pleasure the customary meaning of words in reference to actions." And when the human heart is intent on acquisition, when the highest object of life is money-getting, it is almost sure to do the same thing. Where the strife of trade is fiercest, and where the sordid are most active, maxims and precepts are current, which have doubtless originated with Mammon-worshipers, and which can hardly be traced to the Decalogue. It is an open secret that such worshipers do not pretend to conduct business on the principles of the gospel, but have devised for themselves a gospel of self-interest and overreaching. To create a panic and then ride on its stormy waves to affluence is called "a smart operation," and to acquire a fortune by means which involve the ruin of hundreds, and which beforehand were known to be despicable and pregnant with untold misery, is considered as both legitimate and commendable. And even when companies are formed by speculators, who imagine, and possibly sincerely believe, that their projects are sure to yield enormous profits, but who have not taken sufficient pains to ascertain all the facts in the case, and who by their highly-colored representations draw to their coffers the savings of the industrious and helpless, when they explode and the victims wring their hands with sorrow, instead of being denounced, are spoken of simply as "somewhat questionable affairs." To take contracts for public buildings or other improvements and execute them in such a way as to jeopardize health, property, and life, and to slaughter thousands of the country's defenders by shoddy supplies and grow fat on the spoils, are not looked upon as practices which should entail on the offenders the indignation of the plutocracy. But what a moth-eaten, fly-blown and gangrened conscience must such conceptions of right produce? They may lead to material affluence, but they foster irreparable moral indigence.

Similar must be the effect of the petty tricks and deceptions perpetrated by small dealers and tradesmen on their unwary customers. While many among them are above reproach, not a few, in whom the instinct of gain drowns every other feeling, are guilty of systematic and continuous meanness to avoid giving a fair equivalent for the money they receive. As the ceaseless dropping of water wears away the solid rock, so these repeated acts gradually destroy the moral life, and prepare the way for greater recklessness in the pursuit of wealth. Lured by this glittering idol, men of this type engage in the nefarious rum traffic, in gambling, horse-race betting, lotteries, and in other evils by which the hopes and happiness of thousands are blighted. They have determined to be rich; they are indifferent as to the means. No matter what laws are violated or hearts broken, what wrongs are committed or rights ignored, what innocence is sacrificed or guilt incurred, they will be rich,—honestly if they can, dishonestly if they must. To the attainment of this one object they have devoted everything,—strength, health, body, soul. At this altar they are prepared to immolate all that they are and have,—even to their conscience. That they bind, strangle, slay, and present as a whole burnt offering to appease the insatiableness of the yellow, dusty, dirty deity whose golden smile they covet.

And just here we have the explanation of some of the evils under which the working classes groan. Mammonism having no conscience, no truth, it regards those whom it uses for its own advancement as having no soul. Long hours, short pay for the laborer, short hours and long pay for the capitalist, is its doctrine. It believes in the divine and exclusive right of money. Full banks, surplus cash and driving commerce are of more importance in its estimation than human amelioration. If to secure these ends entire populations must be oppressed, starved and degraded, so much the worse for the populations, but they must nevertheless submit to the inevitable. It is blind and deaf to the fact that no eternal law devotes nine-tenths of the race to drudgery; that no divine policy of economics discriminates against labor, and that no heavenly or earthly reason exists why it should be so wretchedly rewarded as to render the poor-house, or something worse, its final haven. And it stupidly fails to perceive that the science of worldly interests, as now understood, is a monstrous piece of botching, as absurd as it is inhuman, and that as long as it is relied on we need not expect to see any radical abatement of evils which are perpetuating barbarism and breeding dissensions.

But Mammonism also debases the affections. It tears from the heart the image of wife, children, country, home, and even God, and rears instead the bejeweled and bedizened image of itself. The faith, trust and love due humanity, and supremely due the Almighty, it appropriates to its own service, and demands that they shall lavish all their strength and beauty on its repulsive charms. What is home or country to the man who is intoxicated with the gold poison? He will neglect the one and sell the other. His children may grow up uneducated or miseducated for all he cares, and they may be as naked in body as they are beggared in mind for all he thinks or heeds. He loves money with a love that will not brook a rival, and his own flesh and blood is but as dull clay in comparison with the diamond worth and brilliancy of his idol. Hence the number of families in our day who are totally neglected by their fathers, and permitted to grow up as they please; and hence the increasing recklessness, insubordination and lawlessness among the young.

Perhaps the more terrible illustration of the power of this vice is furnished by those who profess to be the children of God, to love Him and their fellow beings, and who are continually confronted by the realities of eternity, and yet cling to their money as though it were their Savior, or dole it out as though it were the life drops from a martyr's veins. Though a world lies in ruins, though humanity is cursed with sin and sorrow, and though they are being whirled with the velocity of earth's diurnal revolution toward the judgment bar, they cling to that which if wisely used would bring salvation to all mankind. They stint their own spiritual nature, begrudging the paltry dollars which decency compels them to offer in return for the bread of life, and seem more inclined to see the souls of others starve than part with their hoarded wealth. They love the image of liberty on the golden coin more than the image of God in the human heart. Such professors are like Mont Blanc, stately, imposing to the eye, lustrous outwardly, but frigid at heart, holding their treasures as that giant mountain hoards its snows, originating no rivers, nourishing no waste places, but simply filling the atmosphere with inhospitable cold. It seems to me that every time they think of themselves they must be overwhelmed with shame, and that "were it not for the interposition of sleep," which, as it has been said by a quaint preacher, "separates all men once in twenty-four hours from the consciousness of their own meanness, they would die of self-contempt."

Am I not warranted, then, from these facts in charging upon this miserable vice the savageness that fills our civilization with sorrow and with suffering? From this source does it mainly spring; and ought we, therefore, to be surprised that the Savior should positively assert the irreconcilableness of Mammonism with the service of God? Surely not. Ruskin has said, sharply but truly: "The immediate office of the earthquake and pestilence is to slay us like moths, and, as moths, we shall be wise to live out of their way. So the practical and immediate office of gold and diamonds is the multiplied destruction of souls, in whatever sense you have been taught to understand that phrase." How can it be otherwise? A passion that perverts, corrupts and debases, that blinds the mind, deadens the conscience and degrades the affections, is necessarily soul-destroying. It has no welcome for God, no desire for His blessing, no joy in His service; but gradually paralyzes the religious nature, and consumes all spiritual susceptibility. Before heaven is reached this fever has burnt up everything that fits for heaven, and before hell opens wide its ponderous gates this frenzy has plunged the shriveled spirit into the depths of deepest fire.

> "Oh, cursed lust of gold! when for thy sake
> The fool throws up his interest in both worlds
> First starved in this, then damned in that to come."

Mammon may be a good and useful servant, but he is a foul and tyrannous lord. His shackles no true man should consent to wear. They may be broken, they should be despised. When Camillus found Sulpitious trying to rescue Rome from the barbarian by large sums of money he proudly exclaimed: "It is with steel, not gold, that Romans guard their country." And it is with the sword of the Spirit, and not with paltry pelf, that our nation is to be helped and delivered from savagery. That sword in the hands of Christ can free the people from the disgraceful semi-barbarism which now afflicts. Take the Word of God, accept its teachings, make its Divine Author "Master," and in submitting to His authority, that which is now your lord will become your slave. All you now possess in this world you may continue to possess; but with Christ in your heart its relation to you will be changed. It will be your servant, not your sovereign, and you will send it on messages of peace and mercy to the ends of the earth. And with the sense of emancipation will come the feeling of proprietorship in more than silver can buy or gold secure. However poor you may be in the perishable riches, you will realize that you own all things. Looking up into God's face you will be able to say "My Father"; the universe will be yours in the highest sense, for you will have attained the art of appropriating its inner treasures. Christ yours, the church yours, heaven yours,— what more can be needed to complete your felicity? Here have we true riches; blessed is he who finds them!

> "Leave wealth behind; bring God thy heart-best light
> To guide thy wavering steps through life's dark night;
> God spurns the riches of a thousand coffers,
> And says: 'My chosen is he, his heart who offers;
> Nor gold nor silver seek I, but, above
> All gifts, the heart, and buy it with my love;
> Yes, one sad, contrite heart, which men despise,
> More than my throne and fixed decree I prize!'"

PAUPERISM.

"Ye have the poor with you always, and whensoever ye will ye may do them good." *Math. xiv*, 7.

"All the care
Ingenious parsimony takes, but just
Saves the small inventory, bed and stool,
Skillet and old carved chest, from public sale.
They live, and live without extorted alms
From grudging hands, but other boast have none
To soothe their honest pride that scorns to beg."
Cowper.

I AM reminded by the breath of autumn, chill prophet of winter's approaching frost, and by the tattered forms of trees, gaunt harbingers of earth's melancholy season, of those sad classes against whose doors the snow forever beats and drives, and through whose "looped and windowed raggedness" the biting wind too freely blows.

"Take physic, pomp;
Expose thyself to feel what wretches feel;
That thou may'st shake the superflux to them,
And show the heavens more just."

Christianity is the eldest and only born daughter of that venerable religion whose care for the poor was among the chiefest of its glories. Whatever may be said to the discredit of Judaism, it cannot fairly be charged that the unfortunate were neglected in its ministrations. It was a thoroughly humane system, seeking to shield the weak from the strong, and to protect the indigent from the rapacious exactions of the affluent. Pinched want and heaped plenty were never known during its sway, as they have been since, and under dispensations reputed to surpass it in philanthropy. Rarely were men seen in Israel who had been fleeced, stripped, and beggared by the heartless schemes of capitalists and monopolists; and only toward the close of its history was such a contrast possible as that which Jesus painted in the parable of Dives and Lazarus. Pauperism and mendicancy were not among the crying evils of the nation in its palmy days, in the days when its people were free, and when princes of the house of Judah reigned. In those halcyon times, from psalms of praise and from sacred statutes continually was heard the voice of God befriending the friendless and pleading the cause of the necessitous. "Blessed is he that considereth the poor; the Lord will deliver him in time of trouble;" "The needy shall not always be forgotten, the expectation of the poor shall not perish forever," chanted the singers; "Whoso reproacheth the poor reproacheth his Maker," echoed the teachers. "When thou goest into thy neighbor's vineyard," the law enacted, "thou mayest eat grapes thy fill, but thou shalt not put any in thy vessel;" and it commanded the landowners to leave standing the corn in the corners of the field, and not to turn back to gather in the gleanings. These were for the foodless and the destitute. The law likewise forbade the rich to impose charges on the poor for money lent; and, if a garment had been pledged for security, it decreed: "In any case thou shalt deliver him the pledge when the sun goeth down, that he may sleep in his own raiment." Such provisions as these, and others that I care not to recall, prove that the mother of Christianity looked tenderly on poverty, did not stigmatize it as a crime, but regarded it as a misfortune to be treated with with the most generous compassion.

But what of the daughter? Has she inherited these traditions and this spirit? That it was the Lord's will that she should do so is evident from His own ministry. It is said that "the common people heard Him gladly," and their attention to His words may have been largely secured by His thoughtfulness of their bodies. Wherever He went He healed the sick, restored the lame, opened the eyes of the blind, fed the starving multitude with miraculous bread, and in these various ways evinced His interest in their temporal well-being. Even in "preaching the gospel to the poor," which He adduced in support of His Messianic claims, He sought to deliver them from the evils of this life almost as much as to prepare them for the life to come. He was not only the Savior of the lowly, He was their Benefactor as well. And that His disciples were to share with Him in this mission of philanthropy is intimated not only in the kindly words of the text, and in the command, "Freely ye have received, freely give," but by the fact that one of His little company carried "the bag," whose scanty contents were devoted to the worthy indigent. Thus was He understood by the primitive church, and hence in her early history, to meet peculiar or pressing exigencies, all possessions were held in common, and to secure equality of distribution a special office was instituted. While this Christian communism speedily passed away, the apostles did not hesitate to enjoin upon the churches the most liberal charity. Contributions were called for in aid of the more destitute brethren, and were cheerfully given by the more prosperous. In Paul's second letter to the Corinthians considerable attention is paid to this subject, where a few comprehensive and wide-reaching principles are laid down for the regulation of benevolence, and in other portions of the New Testament its exercise is made the test of true discipleship. There it is written: "Whoso hath this world's goods and seeth his brother in need, and shutteth up his bowels of compassion from him, how dwelleth the love of God in him?" And even when the object of compassion is not a brother the law of Christ reads: "If thine enemy hunger, feed him; if he thirst, give him drink, for in so doing thou shalt heap coals of fire on his head." In this manner we perceive that the new religion went forth charged with the spirit of the old, and that large-heartedness and open-handedness were to be its distinguishing features perpetually. Whatever changes might overtake it, however its doctrinal conceptions might be modified or its ecclesiastical government be altered, its beneficence was to be abiding. To ignore its relations to the poor or to neglect its duty to the indigent would not only falsify its character, but would strip it of its most heavenly and convincing credentials.

This was recognized very distinctly by the followers of Christ in the centuries succeeding the first. They cultivated feelings of benignity, kindness, sympathy and bounteousness. Everywhere were they known by their fraternal interest in the suffering and oppressed, by their cordial recognition of the manhood of the slave, and by their humane provisions for the sick and the poor, the homeless and houseless, the fatherless children and husbandless wives. Every Sabbath collections were taken for the unfortunate, and even seasons of sore trial, when the alms-giver was hardly any better off than the alms-receiver, did not hinder the discharge of this sacred duty. Within the church all worshipers were equal. No distinction between the slave and his master, between the high and the low, was allowed in the solemn services of the sanctuary. They met on the same level; they separated on the same plane. Beneath the humble roof of the house consecrated to the glory of God, or within the dreary catacombs, where the outcast sect fled for religious consolation, rank and affluence, genius and learning, received as brethren the obscure, the ignorant and the moneyless. In those days the church was a refuge, an asylum, a retreat, a fortress and defense. There the victim of cruelty was comforted and protected, and there the wayward and fallen were welcomed to penitence and hope. The altars of the church covered the nakedness of the orphan, rejected the offerings of the violent and vicious, repelled the homage of the unjust and luxurious, and wreathed a blessing in their holy incense for the souls of all who emancipated the bondsman, delivered the captive, and defended the friendless. This spirit of philanthropy, which led a Christian woman to found the first public hospital, which constrained Constantine to abolish crucifixion, and which impelled Justinian to encourage manumission, was cultivated at every cost and at every hazard. The treasures of the church and the lives of her members were devoted to its service. To redeem the people who had become prisoners to the Goths, Ambrose sold the ornaments of the altar at Milan; and Acacius, to free seven thousand Persian captives, satisfied the triumphant Romans with the precious vessels and golden plate of the Basilica. To these ecclesiastical worthies a man was worth more than a miter, a soul was more than a triple crown, and beneficent acts higher signs of their vocation than pallium, stole and scapulary. During the ravages of pestilences, such as depopulated Carthage, Alexandria and Edessa, the disciples of Christ cared for the sick and dying who had been abandoned by their heathen relatives, and during the devastations of war such as desolated the fair fields of Italy they were ever the mediators and the fearless ambassadors of peace. Ministers of mercy, friends of humanity, they made the impression on society that religion is essentially philanthropic, that it had come to assuage grief, relieve poverty and succor helplessness. To this Julian, the emperor, traced the prevalence of their sentiments, and to this may be attributed the rise of the myriad charities which beautify and bless both Europe and America. As Lecky says of Christianity, and says truly, "It has covered the globe with countless institutions of mercy, absolutely unknown to the whole pagan world. It has indissolubly united in the minds of men the idea of supreme goodness with that of active and constant benevolence. It has placed in every parish a religious minister, who, whatever may be his other functions, has at least been officially charged with the superintendence of an organization of charity, and who finds in this office one of the most important as well as one of the most legitimate sources of his power." A sublime fact, which, however, in our day unhappily must be qualified, as the average minister does not seem to be particularly devoted to this part of his heavenly mission.

The Earl of Beaconsfield, no mean critic of his period, seems to regard it as very questionable whether society is any happier now, and the masses of the people more prosperous and freer from the curse of poverty, than they were in the olden times when the church watched over them and cared for them in this spirit of beneficence. There are passages in his romance entitled *Sybil* which appear to intimate that the poorer classes in our day are more wretched and helpless than in the past. For instance, in one place he says, referring to the monastic age: "There were yeomen then, sir. The country was not divided into two classes, masters and slaves; there was some resting-place between luxury and misery. Comfort was an English habit then, not merely an English word"; and at another point in the story he adds: "Christianity teaches us to love our neighbor; modern society acknowledges no neighbor." Still more unequivocally he writes in another connection: "There is more serfdom in England now than at any time since the Conquest. I speak of what passes under my daily eyes when I say that those who labor can as little choose or change their masters now as when they were born thralls. There are great bodies of the working classes of this country nearer the condition of brutes than they have been at any time since the Conquest. Indeed, I see nothing to distinguish them from brutes, except that their morals are inferior." However harsh and censorious these views may sound, they are not without supporters. Not a few candid thinkers sympathize with them, especially in the Old World.

It is insisted by many that in our age "the rich are growing richer and the poor are growing poorer." Mr. Thornton, an English writer, in his book on *Over Population*, maintains that the condition of the working classes to-day is worse than it was in the middle ages. He condemns, in common with Mr. Wright, author of *Our New Masters*, "the ignorance of those who argue in the face of facts that the English peasantry of the middle ages were less comfortably situated than their living descendants because they used barley instead of wheaten flour, ate off wooden platters, never knew the luxury of a cotton shirt or of a cup of tea, and slept on straw pallets within walls of wattled plaster," and concludes with the statement: "Although ruder means were employed to supply the wants of nature, every want was abundantly satisfied, which is far indeed from being the case at the present." These gentlemen show that Hallam and Froude are more than inclined to this view, incidentally confirming it in their histories. Hallam distinctly says: "I find it difficult to resist the conclusion that, however the laborer has derived benefit from the cheapness of manufactured commodities, and from many inventions of common utility, he is much inferior in ability to support a family than were his ancestors four centuries ago." But taking for granted that these writers over-state the case, there is still abundant reason for looking on the present condition of society with solicitude.

Vast estates are accumulating in a few hands, and only the extent of our territory averts from the New World many of the land difficulties which distract the Old. Monopolies and gigantic capital lord it over labor and hold millions of human beings in a condition approaching that of serfdom. Wages are precarious, and sometimes depend on voting the political ticket of employers,— so farcical is our boasted right of suffrage,— and they are pitiably scant, considering the extravagant prices that are demanded for the common necessaries of life. In England the number of paupers steadily increases; in France, also, after vigorous and partially successful endeavors to reduce it, again it is multiplying. In Holland and Belgium, formerly comparatively free from mendicity, beggars and beggary are becoming more general, and even in this country, although wonderfully favored and prosperous, these evils are enlarging and are rapidly attaining to portentous proportions. That in Europe there are millions of peasants who have little else than black bread to eat, and that there are thousands in every great American city who can scarcely find a crust to blunt the hungry edge of appetite, and that there are other thousands who, strive as they may, can hardly keep the wolf from the door, and who, to drown the sense of overhanging doom, snatch a fearful joy from restless dissipation, are among the commonplaces of daily observation. With untold multitudes of our fellow-beings existence is a tragedy composed of accumulating evils, unsatisfied desire, impatience with the present and weariness of the past, whose brief pauses between the acts are uncheered by the excruciating efforts which the orchestra makes toward music, otherwise known as pleasure. Not veiled as at Egyptian festivals does a specter sit to remind them of life's hollowness, but at every scant meal does it preside, uncovered in the light of day, its fleshless lips deriding their despair, and its hard, cold fingers paralyzing their strength. Nothing brought they into the world, and nothing have they in it. Like the Phrygian Tantalus, they are overwhelmed, but not in water, and they starve with the rich clusters of plenty hanging in their sight. Their efforts to win a living are Sisyphean in their futility,—the stone rolls back only to crush them. Everywhere between Jerusalem and Jericho humanity is found mutilated by its own vices or plundered by its enemies, naked, famished, bleeding, and the good Samaritan at his wit's end to discover a remedy. Now it is a laboring man trying to support a family on a miserable pittance, disheartened by disease and the precariousness of employment; or it is a widow woman with helpless children and failing health; or it is a household cursed with drunken parents and maddened by repeated disappointments; or it is a wretched girl cheated of her earnings that the coffers of soulless affluence may be filled, and driven by beggary to crime; or it is the untutored and fatherless boy, hungry, weak, and ragged, pinched with cold and foul with dirt, that lifts up the imploring voice: "Have compassion,—have compassion on me, fine ladies and gentlemen!" Multiply these cases by the hundreds, and then add to them thousands of others, burrowing in cellars and shivering in garrets, miseducated, uneducated, incompetent people, who have been sent into the mad conflict of life like soldiers uniformless and weaponless; and supplement these helpless crowds with the victims of our rapacious, grinding, heartless civilization, among whom can be found a host who have been maimed, disabled, and mutilated in its service, and you may form a faint idea of the dimensions of the unfortunate and melancholy army that staggers on its way to the grave under the tattered banner of poverty.

No wonder that the tender heart of Philanthropy is appalled at such a sight; no wonder that at times she sits with folded hands in utter hopelessness of ever being able to remove the evil, and no wonder if, choking with sobs, her gloom rises into a wail, and she hoarsely sings:

> "These things confound me,
>   They settle on my brain;
> The very air around me
>   Is universal pain.
> The air is damp with weeping,
>   Rarely the sun shines clear
> On any but those sleeping
>   Upon the quiet bier."

And yet she should not despair. Poverty is neither indestructible nor inevitable. We have fair promises from heaven pointing to its extinction, and we have sweet visions seen from of old of teeming millions rejoicing in abundance, and crowned with prosperity. Better believe that we have failed to discern or wisely to apply the means for the fulfillment of these predictions than that they shall utterly fail, and the earth be perpetually afflicted. Undoubtedly there are errors and mistakes which measurably account for the present deplorable state of things, which, if they could only be distinctly seen and remedied, the way would be prepared for better times. What the gravest of these are I desire to point out, not to discuss them in full, and if I am successful in my humble endeavor I may at least do something toward the ultimate solution of the grave problem that now burdens the thought of every enlightened and loving soul. And I address these reflections especially to the church; for, as we have seen, God committed to her the poor, and she is certainly more responsible than any other organization for their condition.

In my judgment the continuance of poverty and the spread of Pauperism are largely due to the selfish principle which underlies the structure of modern society, and which permeates and ramifies through all its departments. Self-interest is the supreme rule everywhere. Men are in haste to be rich. The end of their striving is wealth; as money in our age is the representative of ease, respect, homage, and even of political preferment, they rush madly toward it, careless of the thousands they may trample beneath their feet in the race. Finance is the god of the present, and there seems to be no pity in the heart of its worshipers. The influence of the commercial idea, elevating in some of its aspects, and beneficent, has been demoralizing and disorganizing in others. It has created the impression that everything has its price, and that even faith, honor, patriotism, justice, chastity, the esteem of men, and the grace of God, are objects of trade and barter. The result is that the calculating spirit is dominant, and it has passed into an axiom that the employer should give as little as possible to labor, not as much as he can reasonably afford. Over-reaching has quite thrust aside as antiquated and impracticable the old law of "do as you would be done by," and it is generally voted inapplicable to modern times. The current maxim is, Get as much for as little as possible; and the workman naturally adopts it, and renders as little as he can for as much as he can get. Consequently there is at bottom no good feeling between these classes, neither confidence nor sympathy, respect nor love. They are preying on each other, doing their best under forms of law to plunder each other, and in the tussle the laborer generally comes out second best. The struggle for existence between them is deadly and fierce, and unfortunately the fittest does not always survive. From the unequal contest the lowly emerge disheartened, and frequently disabled. Fifty cents for writing all day, fifty cents for plying a sewing-machine ten hours, fifty cents for bending over some sickening task, fifty cents the total earnings of a woman trying to guard her little ones from starvation, and but little more to be earned by famished hundreds in the largest business establishments.

Are you surprised that there is poverty? Are you surprised that the multiplied horrors of their life should drive many to intemperance, thence to more bitter poverty still? Are you amazed, even when wages reach the munificent sum of two or three dollars a day, employment being irregular and family sickness frequent, that it is not easy to lay anything by, and that the hopelessness of the fight should induce recklessness and despair? I cannot say that I am. I am rather persuaded that much of the prevalent indigence and appalling destitution may be traced to the mistaken notion that social and economic laws teach that capital in its own interest must wring from labor all that it can get. There never was a greater delusion; for, as I have already argued, there is no law human or divine, that countenances such insane and barbarous inequalities.

If it shall be said there is no help for what appears to be so hard on labor, I deny it. The study of Sociology is yet in its infancy. There must be an outlet from the present confusion and muddle. After ages of pain and thought we have reached the conclusion that government is for the well-being of the many, and that the ruler of a nation is the servant of the people, not their dictator; and in time to come we shall be able to formulate a similar organizing principle for society, which, while discarding the blunders of Communism, will direct the energies of commerce and trade in every department toward the happiness of the many, not as at present, for the lordly affluence of the few. Then capital will be the brother of labor, not its king; and then labor will be the friend of capital, not its slave. Another Adam Smith will in coming years assuredly arise, and in a work grander than the *Wealth of Nations* will discourse on the true relations that exist between the employer and the employed; and will point out how the rich gifts of providence can be distributed more equally among all classes. He will doubtless show that a State cannot afford quietly to look on and see its citizens pauperized; that it must legislate in the interest of the masses for the sake of its national spirit; and he will unquestionably demonstrate that capital and labor can coöperate to the advantage of both, and that by regulating competition, and by educating and even providing for the young, so that they do not, as at present, enter into disastrous rivalry with their seniors, many of the accursed evils which have domesticated themselves among us may be cured at least in part, if not altogether.

In the meanwhile is it suggested that wealthy employers must give to charitable institutions for the amelioration of crying evils? If they can do nothing better, let them do that. But let it not be forgotten that what the working classes require is ampler remuneration, not charity, a fair equivalent for service rendered, not an alms. They demand what belongs to them as men, not what is due the infirm and helpless. Take the money that might be given to benevolent organizations and pay honest toil a better price, and you will soon render their existence unnecessary. Christian capitalists should do this, even if none others do. While our public charities are in one sense our glory, in another they are our shame; for they proclaim the vice, injustice, stupidity, and oppression that have rendered their existence imperative. Get rid of them as rapidly as possible by a new and wiser course toward the dependent. If men of means would incorporate their private donations and their public contributions into their wage list they could abate their own taxes, and they would at the same time abate Pauperism and contribute to the permanent prosperity of society.

Another source of the evil we are considering can be detected in the blundering, undiscriminating methods of charity which we have adopted, and which we adhere to in the face of protests uttered by observation and experience. History confirms with its testimony the fact that lavish and unguarded benevolence tends to pauperize a community. Lecky shows that among the Romans corn was freely distributed to the people, and that under Caius Gracchus it was sold by the government at a merely nominal rate. These measures were corrupted by conscienceless men who sought the popular favor, and in the time of Julius Cæsar three hundred and twenty thousand persons were recipients of state assistance, and the number increased to eight hundred thousand under the Antonines. The result was demoralizing; industry was paralyzed. The people were not satisfied with the corn; they demanded and received oil and meat in addition. In time they looked upon these gratuities as their right, and, in proportion as they did so, they fell away from that self-reliant manhood that had formerly been their country's glory. Similar results followed the excessive and inconsiderate charity of the church of the middle ages, so that at the dawn of the Reformation Europe was an extensive poor-house. It had destroyed forethought and prudence, had multiplied religious impostors, and established begging fraternities. Spencer, in a few sharp sentences, shows the baleful effects of the Elizabethan poor-laws— 1601,— and it is well known that these and other public and private benefactions entailed such frightful evils on England that they had to be made the subject of Parliamentary inquiry, and so grave have been the disclosures that various writers, reviewing the past and the present, have come to the conclusion "that charity is the real cause of Pauperism." While I cannot go as far, I yet firmly believe that when it is indiscriminately administered it fosters the evil it ought to allay. In France, after many bitter experiences, especially from the years 1693 to 1793, legislation succeeded in reducing Pauperism by enforcing the principles of industry, and in my opinion it can be restrained only by the adoption of similar measures.

There are two classes of poor, the worthy and the unworthy, or, as they have been distinguished by some one, "the Lord's poor and the devil's poor," "the poor of providence and the poor of improvidence." As a rule the latter always get whatever the generous have to bestow. If you have a relief society you will find it taken possession of by those who have no claims on its bounty. They crowd the worthy out, and systematically deceive the benevolent. Much money is daily given away to unknown applicants by individuals who have not the leisure to scrutinize their character. It is bestowed in the hope that it may not be misapplied, and yet frequently this liberality is guilty of a double wrong,—it encourages the improvident, and by consuming the means that might have relieved the deserving robs them of what God ordained as their portion. The only safety lies in rigid, though kindly, examination of all persons who desire assistance. To render this effectual there should be an organization and unification of all charities. The community should be districted, and after proper care the names enrolled of all who are deserving of help. This course has been pursued in several cities with marked success. It has found out the worthy who really needed help, and it has exposed the worthless who were following mendicancy as a business. Wherever it has been adopted Pauperism has declined, and the community been purged of its worst and most demoralizing elements.

In this connection I am constrained to say that the failure to keep before us the true end of charity has militated against its efficacy. Discrimination is imperatively demanded here. The design of benevolence is not merely to mitigate present misery, but rather to help the unfortunate permanently to help themselves. Christ, in His ministry, restored to the helpless their sight or their strength, so that they could independently earn their bread, and in so doing He has given us an example to follow. While occasions are frequent when temporary relief is needed, and should be given, philanthropy should seek above all else to make the poor self-sustaining. It should seek to awaken feelings of personal dignity and self-respect in their breasts, and encourage them to rely on their own energies. Hence it should always rather provide work than bread, opportunity than clothing, situations in which to toil rather than institutions in which to rest. Were this kind of discrimination practiced, I am satisfied we would soon rejoice in a more provident and prosperous people.

One more thought and I am done. Of late I have come to believe that the thrift of poverty in our times may to some extent be attributed to the church. It seems to me that she has divorced from her altars that work of charity which she received from her Lord, and which in the primitive age was her glory. Understand me, I do not mean that her members do not aid the suffering in private, or fail to sustain public measures by their sympathy and their alms. I presume that they give liberally in various directions and encourage nearly every humanitarian cause. What I complain of is not that, but that as an organization she does comparatively so little for the relief of the destitute. She has handed over this ministry to other bodies. She contributes to the support of these bodies and surrenders to them the field. As a consequence we hear it frequently said that this or that benevolent society is doing more for the poor than the church. A reproach is taken up against us that diminishes our influence on society. That were, of course, a small matter, were the work for which we are responsible accomplished; but it is not, and in my judgment never can be by any other instrumentality. The more dependent classes are drifting away from us, because the impression has steadily grown that the church as such is not interested in them. When they learn that it is sometimes difficult to obtain money to bury her poor, and more difficult to find means to keep them alive, they naturally take it as a hint that they are not wanted. It is impossible to explain that the members are now burdened with the demands of this or that institution, for the unfortunate are not in the mood for drawing nice distinctions. They judge from the surface, and as it appears on the surface that very inadequate provision is made for their class, they look upon themselves as thrust out from the household of faith. Of course they are wrong, but the only way to convince them of the fact is for the church to resume her functions as a philanthropic society.

I am urgent on this point. She has committed her temperance work to reform societies of more or less efficiency; she has surrendered her city missions to the care of independent organizations, and even her members, when they develop marked ability and exceptional zeal, too frequently set up for themselves, or go out and do for Young Men's Christian Associations what they ought to do within her boundaries and for her success. Rapidly she is depriving herself of everything like a distinctive mission among men. Complex union meetings and special evangelistic efforts she substitutes for her own direct endeavors to win souls to Christ; movements to succor penitent criminals or to aid the worthy poor she allows to take her place in bringing help and healing, and what is left to her of actual service to mankind is hardly worth recording. If ever the church perishes it will be because she has rendered herself unnecessary to the world; and if ever she regains her position she must resume her God-given vocation, have less care about being aristocratic and ornamental, and become practical and useful. Nor can she better begin her reformation than by taking up her long-neglected ministry to the indigent, seeking them out and enriching them with her beneficence.

Do you suggest that such a course would call to her a host of impostors and of worthless idlers? Possibly: but she is under no obligation to give her money to them, and a little judicious discrimination would soon disperse them. But supposing that they came, the message of truth from her lips might reclaim many, and the thousands of others who would throng her courts would be stimulated to earnest endeavor and industry. It is her influence on character that renders her so important an instrumentality in curing the evil of poverty. She is able to quicken dormant sensibilities, to arouse slumbering energies, and to awaken manly aspirations. Thousands have received new life at her altars, and have gone forth animated by a new hope to conquer for themselves a support in the world. It is this work that other societies cannot do, and it is this that is especially needed to diminish the proportions of pauperism, and which, in failing to accomplish by alienating the poor, the church stands justly charged with responsibility for its present magnitude and strength.

My brethren, surely the time has come for us to return to the Lord's plan. Among us there are children to be clothed, widows to be aided, and afflicted ones to be cared for. Here and now determine to be mother, friend and benefactor to them all, so that within your ample boundaries no child of God shall cry in vain for bread, and no worthy fellow-being look despairingly for sympathy or succor. A modest sum added to your pew-rent will be all-sufficient, and this supplemented by your prayers and thoughtful love will carry an enduring blessing to many a melancholy home and to many a discouraged heart. Yea, your gracious ministry will return the benediction to your own soul. It will bless the giver more than the receiver.

You will sleep more warmly in the coming winter nights, because of the mantle you have thrown around the form of shivering need; you will tread more firmly the declining years for the staff of support you have placed in the hands of aged distress, and you will sing more sweetly for the melodies you have awakened in the once mute or wailing bosom of gnawing want. Light will have new pleasure for you when it falls radiant from thankful eyes, and no diamond that ever shone on maiden's brow will be to you as precious as the silent, glistening tear of gratitude bedewing your hand of charity. As you draw nearer to the poor, the Savior will come nearer you. In their presence you will feel that you are in His. The legends of Saint Christopher and of Saint Julien will be translated into the vernacular of your experience. The orphan child you carry across the swirling stream in your embrace will grow into the Christ, and the stranger you rescue from the pitiless storm and from the dreary night will be transformed into the Savior; and then will you discern the meaning of those gracious words: "As ye did it unto one of the least of these, ye did it unto me." And then, stealing over your soul like the music of the morning, will sweetly chime the Master's welcome, assurance of eternal rest: "Come, ye blessed of my father, inherit the kingdom prepared for you from the foundation of the world."

ALTRUISM.

"For whosoever will save his life shall lose it, and whosoever shall lose his life for my sake shall find it." *Matt. xvi, 25.*

"Abou Ben Adhem,— may his tribe increase!—
Awoke one night from a deep dream of peace,
And saw amid the moonlight in his room,
Making it rich, and like a lily in bloom,
An angel writing in a book of gold;
Exceeding peace had made Ben Adhem bold,
And to the vision in the room he said,
'What writest thou?' The vision raised its head,
And with a voice made of all sweet accord
Replied, 'The names of them that love the Lord.'
'And is mine one?' said Abou. 'Nay, not so,'
Replied the angel. Abou spoke more low,
But cheerly still, and said, 'I pray thee, then,
Write me as one who loves his fellow men.'

"The angel wrote and vanished. The next night
He came again with a great wakening light;
He showed the names whom love of God had blest,
And lo! Ben Adhem's name led all the rest."

Leigh Hunt.

WHILE with deepest solicitude a serious man will address himself to the question of his soul's salvation, with hardly less earnestness will he seek to know how he may save his life. The two lines of inquiry, though intimately blending, are not identical; for even when anxiety regarding the future world has been entirely allayed, dissatisfaction with the experiences of the present may be sorely felt. Many religious people who have no kind of doubt as to their acceptance with God are painfully conscious that they are of little service to man.

They find no genuine enjoyment in their pursuits, their triumphs and their pleasures. Their daily life is barren, commonplace and uninteresting. They grow infinitely fatigued with its routine, and were it not impious, they could wish for its speedy termination. Their attitude is one of moody resignation and of stolid submission. Life is endured because it would be sinful to end it, and its ghastly possessors smile sepulchrally at each other, and try to make each other believe that it is relished. The thin hypocrisy, however, cannot conceal the truth that a very large number of people, religious and non-religious, have no very distinct idea as to why they were born, what they are here for, or how they are to derive from existence sufficient satisfaction to compensate for the evils they are forced to endure. Life to them is a sky without stars, a star without radiance, a garden without flowers, a flower without perfume, an orchestra without music, music without harmony. Evidently they have missed its secret, have not discovered its art, and are in imminent peril of dying without having truly lived.

When they are oppressed by the consciousness of this fact, and begin to discern and believe that there must be a sweetness and profit in life hitherto concealed from them, and to inquire with reference to it, "What must I do to be saved?" a crisis is reached only second, if indeed it be second, to that which prompted the soul to give utterance to a similar cry when burdened with a sense of guilt. And it is a cause of rejoicing that the Book which furnishes an adequate answer to the appeal of the soul has not failed to supply a principle for the conservation of the life. That principle is stated tersely and paradoxically in the words of the text,—words which we shall do well to lay to heart on the close of this sermon-series,—and which, if fairly interpreted and honestly received, may render our future more useful, and infinitely more gratifying, than has been our past.

George Eliot has given her reading of the problem, representing a school of thought which is entitled to respectful consideration, though it may at times awaken commiseration. In early years, influenced by such books as Strauss' *Life of Jesus* and Feuerbach's *Essence of Christianity*, she drifted away from the faith of the church, and embraced sentiments which are now currently known as "Altruistic." She was undoubtedly the grandest representative and the noblest advocate which these views have ever had, and what she has not directly or indirectly said in their behalf is hardly worth saying. While the essence of Altruism is expressed by Spinoza in the famous passage "He who loves God must not desire God to love him in return," we get a clearer view of its sweep and scope from the works of its acknowledged champion. According to its teachings, the religion of humanity prescribes as its first, and perhaps only, law that we should devote ourselves absolutely to the well-being of others, and should so subordinate every selfish instinct to this supreme object as to be unaffected by hopes of rewards or fears of punishment. Virtue is identified with total disinterestedness, and duty is degraded, loses its character, and is changed to expediency when it is associated with thought of motives. Immortality, the world beyond, the favor of God, and even the happiness of self, are unworthy a moment's attention; for the former are beclouded with uncertainty, and the latter consideration is utterly despicable. Altruism and Agnosticism shake hands, and are in brotherly agreement. The second claims that we are in ignorance concerning everything beyond the range of our senses, and the first declares that we ought not to permit the Unknowable to influence our conduct. Unquestionably George Eliot is correct in magnifying the duty of loving self-sacrifice for others. This is essentially the doctrine of the Bible. We are "to esteem others better than ourselves," we are to "love our neighbor as ourselves," we are "to bear each other's burdens," and so to "fulfill the law of Christ." Nay more, we are also to devote ourselves to God's service, and to surrender all that we have, if necessary, to further His holy will and pleasure. We are to count ourselves least, to hold ourselves as dead to our own selfish interests, and to count not our life dear if we can by any means save others. To this extent Christianity is altruistic, and as far as this central principle of self-abnegation goes I have only words of respect and admiration for this Ism and its advocates. But Christianity does not sanction their wholesale repudiation of motives. While it is far from appealing to selfish fear or mercenary hope, it does recognize the fact that man is susceptible to various influences, and that he is moved by inducements more or less refined and noble. It aims to sway him by considerations which will meet this part of his nature, and yet do so in such a way as to deepen in his heart the spirit of thoughtful love and self-sacrifice for others. In other words, its supreme motive is of such a character that the more it is felt the less will men think of themselves or of their own interests, and the less will they be given to vain egotism and narrow selfishness. This Christian Altruism, if I may be allowed to combine terms usually hostile, is expressed by our Lord in the text, and if seriously pondered and thoroughly comprehended will, I am persuaded, commend itself to every man's conscience in the sight of God.

After the disciples had confessed that Jesus was the Christ, they were startled and overwhelmed by His declaration "that He must go unto Jerusalem, and suffer many things of the elders and chief priests and scribes, and be killed, and be raised again the third day." This voluntary surrender to what seemed unnecessary suffering especially appealed to the feelings of Peter, who immediately and earnestly remonstrated, saying: "Be it far from Thee, Master; this shall not be unto Thee." In our version we have the expression that Peter "rebuked" Jesus, but the original does not convey this impression, and our own sense of the respect in which the disciple must have held his Lord will not permit us to suppose that he presumed to employ language so irreverent. He did not reprove; he rather expostulated with Him, whom he had so recently acknowledged as the Messiah, and sought to dissuade from His fatal purpose. The marginal reading reveals the spirit in which the apostle made this appeal. As there given his language is "Pity Thyself," that is, "Be merciful to Thyself, and do not go to Jerusalem; attain the end of Thine mission without suffering and shame." Alas! Peter, like many of my readers, did not understand the real significance and the strange mystery of life. He seemed to labor under the delusion that Christ could accomplish His sublime purpose of mercy at ease, surrounded with every comfort, in an autocratic manner, and that, as God in the beginning "commanded and it stood fast," so all that the Master had to do was "to speak and it would be done." This seemed to be his idea, but it was not Christ's. Rudely was he roused from his delusion by the stern words of the Savior, almost identical with those addressed to Satan on the occasion of the temptation, "Get thee behind me, for thou savorest not the things that be of God." Just as the devil had tried to induce Him to seek an easy and short road to success by "falling down and worshiping him," so Peter had presumed to suggest the possibility of victory without conflict. In both instances the great law of life was ignored, and the fruitful source of its perversion and failure was insinuated.

Straightway the Savior corrects the error of His servant. He shows that his attitude is not exceptional; that he is neither erratic nor eccentric, but that what is true of Himself is also true of all men. Even as He "to rise again the third day," with power and in glory, and to actualize the sublimest possibilities of His existence, must travel the highway of death, so in a similar, though inferior sense, every disciple, yea, and every man who would save his life from uselessness, perversion and dishonor, must consent to lose it. There is one law applicable to all alike, to the Savior and the saint, to the saint and the sinner. The seed-corn "must die or it abideth alone," but if it die it "shall bear much fruit." There is that "which scattereth and yet increaseth," and there is "that which withholdeth more than is meet and that tendeth to poverty;" and there is that which deals with life as a miser deals with money, and that loses it at the end.

Never has any real benefit been conferred on society, or any permanent advantage been secured without costing somebody suffering and loss. As the old Latin poet sings,

> "Not for themselves birds rear the nest,
> Or bears its woolly fleece the sheep,
> Or builds the bee its honeyed rest,
> Or drags the ox the ploughshare deep."

And never was nest yet built for weary humanity, and never was covering wrought for its infirmities and sins, and never was sweetness extracted from the flower to mingle with the bitterness of its anguish, and never, never, did the share prepare the way for abundance to meet the famine of its mind and heart, without somebody performing exacting labor and enduring exhausting anguish. The names of martyrs, heroes, reformers, explorers, scientists and philanthropists, the Polycarps, the Winkelrieds, the Savonarolas, the Magellans, the Keplers, and the Howards, are perpetual witnesses that no great victory has yet been achieved for the world apart from self-abnegation and self-surrender. Death seems to be the condition of life, and vicariousness the law of progress. If we would deliver others from evil we must be willing to bear evil ourselves; if we would bring others into the light we must consent ourselves to go down into the darkness; and if we would press others upward to the mount of Transfiguration we must be prepared to descend into the valley of Achor. So deeply has this conviction impressed the human mind, and interblended with its thinking, that in the literature, and especially in the religions, of all lands we find it taking shape in some legend or doctrine by which the relation of self-sacrifice to the advancement and well-being of society or the world is maintained and illustrated. Perhaps the earliest of these representations are to be found among the Hindus, and I refer to them particularly as they at once suggest the antiquity and the prevalence of the principle involved. For instance, according to authorities cited by Johnson, the *Rig Veda* is supposed to teach that the Supreme Spirit sacrificed himself to create the world; and Soma is exalted in the " Hymns " as a " healer, and deliverer from pain," the *Sáma Veda* testifying that this deity " submits to mortal birth, and is bruised and afflicted that others may be saved." But the most splendid and thrilling illustration of this doctrine is contained in the *Mahaprasthánika Parva* of the *Mahábhárata*, the " fable of faithful love which is stronger than death." It will repay us to glance hastily at the story, as it is given by Edwin Arnold in his translation published recently in the *International Review*.

The kingly family of the Pandavas, having received from saintly Vyasa a view of the invisible world, became discontented with royalty and determined to journey toward Mount Meru, "where is Indra's heaven," where all sorrows would terminate and union with the Infinite be attained. King Yudhishthira, his sister the peerless Draupadi, and his brethren, Arjuna, Sahadev, Nakula, and Bhimasena, clothed in rough habits, moved forward without faltering or hesitancy, through tangled forests and across the "wide waste of sand, dreadful as death," toward the East, where Paradise blooms. When they came in sight of Meru, Draupadi fell and died because she loved her husband "better than all else," better even than heaven. "That was her tender sin, fault of a faultless soul." Then Sahadev swooned and died, because "wisdom made him proud;" then Nakula perished, because of self-satisfied love; then Arjuna followed, because "once he lied a worldly lie and bragged," and then Bhimasena, too, because he "fainted and stayed upon the way," "too much devoted to the goodly things of earth."

> "Thenceforth alone the long-armed monarch strode,
> Not looking back — nay! not for Bhima's sake,—
> But walking with his face set for the Mount.
> After the deathly sands, the Mount! and lo!
> Sakra shone forth,— the God,— filling the earth
> And heavens with thunder of his chariot wheels.
> 'Ascend,' he said, 'with me, Pritha's great son!'
> But Yudhishthira answered, sore at heart
> For those his kinsfolk, fallen on the way.
> *   *   *   *   *   *   *
> 'They, the delightful ones, who sank and died,
> Following my footsteps, could not live again
> Though I had turned,— therefore I did not turn;
> But could help profit, I had turned to help.'
>   Indra smiled and said,
>   'O thou true king,
> Thou that dost bring to harvest the good seed
> Of Pandu's righteousness . . .
> Enter thou now to the eternal joys.'"

But Yudhishthira replied that he could not consent to tarry where his loved ones were not. He felt that it was his duty to be with them even in sorrow, and expressed a wish to join their company. A golden Deva was therefore sent to conduct him where his kinsmen were. Onward they went together treading "the sinners' road."

> "The tread of sinful feet
> Matted the thick thorns carpeting its slope;
> The smell of sin hung foul on them; the mire
> About their roots was trampled filth of flesh
> Horrid with rottenness, and splashed with gore,
> Curdling in crimson puddles; where there buzzed
> And sucked and settled creatures of the swamp,
> Hideous in wing and sting, gnat-clouds and flies,
> With moths, toads, newts, and snakes red-gulleted,
> And livid, loathsome worms, writhing in slime
> Forth from skull-holes and scalps and tumbled bones."

Thus the king reached Kutasháa Mali, gate of utmost Hell, and for a moment paused; and then pressed on amid piteous groans, bringing by his presence mitigation of suffering to the wretched captives. At last he meets his unfortunate relatives, and ministers some solace to their agonizing hearts. Finding that partnership in their anguish affords them relief, he exclaims:

> "I stand
> Here in the throat of Hell, and here will bide—
> Nay, if I perish—while my well-beloved
> Win ease and peace by any pains of mine."

This readiness to brave hell for love excited the admiration of the "Presences of Paradise," and they told him that all heaven was glad because of him. On his account, and because of his self-immolation, his friends are freed from dread despair, and with him enter the abode of the blessed and saved—"washed from soils of sin, from passion, pain, and change."

Beautiful and impressive as this narrative is, it does not surpass the gospels in their manner of enforcing the indispensableness of the vicarious principle. The entire movement to rescue man from sin and death proceeds on the supposition of its efficacy. Jesus "who was rich becomes poor, that we through His poverty might be rich"; "He dies the just for the unjust that he might bring us to God"; "He redeems us from the curse of the law, being made a curse for us"; and thus these special benefits to us are all conditioned on His becoming poor, being made a curse, and suffering the pangs of death. Explain as we may the precise meaning of these passages, the one dominant thought pervades them all, that to save the life of others Jesus had to lose his own. The same principle reveals itself conspicuously in His followers and in their teachings. Paul could wish himself accursed from Christ for Israel's sake; Peter rejoiced in being a partaker of Christ's sufferings; and perhaps all of the sacred writers in some form recognized the fact that nothing could be done for the world in the spirit of self-seeking or of self-indulgent somnolence. We may, therefore, conclude that on no point in the entire domain of religious and moral thought is there such general agreement as on this; and that, if we would really help the world, we must be ready to surrender self in sacrifice.

To understand what our Lord means by losing life we may with profit consult the force of the prescription contained in the preceding verse. He there declares that His disciples must deny themselves, must take up their cross and follow Him. As this unquestionably is tantamount to "losing life," it is of the highest moment that we should apprehend distinctly the meaning of the language. It may also assist us to remember that He Himself is the clearest exemplification of the principle He inculcates, and that it must aid us to study it in the light of His personal history.

Certainly by self-denial He does not intend to recommend anything of an artificial and perfunctory character. There have always been ascetically-minded individuals who have interpreted our Lord's words as enjoining some self-imposed sufferings. Hence they have afflicted their bodies, have sought out curious means of torturing themselves, as though a man in the discharge of his duty would not encounter trials and pains enough to satisfy the most morbid without taking the trouble to invent them. They have scourged themselves with whips, as though the enemies of righteousness would fail to scourge them with scorpions; they have withdrawn from their families, as though their flesh and blood would not of its own accord raise its hand against godliness; and they have alienated their property and voluntarily become poor, as though there were not worldly cormorants in sufficient numbers, and with appetites sufficiently voracious, to devour all their substance. Saints of a less heroic mood have felt it incumbent on themselves to wear unsightly garments, to look with scorn on the harmless amusements of society, to perform vigils and fastings, and to make themselves as unamiable and as uncomfortable as possible. But Christ never countenanced in His own life any such interpretation of His words. He never formally undertook a fast. When He abstained from bread the stress of His feelings was such that He had no appetite for food. He never withdrew from a pleasure that came not in the way of His work, nor did He wear a robe to distinguish Him from others, and equally far was it from His thought to afflict His body in any way. In other words, He never regarded it as needful to be His own enemy in a world where enemies were thick on every side. Whatever difficulties, whatever sufferings, whatever burdens had to be endured in the course of His ministry, He submitted to unrepiningly and patiently, and these were as much as He could bear. And it is not necessary, nor is it modest, for the disciple to pretend to a higher degree of self-abnegation than his Lord. He, too, will have his trials and his agonies, and if he will only meet them in the spirit of his Master he need not undertake to convert his meager garden into a wilderness, nor his little day into night.

Not infrequently are Christians heard to speak of duties as crosses to be borne, and I am convinced that some among them regard their performance as a complete compliance with the law of self-denial. It is a cross to pray, to speak, to commend Christ to others, to attend church, to frequent the social meetings, and, indeed, to do anything of a distinctly religious nature. By the force of their will and with the aid of sundry admonitions they bring themselves up to the discharge of these obligations, but on the whole they feel that it should entitle them to a place in "the noble army of martyrs." I am sorry to dissipate the comfortable illusion, but I am compelled to assure them that they totally misapprehend the doctrine of our Lord. He said that it was His meat and drink to do the will of His Father, and He never once refers to duty in any other way than as a delight. The cross was something distinct from it, and incidental to it, but never to be identified with it; and if we look upon it otherwise, if we find no honest joy in the service of God, and if we fail to discriminate between that and the pangs and pains to which it may give rise, we shall fall infinitely short of the conception embodied in the language of Christ.

To deny oneself, to take up the cross, denotes something immeasurably grander than self-imposed penance or rigid conformity to a Divine statute. It is the free surrender of self to an ennobling work, an absolute subordination of personal advantages and of personal pleasures for the sake of truth and the welfare of others, and a willing acceptance of every disability which their interests may entail. It is the sacrifice of life, as life is understood among men, of the absorbing care with which it is usually regarded, of the greatness to which it may attain, of the comforts which it may enjoy, and of the honors wherewith it may be crowned. In Christ this spirit prompted, for the sake of human redemption, the abandonment of heaven's glory and the endurance of earthly shame. It constrained Him to become of no reputation, to assume the form of a servant, and to carry His obedience even unto the death of the cross. In such a man as Paul it moved him to seek the world's welfare at the expense of his social standing, his friends' approval, his earthly prospects, and his personal safety. In such men as Bruno and Galileo it inspired, for the emancipation of truth as truth, a zeal and self-forgetfulness, and the sacrifice of ecclesiastical favor, the comforts of home, and the dignities of life. In the mother, for the sake of her children, it leads to wakefulness while others sleep, to solicitude when others laugh, and to an absolute merging of her selfhood in theirs. She carries their burdens, drinks deeper of their sorrows than of her own, and deprives herself of every pleasure that theirs may be increased. In the patriot it creates an unselfish devotion that influences him to subordinate personal preferences, considerations, aspirations and ambitions to the public weal. And in the minister of the gospel it enkindles a flame of love, a consuming passion for the salvation and elevation of humanity, in which all thought of self is burned away, and before which all idea of self-aggrandizement, reputation and honor is brought to naught. Possible in every calling and pursuit, and among every class and condition of mankind, its radical characteristic is a recognition of something in the universe grander than personal well-being, and a voluntary consecration of everything that enters into temporal well-being to the interests of whatever that ideal something may be.

This, in my opinion, is what the Savior meant by "losing life," and doubtless when He laid aside His glory and entered into the world of sin, the angels, who understood not the mystery of redemption, plead with Him, as did Peter, at a later day, "to be pitiful to himself." I can conceive of them as meekly remonstrating with Him not to lose His life, for to their sight, blinded by excess of peaceful blessedness, it must have seemed that His self-sacrifice was indeed the extreme of unthriftiness. But if they never indulged so misguided a judgment, it cannot be said that our fellow-beings have been wiser. Many of them have only seen in self-sacrifice the wildest fanaticism and the most foolish prodigality. To the apostle bound to go to Jerusalem and to Rome, where dangers and enemies awaited him, they have uttered their protest born of worldly wisdom. To the scientist they have said: "Why pursue your investigations at such a cost as your ease and happiness? Why not cherish your opinions in secret, and leave an ungrateful and unsympathizing community to its ignorance? Be merciful to thyself." To the mother they have offered their commiseration, and have not hesitated to express the conviction that she was wasting her life, and that she should eat, drink, dance, and be merry, as on the morrow she would die. And to all others moved by a lofty purpose, and inspired by a great idea, such as patriots and ministers, they have chattered the same expostulations, warning them that if they were not less zealous they would cut short their days, or die in poverty, as though sudden death or lack of riches was the most terrible of evils. "Be merciful to yourselves," echoes the voices of these earth-blinded souls; "be pitiful to yourselves, do not throw away your life, be considerate of your own interests, and mindful of your own welfare. Do not throw away your life, we beseech you; you have only one, husband it, care for it, cherish it, wrap it in a napkin and bury it where it will be safe."

When, two or three years ago, in our religious gatherings we sung the lines,

"Oh! to be nothing, nothing,
 But simply to lie at His feet,
A broken, empty vessel,
 For the Master's use made meet."

the sentiment was received in some quarters with derision. It was said sarcastically, "what have such cities as New York, Boston, or Chicago, in common with such self-abnegation?" "The age," it was declared, "is self-assertive, and the thought of this hymn is utterly foreign to its spirit and its life." Unquestionably the criticism has some foundation in fact; but admitting this to be correct, it does not condemn the sentiment of the hymn, but rather the temper of our times. Unhappy are we if our civilization has so materialized us that no room can be found for the generous devotion of self to a worthy and sublime enterprise, if there is nothing higher for a man on earth than the zealous promotion of his own worldly interests. Christ not only rebukes, but also states the essential folly of such a theory. In His turn He remonstrates with humanity, in substance saying: "Be merciful to thyself; for whosoever will *save* his life shall *lose* it." What the Savior taught upon this point has not only been reiterated by His disciples, but even some of the heathen have recognized its essential soundness. With a clearness that may well put to shame the boasted broadness and discernment of our age, it was perceived by several of the wiser pagans that to be *something* life must be *nothing*, and that to *save* it it must be *lost*. One of these writers I quote, and only one, and he a representative of that Asiatic thought which some restless minds are seeking in our day to array against Christianity, who elaborates into a philosophy what Jesus delivered as an apothegm. I refer to Lau-Tsze, the Chinese, who was contemporary with Confucius, and who excelled that celebrated personage in the grandeur of his teachings. Six hundred years before Christ he gave utterance to the following sentiment: "The sage does not lay up treasures. The more he does for others the more he has of his own. The more he gives to others the more he is increased." On which sentiment the translator and editor of his works offers the following comment from Bunyan:

"A man there was, though some did count him mad,
The more he gave away the more he had."

In another place this ancient sage exclaims: "He who bears the reproach of his country shall be called the lord of the land. He who bears the calamities of his country shall be called the king of the world." . . . "He that makes mars. He that grasps loses. The sage makes nothing, therefore he mars nothing. He grasps nothing, therefore he loses nothing." . . . "When he wishes to be before the people he must, in his person, keep behind them. When he wishes to be above the people he must, in his language, keep below them." He also declared "that he that is diminished shall succeed," and to him may be traced the pregnant suggestion, expressed by Oken, "Zero is the essence of mathematics." Just as we are able by the sign "0" to make the most abstruse and complicated calculations, so when a man descends to that sign of nothingness is he able to rise to the sublimest heights of potency and greatness. As zero is the very substance of mathematical science, so self-denial is the very substance of personal usefulness. Or, as the Talmud has it: "Whosoever runs after greatness, greatness runs away from him; whosoever runs from greatness, greatness follows him." Which is just equal to saying: "Whosoever will save his life shall lose it, and whosoever will lose his life for my sake shall save it."

While it is well to recall the fact that thoughtful souls of pre-Christian ages have approved the principle commended by the Savior, we should at the same time realize that it is not only attested by evidence, but is grounded in common sense. What more reasonable than the belief that life becomes broader, deeper, fuller, more abundant, in proportion as it is concerned with the interests of others? By identifying itself with the lives of many, by making their cause its own, by entering sympathetically into all their sorrows, hopes and fears it must inevitably enlarge its own capacity and elevate its character. Just as the heavens increase in radiance proportionate to the multiplication of stars that gleam in their vault; just as the winds increase in fragrance according to the extent of sweet-scented fields over which they blow; and just as the river grows in fullness, the greater the number of streams that flow into its bosom, so life must become more luminous, more fragrant and more complete the more it admits the hopes of others to a place in its sky, and mingles the griefs and cares of others in its floods. The mother is conscious of an expansiveness of soul, and of a peculiar personal elevation that comes with her self-surrender for her child. And the more she denies herself the pleasures of society, when they seem to conflict with devotion to her offspring, the more ennobled does she feel, and, in reality, the more ennobled she is. Another star glitters in the azure of her love, and though a tiny one, it brightens the path of her feet. The man who is entirely absorbed in business, who has no thought beyond its marts, and no ambition higher than its gains, may, in many respects, be very estimable, but obviously his spiritual stature cannot be as great, nor his capacity for enjoyment be as large, as they would be were he steadfastly to make his temporal affairs directly tributary to the well-being of humanity. In the former case he becomes gradually assimilated to the dryness, hardness and narrowness of his pursuits; but in the latter, like Lorenzo De' Medici, he grows toward the fair or grand ideal for the actualization of which he cheerfully endures the daily round of monotonous toil and care. Hence it is that in trade and commercial circles we frequently meet with men who tower above their associates, and whose presence carries with it sunshine and peace. They are poets, artists, saints or scholars in their instincts; they desire to beautify, sanctify and enlighten the race; and swayed by this passion they rise early, retire late, and submit to all kinds of self-denial that means may be procured for its gratification, and in doing this they themselves become beautified, sanctified and enlightened.

During my various wanderings in the old world I have frequently been reminded of this truth. There are ancient churches in Europe which the American traveler soon learns to venerate, not merely because they are the shrines of Deity, but because they have become the memorials of human greatness. Indeed, God is less thought of than man within the sacred walls of Westminster, Santa Croce, and the French Pantheon. There, mingling with the dust of kings and princes, rest the honored ashes of the martyr-heroes both of science and religion, the explorers of nature's mysteries, the prophets of the world's progress. And yet these were the very men whose names were cast out as evil by their own times, who were derided as fanatics and dreamers, who were denounced as disturbers and iconoclasts, who were pitied by friends and hated by enemies, whose senseless remains are now entombed in so much state. Verily, the fanatics of one age become the gods of another, and the dreamy enthusiasts of the past are the sober commonplaces of the present. In London, Paris and Florence the same moral appears between the lines of epitaphs penned by the descendants of persecutors in commemoration of the persecuted: "Whoever will lose his life shall save it"; for who can doubt that Dante, Galileo, Copernicus, Bruno, Columbus, and the rest of their fraternity, gained more in their consciousness of personal superiority, and derived more satisfaction from their exalted thoughts, than they sacrificed in temporal estate, even as they have risen to such a height of dignity and power as more than compensates for all they surrendered or endured.

Conversing recently with an acquaintance at Dresden on continental habits, surprise was expressed that Americans were so indifferent to the attractions of the café and the open-air concert. It was said that they made life too serious, and deprived themselves unnecessarily of many of its pleasures. The criticism and the censure on the surface seem to be just, and yet they are not as conclusive as they appear. Compare life on both continents, and the opinion of our critic will hardly stand. In reality he assumes that the end of human existence is the café or the concert-garden. The average European performs his appointed task patiently, if not cheerfully, and if he can sip his wine or beer and hear music,— music, by the way, not infrequently of an excruciating type,— he is satisfied. *That* he calls "living," and, in the meanwhile, he permits himself to be drafted into armies, consents to pay enormous taxes for the support of senseless royalty, and grubs along from the cradle to the grave with a benumbed consciousness of what he is and what he should be. Such people may live more years than the average American, but they do not live as much in any or all of them as he. He does not regard amusement as the chief end of man, but liberty, culture, mental and spiritual growth, the service of God, and the elevation of his fellow-beings. As a consequence, his experiences are more diversified, his resources more varied, and his existence more complex and complete. What he loses is not worthy of consideration in view of what he gains. Better, far better, sacrifice seductive pleasures, pleasures that emasculate, and that perpetuate dull submission to oppressive systems, if by doing so the sense of freedom, of personal independence, and of responsibility for the condition of others may be won. This is the choice of our people, and I think history proves that it is never successfully made where time and thought are to any extent bestowed on sentient indulgencies and dissipating follies. If the citizens of any country would save their highest life, and the only life worth living, they must be willing to lose their lowest, and which, after all, is not worth preserving. I need not attempt to show you how this principle is confirmed in our Savior's history, or that it is the most obvious teaching of the New Testament. He who was made poor is now rich; He who bore the cross on earth is now seated on the throne in heaven; He who was embraced of death is now alive forevermore; He who, in Peter's judgment, ought to have had more mercy on Himself has convinced His erring servant that He really did compassionate Himself when He chose to ascend the hill of shame; for that, and that alone, led to the height of glory.

From this line of thought it is not difficult to perceive that a man can come to feel real delight in the gift of existence, and can attain to conscious enjoyment of the life to which he has been called by God. Of the refined and elevating nature of this enjoyment there can be no doubt, and the only question that remains to be considered is whether as a motive to action it is commendable and legitimate. Or, to frame the inquiry differently, whether we may with propriety be influenced by considerations of our own well being to seek the well being of others? Altruists think not. They argue that a subtle selfishness is interwoven with all such considerations; that every kind of motive impairs the character of virtue, and that duty should be performed simply because it ought to be performed. To Christian people this seems to be an extreme view to take of the matter; nor can they see how the idea of motive is to be eliminated from right conduct. For instance, is not the very sense of *oughtness*, on which the Altruist lays so much stress, in itself a motive of the weightiest kind? If that ceased to control, would not practical righteousness fall into decay? But whether we regard it as a motive or not, we believe that it is right to do good to those around us; and it cannot be denied that the reasons we have for this belief are equally conclusive in favor of our doing good to ourselves. Altruists and all agree that it would be contrary to nature for us not to have concern for the happiness of the race, and it is equally evident that it would be no less contrary to nature for us to be indifferent to our own. The instinct of self-preservation, the horror we have of suicidal recklessness, and the contempt we feel for those slatternly individuals who are heedless of their standing and influence, sufficiently prove that the obligation to seek in some sense our own is an everlasting reality. It has always been more or less of a problem to know how this can be done, and the individual at the same time be preserved from utter and irremediable selfishness; and when it is shown that it can be effected by devotion to the interests of those around us the practical philanthropy involved in the method certainly justifies and glorifies the motive. Therefore I am convinced that this motive is not fairly open to the objections which are so freely pronounced by Altruists, and that in being influenced by it we are neither degrading ourselves nor corrupting the idea of virtue.

Thomas à Kempis, writing on the duty of self-renunciation, exclaims: "O Lord, this is not the work of one day, nor children's sport; yea, rather in this short word is included all perfection." It is well that we lay this thought to heart. With honesty of purpose we may decide henceforward to practice the law of self-denial, but never having measured the difficulties in the way we may speedily be discouraged. Our egoism, our self-love, and the example of multitudes around us, may suggest the hopelessness of the undertaking, and we may be driven back to our old self-seeking and to the degradation of self-worship. We may escape this sad experience if we will but remember what à Kempis teaches, that such a life is "not the work of one day," and that, consequently, we should not abandon our sublime task because we meet with defeats and failures in its performance. Persevere; exercise yourselves continually unto self-renunciation, and gradually will you overcome all obstacles to a complete conformity to Him who "loved us and who gave Himself for us."

If you can only be persuaded by what has been said to undertake this, "the life of the Son of Man in the flesh," you will soon cease to question its moral grandeur. The staleness and monotony will speedily disappear, and you will realize that you have at last discovered the secret of its profit and its power. Instead of being a burden it will be a blessing to you; the bloom will return to its cheek, the luster to its eye, the dew to its forehead. You will rejoice to possess it; you will delight in its experiences; you will be glad in its trials. Life will be to you entirely different from what it has been; it will be invested with a new charm, a fresh beauty, a solemn glory. Yea, you will be led repeatedly to exclaim: "That which was lost is found, and the dead is alive again." Rejoicing in its salvation, you will contemplate its close with hope, believing that that which has yielded you so much satisfaction here will multiply your joys hereafter. You will look for the life on earth to wreathe crowns for the life in glory, and you will part from it below sustained by the prospect of greeting it above. In this sweet confidence may you abide, my reader; may each day be filled with music, and each night with peace; and when the hour of separation comes may your blood-washed soul chant in tenderest strains the fond adieu:

> "Life! we've been long together,
> Through pleasant and through cloudy weather;
> 'Tis hard to part when friends are dear,—
> Perhaps 'twill cost a sigh, a tear;
> Then steal away, give little warning,
> Choose thine own time;
> Say not "Good Night"—but in some brighter clime
> Bid me "Good Morning."

www.ingramcontent.com/pod-product-compliance
Lightning Source LLC
Chambersburg PA
CBHW020220240426
43672CB00006B/368